Jesus and the witchdoctor

Jesus
and the witchdoctor

an approach to healing and wholeness

Aylward Shorter

Geoffrey Chapman, London
Orbis Books, Maryknoll, New York 10545

A Geoffrey Chapman book published by
Cassell Ltd
1 Vincent Square, London SW1P 2PN

Orbis Books
Maryknoll, NY 10545

The Catholic Foreign Mission Society of America (Maryknoll) recruits and
trains people for overseas missionary service. Through Orbis Books Maryknoll
aims to foster the international dialogue that is essential to mission. The
books published, however, reflect the opinions of their authors and are not
meant to represent the official position of the society.

First published 1985

British Library Cataloguing in Publication Data

Shorter, Aylward
Jesus and the witchdoctor: an approach to healing and wholeness.
1. Faith-cure 2. Healing—Developing countries—Religious aspects
I. Title
615.8'52'0924   BT732.5

Geoffrey Chapman ISBN 0 225 66431 3

Orbis ISBN 0–88344–225–6

Printed in Great Britain

Dedication

To all who are engaged
in the medical apostolate
particularly in the countries
of the Third World

For you who fear my name, the sun of righteousness will shine out with healing in its rays.

Malachi 4:2

You see this city? Here God lives among men. He will make his home among them; they shall be his people, and he will be their God; his name is God-with-them. He will wipe away all tears from their eyes; there will be no more death, and no more mourning or sadness. The world of the past has gone.

Revelation 21:3–4

Contents

Preface

In a certain sense Jesus was a medicine-man, but he was far from being just that. He went beyond all forms of healing, scientific and pre-scientific, known and unknown, to offer a new perspective on wholeness itself. Wholeness is experienced by human beings at various levels—in a rapport with nature, in bodily health, in expectation of survival after death, in social and psychic integration and in the sphere of human morality and the world of cosmic forces. The ambivalent experience of health and sickness at all these levels beckons us to the final wholeness proclaimed by Christ.

In the service of final or transcendent wholeness every available means of healing must be considered—scientific medicine, supplemented on due occasion by so-called alternative medicine, but accompanied by the refusal to yield to irrational magic or social paranoia. There must be a rational approach to psychic healing, but above all the value of prayer has to be upheld and the healing gifts available in the Christian community integrated in worship and pastoral action. The sacraments also have to be revalued as channels of healing and the medical apostolate seriously organized. Only with healing seen as a unified process can the Church of today, challenged by the demands of the Third World, continue the mission of Jesus to the sick, the disabled, the deprived and the diminished.

This book falls into two parts. Part One deals with the darkness constituted by environmental pollution, sickness, the fear of death, the breakdown of relationships, psychic disorders and sin. It also considers human speculation and beliefs about the sources of evil. Physical, psychical and moral healing are not enough to dispel this darkness. Humanity looks towards wholeness on a higher plane, a new plane of existence in which evil has no part and healing is redundant. Part Two concentrates on the Light that shines in the darkness, Jesus as the source of all healing power and as the guarantor of transcendent wholeness. Medicine is a part of God's providence and is necessarily linked to the power of prayer—prayer purified of magical and manipulative temptations. This explains the presence of chapters on magic and millenarianism in this part of the book. Nevertheless, the sub-conscious has to be taken seriously, which is why a chapter is devoted to dreams. The appearance and popularity of spirit-healing and mass exorcism compel the Church to consider how such practices can be reconciled with liturgy and pastoral minis-try. The last three chapters deal explicitly with the question of the sacraments in a context of healing, with the integration of healing gifts in the Church's ministry and with the organization of the pastoral care of the sick as a real foretaste of transcendent whole-ness.

For more than twenty years I have been conducting anthropo-logical research, doing pastoral work as a Catholic missionary, writing and teaching in universities and places of higher educa-tion in the three countries of East Africa, Kenya, Tanzania and Uganda. I know these countries well and I have also made short visits in the course of my work to some twenty other African countries. I recently had the opportunity of enlarging my hori-zons by visiting Australia, New Zealand, Papua New Guinea and Brazil. The bibliography at the end of the book is an indica-tion of the reading on which it is based, but I have tried to introduce as much narrative material as possible. Much of this is autobiographical experience, and perhaps I should apologize for this. I can only say that my experience has been providentially varied and that I have the habit of recording cases and experiences in field diaries. It is from these (stretching back to 1964) that most of the stories come.

Many people, mostly my confrères in the White Fathers of Africa, have offered advice during the writing of the book for which I am grateful. I wish also to acknowledge one very helpful and affirming experience, the chance to communicate some of the ideas contained in the book to a class of catechumens and newly baptized at St Teresa's Parish, Eastleigh, Nairobi, using the Swahili language.

Feast of the African Martyrs   Aylward Shorter WF
of Uganda, 3 June 1984

                                              Catholic Higher Institute of
                                              Eastern Africa, Nairobi

Part One

The Darkness of God

I said to my soul, be still, and let the dark come upon you
Which shall be the darkness of God.

T. S. Eliot, *Four Quartets: East Coker III*

Introduction

It is not illnesses that are healed but people. In the human person there are many levels of being: the physical, the psychic, the social, the moral, the spiritual. The human person may be afflicted at one level more than the others, but all the levels are affected. There is a lack of wholeness. It is for this reason that the traditions of integral healing practised in the Black cultures of the Third World have so much to teach us. The integral approach to healing will also lead us to a better understanding of the Christian healing ministry and of Christian ideas about final or transcendent wholeness.

Chapter 1 begins by considering the tradition of integral healing associated with the African medicine-man and attempts a Christian reinterpretation of this much maligned figure. Jesus was a medicine-man in his own culture and a worker of wonders. He saw physical sickness and misfortune as an image of world-sickness or sin, and he offered a comprehensive redemption from it. This redemption stems from the restorative power of God's love and it is available to those who have faith in Christ's healing power. Christ cured the sick, but he also showed that suffering was a means of transcending human limitations. The Beatitudes are a charter for the transcendent wholeness proclaimed by Jesus, but they are also an index of suffering. In Christ, God offers a whole new possibility through the Cross which is the 'scandal' of a suffering God. Since all healing yearns for, and is connected with, the comprehensive redemption wrought by Christ, the Church has to recover a unified view of healing.

In the second chapter the human relationship with the physical environment is studied. The physical world speaks to us of a divine order, and the ethnic traditions of the Third World evince a symbiosis with nature—the faith in an organic link between human beings and the world of nature. Modern industrialized society is distanced from nature. Worse still, it abuses nature.

Ultimately this is due to an internal mental conflict. Society must learn to inhabit a larger world of first-hand experience and must acquire a sacramental cast of mind. Medicine is the produce of the earth, and healing necessarily includes being at rights with the physical environment. Through such a reconciliation human nature is set at rights with the world of the Spirit. Jesus used the whole of nature as a parable of the transcendent wholeness he proclaimed, and he revealed that the physical world shares in this same destiny of positiveness and goodness, growing towards it in the power of the Spirit.

Physical suffering and disability is part of the human condition. Chapter 3 notes that, in the religious traditions of the Black Third World, human beings are a synthesis of all that is found in the universe. They stand at the centre, containing in themselves all that is creative and destructive. These traditions also recognize the sublimation of pain and the value of asceticism. Sickness and disability are life-diminishing only in so far as they are deprived of meaning. Suffering belongs to transcendence and it is this 'beyondness' which gives it meaning and makes it bearable. There is no adequate answer to the question: Why does suffering occur? It is there. But paradoxically it reveals the goodness of God. Faith offers scope to sickness and makes it constructive of transcendent wholeness. Sickness, like the value of 'liminality' (state of being on the threshold) in African rites of initiation, is a mirror of that wholeness at the very moment when it is also a symptom of world-sickness or sin.

In Chapter 4 the world is seen as a theatre of death, the ultimate misfortune. African traditions provide a catharsis for human grief, and their funerary rituals offer the mourner a role to play in the continued existence of the deceased. Death cannot be conceived psychologically by the individual, but it represents the consummation of life. Death has its own appropriateness. In this way of thinking, we rejoin African concepts of social growth. However, attempts at transcending death through physical generation or through concepts of reincarnation are unsatisfying. Healing the state of bereavement and the fear of death depends on a positive attitude of faith that transcendent wholeness is already experienced to some degree in life. This is the power of the resurrection—the recognition of God's presence in the darkness.

Physical sickness is aggravated or alleviated by social factors. This is a conclusion of Chapter 5. The ethnic traditions that we are considering understand this very well. Not only is illness connected with unhappy human relationships, but social deprivation is itself a form of illness. We can even go further and note that societies in a state of upheaval can become 'sick societies' of which the physically ill may be effective symbols. Social harmony and reconciliation are therefore an important part of healing and the comprehensive wholeness taught by Christ is a final and total reconciliation.

Chapter 6 shows how psychiatric disorders which cause fear and embarrassment are a result of failed relationships. Emotional distress can also be a cause or consequence of physical illness. At times madness appears to be a form of unreality, but it is often a striving towards normality or even a prophecy of inner truth. Both private and shared fantasies have this ambivalence. All that happens to us is either gift or curse in so far as we make it so. Healing the depressed and the disordered comes about primarily through loving relationships and through the controlled expression of the emotions. Jesus' own emotional life can be our guide in achieving a greater expression of feeling in religious worship and practice.

African and other peoples of the Third World have been taught by the missionary to apply their taboo mentality to the concept of sin, but they originally possessed a perfectly adequate notion of sin. This is the conclusion of Chapter 7. Sin destroys relationships between people, and between human beings and God. Sin is sometimes related directly to the physical illness and misfortune of individuals, but its essential character is social. Moreover the sin of the individual contributes to social sin, the reign of sin or world-sickness, as we have called it. Modern societies tend to divorce the concept of crime from that of morality, but human responsibility cannot be finally ignored. Healing the sinner and the criminal involves both a sense of sin and a sense of God. Sin is, after all, the final evil, and the inner conflict of the human conscience, the final scandal. Yet even sin—one should say, especially sin—reveals the mercy of God who can alone forgive sin and who offers a definitive wholeness in which sin is definitively destroyed.

Chapter 8 considers the social paranoia of witchcraft beliefs and belief in the power of evil magic or sorcery. Such ideas are prevalent in many Third World societies. They are based on an unacceptable moral dualism and on the usurpation of the place of God by the witchfinder. Europe has the terrible example of the medieval witch craze from which to learn. Where health and health behaviour are linked to such fears, Christ's repudiation of vengeance and retaliation is the only answer. Human society has to reflect already the definitive wholeness of Heaven—the Kingdom of love, love of God and neighbour, love of God in neighbour.

The final chapter in this first part of the book deals with the source of evil in a personal Devil. Neither a thoroughgoing moral dualism nor a thoroughgoing moral monism is tenable. Africans and others in the Third World tend to personalize misfortunes and psychosocial realities in general. These are not cosmic forces of evil like the Devil. Just as there must be limits to a healthy speculation about the Devil, there are also limits to the demonization of experience. Otherwise God's victory in Christ is jeopardized. If evil is dissociated from God, as it must be, the victory of God entails the complete swallowing-up of evil and the redundancy of healing. The light finally dispels the darkness.

1

Jesus and the witchdoctor

Christian missionaries at the turn of the nineteenth century often saw their work in the context of a cosmic struggle between the forces of good and evil. Mission literature of the time is filled with colourful accounts of a local witchdoctor or diviner being vanquished by a missionary or an evangelist, and the stories are told with simplistic self-confidence. An example of the genre is provided by J. M. Robert.[1]

In around 1902, on the Fipa plateau [in modern Tanzania] where the people were still pagan, the diviner Ntekilomo was a source of wonderment because he made his clients rotate on a magic stool, during his consultations. Two intelligent and educated catechists, graduates of Karema catechist school, Paolo Songola and Leopoldo, resolved to investigate the facts and catch the charlatan red-handed. . . .

The two catechists arrived at Ntekilomo's homestead. First of all they carefully examined the stool on which the clients were invited to sit. It was constructed out of a three-legged stool, incorporating magical charms, and an up-turned pot, placed on the stool and covered with the skin of a wildcat.

Having uttered his spells, the diviner invited his client to sit on the skin, and shaking his gourd-rattle he put the usual questions: 'Is it the water-spirits, the benevolent dead, the malevolent dead, witches . . . who have caused this accident, sickness or failure?' When there was a positive answer, the client rotated in spite of himself.

Several clients submitted to the experiment and all of them rotated helplessly on the diviner's stool when the answer was in the affirmative. The facts were undeniable, as was the sincerity of the clients, among whom were several of Paolo's friends. 'Our spirits are powerful!' exulted the diviner.

'Your spirits?', exclaimed the catechist Paolo with a loud voice. 'They are not your spirits who help you, but Satan!'

The diviner, who was without doubt hearing the name Satan for the first time, misunderstood the catechist's remark. He thought that Paolo was accusing him of witchcraft, and replied excitedly, 'I call upon the water-spirits and the spirits of the dead, not Satan. I am a diviner, not a witch.'

'Can my friend also sit on your stool?', asked Paolo. 'If you succeed in making him go round, I will accept that Satan is not your helper.'

'Agreed!', said Ntekilomo.

Then the two catechists prayed to God, and Leopoldo, putting his crucifix on the stool, sat down on the skin.
The diviner for his part began to invoke his divinities, and taking his gourd-rattle, shook it with a will. All in vain! Leopoldo did not move round. On the verge of humiliation, the diviner who wanted to escape the accusation of being a witch at all costs, shook his rattle even harder, calling upon his gods. He struggled and sweated, but all in vain. At last, he gave up and in order to save his reputation produced the following explanation: 'Ah! You people who wear a crucifix, you are not like other people!'

This type of story, one instinctively feels, is a direct descendant of the story of Elijah and the priests of Baal. However, it contains—unlike Elijah's story—a number of spoken and un-spoken implications: the easy identification of traditional African spirits with Satan, the possibility of inexplicable psychological factors, the crucifix as powerful and visibly triumphing. Elijah triumphed over the discomforted priests on Mount Carmel, but how much has such a victory in common with that of Jesus Christ, and especially with his power-through-weakness on the cross? Missionary apologists were, in fact, a little premature in announcing the defeat of the witchdoctor. Under the picture of a somewhat terrifying Ugandan diviner or spirit-medium, loaded with amulets and charms, Julien Gorju wrote in 1920: 'The last (?) medium of Nkulo during a consultation'.[2] The question-mark is his.

The popular term 'witchdoctor' is misleading anyway, since it suggests that the person so called is mainly or exclusively in-volved in anti-witchcraft activities or is perhaps even a witch himself, an idea indignantly repudiated by Ntekilomo in Robert's story. The term is used to refer to traditional diviner-doctors in pre-literate societies, particularly in Africa. Divination is a form of revelation. It goes beyond mere diagnosis, the examination of the patient and the knowledge of natural cures and remedies, to include the analysis of dreams, the restoration of mental hygienic balance and the dynamics of human and supra-human relationships. The healing performed by a traditional diviner-doctor is carried out at various levels and by various means. There may be a greater or lesser proportion of treatment of physical ailments, using herbal remedies. There may be a care and respect for the natural environment and a preoccupation with social reconciliation as a prerequisite for healing. Attention may be paid to the effects of human enmity, to cursing, to witchcraft and sorcery, as well as to the intervention of ancestral spirits and non-human or supra-human agencies.

The divinatory process may be an impersonal ritual, or it may claim to invoke and tap the wider knowledge of spirits who may or may not be objects of religious faith and worship. In any case, it operates as a kind of 'switchboard', offering the client an appropriate course of action, ritual or therapy. Some diviner-doctors would seem to possess parapsychological powers of clairvoyance or healing, even healing at a distance. It is easy to see how divination is related to forms of prophecy and to questions of religious interpretation of experience. It is also understandable that early missionaries and evangelists should have clashed with these exponents of divination, since their mission involved a competing form of healing and revealing.

The witchdoctor not only did not disappear, on occasion he has even reappeared with a Christian messianic character, and his public humiliation at Christian hands may have stimulated this development. The power of the cross is a power-through-weakness, a fact that may have been momentarily forgotten by the latter-day Elijahs. Jesus Christ, to quote T. S. Eliot, is 'the wounded surgeon', 'the dying nurse', 'the ruined millionaire' who has endowed our cosmic 'hospital'. It is with 'bleeding hands' that he heals. Not only have new healers and prophets arisen in such places as South Africa or Papua New Guinea, proclaiming themselves to be 'Black Messiahs' or 'Black Christs' who have experienced rejection as Jesus did and who have re-enacted the drama of passion, death and resurrection, but even traditional sacrificial figures, such as the deified M'Bona in the Zambezi valley of Central Africa,[3] or relegated ancestral divinities like those of Uganda have received a new lease of life from the Christian model.

On 31 July 1975 I took part in a séance with a Ugandan traditional medium in Kampala City. I removed my shoes and entered the divining-house or temple. The floor was covered with mats and there were numerous small baskets for offerings. My host and his companions wore pieces of bark-cloth over their everyday clothes. Opposite us, with her back against the wall facing us, squatted a young woman, also clothed in bark-cloth. This was the medium. She had a baby whom she set down on the floor before going into her state of spirit-possession. Presently, she began to belch, at which my host whispered: 'The spirit is here'. Looking straight ahead, and speaking very slowly and deliberately without any hesitation, the medium preached me a fine homily about God the Creator, about the universal relevance of traditional Ganda religion and about the cultic significance of bark-cloth. 'Who are you?' asked one of those present, with noticeable reverence. 'I am the hero-spirit Kiwanuka' replied the medium. After the séance, when we got outside, my host explained the phenomenon we had just witnessed with reference to Christ. The Spirit had rested upon the medium as upon Jesus Christ and had transmitted God's message to humanity.

If the despised and vanquished diviner-doctor is undergoing a Christian 'resurrection', there is an even more fascinating question of how far the role of the so-called witchdoctor helps us to understand Jesus himself as a healer. The tradition of the witch-doctor is one of integrated healing, healing at every level, healing using different available means and healing as related to, or consequently upon, a process of revelation. Was Jesus some kind of witchdoctor?

Jesus of Nazareth certainly conformed to the type of itinerant healer-exorcist of his own day in rural Palestine. We do not see Jesus in the Gospels carrying out a medical diagnosis of sickness or examining patients. We do not see him treating the sick, administering medicines, or even massaging limbs or binding wounds. We do, however, see him imitating the 'mumbo-jumbo' of contemporary healers. Saliva was frequently used by pagan healers as a symbol of the healer's life. Jesus touched the tongue of a deaf-mute, having spat on the finger.[4] He also made a kind of primitive poultice out of mud mixed with his own spittle for a blind man.[5] He usually touched or manipulated the affected part of the body. At times he made a noise, variously interpreted as a 'sigh', a 'groan' or a 'snort' which may have been characteristic of an exorcist and which was recommended as a potent action in several ancient magical texts.[6] Perhaps it was comparable to the belching noise made by my Ugandan spirit-medium. At times, Jesus allowed healing power to pass through his clothes, as is also alleged for certain ancient healers, and is recorded also for the apostles in the New Testament.[7] Jesus certainly told his followers to use oil in healing, and it seems from the story of the Good Samaritan that it constituted a simple dressing for wounds.[8] Finally, the characteristic gesture of laying hands upon the sick was so common among healers as to be a synonym for healing itself.

Modern scientific medicine is scarcely two hundred years old. For centuries in Europe medical practice was based upon theories such as those of the four humours or the signs of the Zodiac. One could say that, until systematic medical science was born, all medical practice was 'alternative medicine'. In Jesus' time there were no very precise ideas about sickness. The term 'leprosy' covered a wide range of phenomena relating to the skin, and not only were psychic states attributed to possession by evil spirits, but so also apparently were epilepsy and dumbness.[9] It would be going too far to say that a 'spirit theory' of disease took the place of 'germ theory', but there was no germ theory in Jesus' day and spirits were very often identified as the cause of disease. Moreover, cures often took the form of exorcism during which a dialogue took place between Jesus and the spirits who were accounted responsible for the sick man's condition.

Jesus did not go in for divination as such, but he possessed a mysterious knowledge about the conditions of people he healed. He knew that the woman with the haemorrhage had touched his clothes,[10] even though a large crowd was pressing round him. He knew that the paralytic was in need of moral healing.[11] He knew that the sick man at the pool of Bethesda had waited a long time to be cured[12] and that Lazarus was already dead before he reached Bethany.[13] Above all, Jesus viewed his healing as a means of inaugurating the Kingdom or Reign of God. Curing the sick was a sign of the more fundamental restoration of health and wholeness, of forgiveness and reconciliation which typifies God's reign. It is the most complete fulfilment possible, and it necessarily entails the conquest of human suffering and human wickedness. We will return to this point later. For the moment we are simply noticing that Jesus revealed, as well as healed, and that the two activities necessarily went together in his ministry.

Jesus is presented to us as a wonder-worker and a worker of wonders that were also *signs* of an inner, spiritual reality. There were other wonder-workers in the culture histories of the ancient world, both Jewish and pagan. Some, like Aesculapius who was a historical person before he was deified, are credited with even more wonders than Jesus. When we look at the miracle stories of the Gospels in the light of modern Biblical criticism, we notice that several are doublets, that others are modelled on legendary miracles performed in the Old Testament, that others are 'popular' in style and may well have been embroidered. However, when the form-critics have done their work, we are still left with a body of miracle stories which testify to the reputation of Jesus as a wonder-worker and to his contemporaries' experience of him as such. It is impossible for us to say precisely what grounds of historical fact underlie these miracle-stories. It is equally, if not more, difficult for us to judge whether these cures defied the explanations of modern medical science. There were no such explanations in Jesus' day, and even today when these explanations are available, scientifically inexplicable cures still take place. Some of these happen in a strictly religious context, like the medically attested cure of Dorothy Kerin from tubercular peritonitis in England in 1912,[14] or the more than 65 cures accepted by the medical bureau at Lourdes from among the 4,000 or more cases recorded since 1858. It is not very profitable perhaps to speculate whether such experiences release a potentiality for recovery within the sick person or whether processes of natural deterioration are inexplicably halted or reversed by an external power. In the Christian context a sudden cure, especially a cure that defies medical explanation, is an effective sign of the power of God's love and the point about Jesus' cures was precisely that God's love was infinitely more powerful than all the suffering and all the evil in the world.

How then did Jesus connect physical suffering with human moral wickedness? Jesus certainly saw a general connection and he intended his miraculous cures to be signs of the cosmic battle between good and evil. He did not deny that repentance for sin could have a bearing on physical healing, but he rejected the idea of a specific causal link between sin and human disability or suffering. In the case of the man born blind he repudiated the idea of his followers that either the man himself or his parents had been guilty of sin,[15] and he told others that the Galileans killed by Pilate and the victims of the disaster of the Tower of Siloam were not greater sinners than those who were unaffected.[16] However, he saw such suffering and such disasters as an invitation to repentance in general and to the recognition of God's healing and liberating love. For Jesus physical healing from sickness and suffering was an outward sign of the more profound inner healing wrought by human repentance and divine forgiveness. Jesus did not offer a total explanation of evil and suffering, but he offered to break their power. This is clear in such accounts as that of the cure of the paralytic at Capernaum.[17]

Jesus, therefore, used the techniques of popular healers and exorcists of his time, and to that extent, at least, he was like a traditional diviner-healer or witchdoctor. Scientific medicine was not a possible option in his lifetime, or for many centuries afterwards. Nevertheless, in antedating medical science, Jesus also escaped its limitations, notably its comparative lack of interest in the environmental, social and moral aspects of healing. Jesus shared the integrated approach to healing which characterizes the so-called witchdoctor, but he carried it infinitely further in every dimension. In his own life he offered a comprehensive redemption from the world's sickness, and in his own person he offered a release for the sick, the sinful, the sad, the aliens, the outcasts, the poor and the ritually unclean. In Jesus' message there was no condition of diminished humankind, no sickness, disability or guilt which was impervious to the liberating and restorative power of God's love encountered in his own life and person.

It was for this reason that Jesus placed so much emphasis on faith. Many times, Jesus told a sufferer whom he had healed: 'Your faith has saved you'. Faith is one fundamental aspect of the personal relationship which a believer has with God. Faith is not possible without an object, the God in whom believers dwell and who invites them to respond to his self-revelation. Faith is a kind of 'falling in love' with God. It is not at all some kind of independent stoicism or esoteric knowledge, still less is it a presumption or unjustified claim on God. It is an entry into God's way of thinking, an alignment with his will. When Jesus said, as he frequently did, to people he healed: 'Your faith has saved you', or 'Your faith has made you whole', he was not referring to the theory known as 'faith-healing'. His words did not mean that a person's own disposition saves him, his own theory of the unreality of sickness or pain, or even his own virtue of faith. He simply meant that people had responded to God revealing himself in the healing power of Christ and that this faith had brought them to Jesus for healing. We must have the right ideas about God, about ourselves and about our relationship with God. We must approach him confidently, but not presumptuously, and then he will heal us. 'Your faith has saved you' means simply 'Your faith has brought you to me for healing'.

Suffering is a wider concept than sickness and there are many causes of suffering in the world. Some of these are due to human wickedness and some appear to be inherent in the nature of human beings and the world they inhabit. People suffer through loneliness and separation from those they love, through having no children, through exile and persecution, through their own sense of failure, through remorse of conscience, through war and violence, through natural disasters such as earthquakes, famines, droughts, volcanic eruptions, cyclones, storms at sea, floods, through poverty and social deprivation, through accidents when travelling or working, through disabilities which are congenital or acquired later in life, through old age, anxiety, depression and emotional anguish—as well as through sickness of mind and body that may befall them at one or another time of life. Suffering is deeply rooted in human nature and human experience. It cannot be satisfactorily explained, even in terms of punishment, trial or discipline, and Jesus, as we have seen, did not attempt such explanation. Jesus relieved suffering through his healing activity because it was a symptom and a symbol of the world's sickness, the definitive suffering which is the loss of eternal life. Jesus came to break the power of suffering by means of the infinitely greater power of God's goodness and love, revealed in his own life and person.

That is why he was not content merely to heal physically. He drew near to the world of suffering, for suffering belongs to human transcendence, to the call to go beyond ourselves and our own self-centred interests, to go beyond the limits of human life and experience. Jesus offered a way of overcoming the sense of uselessness of suffering and he even went so far as to call sufferers 'blessed' or 'happy'. The Beatitudes are, as Pope John Paul II has said, 'an index to suffering':[18]

How happy are the poor in spirit;
  theirs is the kingdom of heaven.
Happy the gentle:
  they shall have the earth for their heritage.
Happy those who mourn:
  they shall be comforted.
Happy those who hunger and thirst for what is right:
  they shall be satisfied.
Happy the merciful:
  they shall have mercy shown them.
Happy the pure in heart:
  they shall see God.
Happy the peacemakers:
  they shall be called sons of God.
Happy those who are persecuted in the cause of right:
  theirs is the kingdom of heaven.[19]

The Beatitudes—and indeed all of Jesus' teaching—suggest that suffering is itself creative for bringing about salvation or world 'wholeness'. People are called to accept, as well as to relieve, suffering, even to deny themselves by suffering voluntarily and innocently. Physical suffering is linked to moral conversion and spiritual maturity and 'to suffer means to become particularly susceptible to the working of God's saving power'.[20]

The wholeness to which Jesus called the world is the pure positiveness of God, the transcendence of a human nature susceptible to pain and decay. It includes bodily health and integrity, but it also looks forward to peace and well-being, to perfect relationships, to the forgiveness of sin and enlargement of soul, to recapitulation or summation in the wholeness and holiness of God himself. This is the reign or kingdom of God which Jesus preached and of which his healing was a sign. That kingdom spells liberation from every kind of evil, a new possibility from God, hope for every category of sufferer, even for the dead.

The way in which God-in-Christ brings about this definitive wholeness and effects the healing that anticipates it at other levels, is through the principle of power-through-weakness, already exemplified in the Beatitudes. Jesus lived this principle to the full. His own life-style of poverty and nomadism, his preference for marginal people and the ritually unclean, his celibacy and total availability culminated in a disregard for his own safety and a refusal to run away when his life was threatened. Eventually, it was through the destruction of his human existence on the cross that he 'was made perfect' and that his humanity was transformed by the Resurrection into a vehicle of salvation for the whole world. His personality received its fullest expression for us and his presence to us became unlimited. Jesus' love for us, even to the point of death, has now become an all-embracing means of salvation.

On him lies a punishment that brings us peace,
and through his wounds we are healed.[21]

Jesus Christ is the wounded healer, the one who has proved the truth of God's love by the truth of his suffering. In him God suffered as a man.

A suffering God is a scandal for monotheistic religion and for religious philosophy, but the fact remains that for Christians God revealed himself finally and most completely through the experience of human suffering. Divine impassibility is challenged by the incarnation. We glibly say that the divine subject of Christ's human acts really suffers, but only according to his human nature, yet we are limited in our modes of thinking and speaking about the mystery that is God. Paradox may not become contradiction, and yet to be true to Revelation we must automatically unsay everything we say, when we talk of God. Jesus Christ really revealed God when he suffered, and yet God is not affected by anything that originates in his own creative act. God, as God, can feel compassion for human sufferers without himself experiencing their passion. Yet, theologians continue to ask, what is left of compassion, as a personal quality, if it is detached from passion? Suffering, at any rate as we know it, is God's chosen means of salvation and wholeness. Suffering *is* creative even though it results from the limitation of a good.

Human beings are called not only to share in Christ's sufferings but even to 'complete' them, to make up in their own sufferings what is needed 'to be undergone by Christ for the sake of his body, the Church'. Human suffering is then far from being useless. Pope John Paul II has written: 'To a suffering brother or sister Christ discloses and gradually reveals the horizons of the kingdom of God'.[22] Moreover, when suffering is accepted and its saving role understood, there is even joy in suffering. 'It makes me happy to suffer for you', says St Paul. It is not because suffering is enjoyable in some inverted or perverted way, but because weakness—in God's dispensation—becomes a source of ultimate strength.

We began this discussion of Christian wholeness by asking if Jesus had anything in common with the witchdoctor. Jesus *was* a kind of witchdoctor, if only because he adopted the practices of traditional healers of his own time. There is, however, another resemblance which has already been hinted at. The traditional diviner-doctor in the cultures of the less-well-developed countries of the Third World offers a healing 'package', as it were. His approach to healing is multidimensional or integrated. He does not make very clear distinctions between the different levels at which healing operates—physical, emotional, psychic, social, religious. He is content to operate on several levels at once. This is definitely one of his great strengths. Jesus also, as we have seen, operated on several levels—the psycho-physical, the moral and spiritual, the eschatological, or level of final fulfilment.

This unified view of healing was bequeathed by Jesus to the early communities of the Church, and the ministry of Jesus was reproduced in the ministry of the apostles and their helpers. Unfortunately, as time went on, it was lost sight of. The sacraments and sacramentals of the Church tended to be seen in terms of mainly moral or spiritual healing. Miraculous cures came to be associated with shrines and places of pilgrimage and with people of outstanding holiness, usually after their death and canonization as saints. There was little in the way of personal ministry or the holding of healing services. Moreover, the Church tended to approach its members more and more as individuals and the social character of many of its celebrations was lost. In this way it came to contribute less and less to social healing. Healing thus came to be more and more departmentalized and differentiated.

In addition to these trends, the Church also became alienated from contemporary medical practice. This was not surprising as long as medicine was rudimentary or even dangerous. Priests and religious were strictly forbidden by Church law to practise medicine which was practically synonymous with 'the shedding of blood'. The rapid development of scientific medicine in the last two centuries has even rendered the departmentalization of healing more absolute. When medical practice was primitive, the Church could afford to subordinate the cure of bodies very firmly to the cure of souls. When it developed through multiple specializations and through its own inventive momentum to become an effective science and art, the Church was happy to invoke a separation of corporal and spiritual spheres, leaving medicine to the specialists. The Church was nevertheless able to enter the sphere of bodily healing through the foundation of religious nursing orders and hospitallers and through the setting up of hospitals, clinics, hospices and medical programmes of all kinds, particularly as part of its mission activity in Third World countries.

However, it is in these very countries that the separation of healing powers is most vociferously challenged. We are back with the witchdoctor again! The new Christians of Africa, Asia and Oceania are unhappy about such a separation of healing processes. In Latin America too, there are unassimilated views on healing which have much in common with those of Africa and Oceania, and some of which are a direct legacy from the trans-Atlantic slave trade. In many places, new healing processes are coming into existence that are often syncretist, or at any rate deviant from the Church's recent practice. Unauthorized healers and exorcists are appearing who offer traditional-African (as opposed to traditional-Christian) explanations of disease or deprivation. The Church's own sacramental life appears to make little impact, or at least to have little apparent relevance to the multidimensional needs of the new Christians in the sphere of suffering and relief from suffering. Existing liturgical and canonical forms make it difficult to incorporate the new healing gifts and healing traditions that are springing up, and there is real danger of heterodoxy or even schism.

Large numbers of so-called independent churches and new religious movements are coming into existence. As long ago as 1968, David Barrett identified as many as 6,000 such movements in Africa alone.[23] There must be many more by now. In addition to these, and to a certain extent connected with them, is the profusion of evangelical Pentecostal churches, many of them taking their origin early in the twentieth century among Black American communities in the United States. These have spread with surprising rapidity in many countries of the Third World. Their millenarian teachings and their other tenets concerning demonic illness and faith-healing are often attractive to Christians who are dissatisfied with the attitude of the main-line, mission-related churches, Catholic included, towards healing and exorcism.

It is not only in the Third World that Christians are dissatisfied with the Church's approach to healing and with departmentalized healing in general. The impersonal approach of scientific medicine and its agnosticism towards social and moral needs (even, until recently, its agnosticism towards the area of psychic and emotional needs) frequently leads to alienation and emotional distress which adversely affects the physical health of the patient. The separation of healing spheres and the concentration by the Church on the spiritual and moral aspects is equally unacceptable. The growth in popularity of charismatic prayer-groups and charismatic healing has gone far towards catering for a unified approach to healing in the western world. However, these trends are not without their own problems—particularly the tension between them and the formal liturgical celebration of sacraments.

It is clearly inadequate to concentrate on any one aspect of healing to the exclusion of others. Medical science especially has its limitations, so does the approach that seeks immediate explanations, predictions or forms of control—or results taken in isolation from other healing dimensions. Above all, it is ultimately unsafe to ignore the link between suffering and transcendence, the goal of ultimate wholeness to which Jesus testified by his life and death and which, through his life and death, he accomplished and revealed. Christians in the Third World must go back to the despised witchdoctor to find the answers to many of the questions being asked today about healing and to see how compatible they may be with the teaching and witness of Christ. Was he so wrong after all—that diviner and his mysterious switchboard?

2

Flesh of the flesh of the world

Probably there has been no people on earth that has had such a close rapport with nature as the Australian Aborigines. For forty thousand years these Australian tribes lived out an unwritten compact with their own harsh environment, with fire and water, rock, desert and forest. Theirs was an uneasy truce. They did not have time to build, or to create an elaborate material culture. Their full-time occupation was survival and it is one of the great triumphs of human achievement that they did survive against appalling odds. The survival of the Aborigines is founded on their respect for the environment, the world of nature by which they were surrounded. They were wandering hunter–gatherers, participating in the very natural processes themselves. They took what nature provided in the way of fruit and game, but did not cultivate or raise livestock. They moved lightly over the vast, empty continent with fire-stick in hand, helping to precipitate the fire-storms which released the seeds and the new vegetable life in the wilderness.

Their relationship with the world of nature was also essentially religious. Their totemic system ensured a living link with the species on which they depended and a link with the totemic ancestor-creators whom they worshipped. They believed that they could increase or re-create these natural species and that, being themselves totemites, or incarnations of the totem, the shedding of their own blood was sacrificial. In this manner, natural phenomena entered into their whole social and psychological experience and their involvement with the world of nature was thought of as organic.

Australian Aboriginal religion represents an extreme formulation of a profound truth—the recognition that the world of nature is both a symbol and a vehicle of the transcendent power which transforms us and restores us to our true wholeness. The traditional ethnic religions of the Third World have realized this because they have arisen in societies where life is lived in continuity with the world of nature. The western mental approach to nature, however, has been quite different. It has been the approach of those who come to exploit natural resources, to isolate themselves from the world of nature by creating cities and to free themselves from dependence on nature through technology. The clash between the Aborigine and the British settler in Australia was one of total mutual incomprehension. Neither race could possibly conceive the other's philosophy of life. It is only now, nearly two hundred years after the original impact, that the white peoples have begun to appreciate something of the Aborigine's outlook and to yearn for a healing of the rift between themselves and the environment.

It is likely that every religious outlook must be grounded in a positive attitude towards the natural environment, because it is only this world of nature which can speak to us of a divine order and of a hope of ultimate wholeness. Human beings have their history and their immense technical achievements, but they deceive themselves if they think that these release them from dependence on natural elements. Furthermore, they deceive themselves if they imagine that their own achievements in history carry a significance which can somehow be divorced from the innate meanings of nature. The world of nature is given to us as our life-context. In a sense, everything we make or do is 'natural'. However, religious systems tend to operate with symbols culled from both human history and the world of nature, and they place a varying emphasis on them. Judaism and Christianity are so-called 'historical religions' whose peculiar insight has been to experience God revealing himself in and through human history. History is so important to these religions that they regularly choose historical symbols and even 'mythicize' their history in order to bring out its religious meanings. For all that, the world of nature plays an important role in this process, although natural events are made to conform to the history of God's people. The mountains 'skip like rams'; the Jordan flows backwards and 'flees', while all the trees of the wood 'clap their hands'. God's intervention in the affairs of human beings has a counterpart in the phenomena of nature.

The traditional ethnic religions, by contrast, tend to live out a historicized mythology. The emphasis here is on physical proximity—even continuity—with nature, and human history is seen as a re-enactment of a pattern of relationship with nature that is God-given. It is the world of nature that offers these religions their essential matrix of symbols. Nature is their theological dictionary, as it were, and it is in the experience of nature that their adherents meet divine reality. The historical interaction of a people with their physical environment and the adaptations they have made to it in their way of life constitute their particular 'natural temple', or to use Zahan's colourful phrase, their 'elementary cathedral'.[1] Oddly enough, when temples and cathedrals come to be built of bricks and stone, their purpose is not so much to capture and imprison within their walls an experience of the sacred which might otherwise be lost in a secular or hostile world, as to provide a map or key to a whole physical environment experienced as sacred. Traditional ethnic religions are not 'nature religions', but 'religions of nature'. Their adherents do not worship natural phenomena or mistake them for divine reality itself, but the experience of nature provides them with a genuine experience of the divine.

The physical environment is the ultimate human life-context. It is almost an extension of the human body that breathes its air and walks its earth. The Caribbean poet Aimé Césaire has expressed the idea very beautifully in his phrase 'flesh of the flesh of the world'. That is what we are. The late Joseph Goetz expressed the same idea by his term 'cosmobiology'. He coined the word to convey the outlook which assumes there is a biological connection between the rhythms of the natural world and the cycles of a human being's bodily and even historical existence.[2] In this outlook the immediate environment of the human individual is an 'organic universe'. This phrase is favoured by the Nigerian playwright Wole Soyinka.[3] Traditional ethnic cosmologies and religious systems constitute an organic universe of which the human being is an integral part. It is one of the concerns of the witchdoctor, whom we met in Chapter 1, to see that the harmony of this organic universe is maintained. That is why he always exhibits a great respect for nature and a great care for its products, dealing as he does with an immense array of herbs, roots, fruits and leaves which form the ingredients of his medicines and potions.

The evolution of an organic universe is not due to an ignorant inability on the part of people in the Third World to differentiate between people and things. It is simply that in such a village world people have to do with an abundant nature, an over-whelming environment, at every instant of their lives. They also place a premium on personal relationships, since they live on a comparatively small social scale. It is hardly surprising that they take their analogies from nature and personalize their experience of it. It is worth taking a look at an example of such an organic universe.

The Kimbu people of south-western Tanzania number about 50,000 at the present time.[4] They have traditionally practised shifting cultivation, hunting and honey-collecting in a very large area of heavily wooded and well-watered hills. They are a multi-chiefdom society and, in spite of many social upheavals in colonial times and in the era of national independence, they can trace 38 chiefdoms today. Each chiefdom was an organic universe of its own, the transformation of a pattern shared with its neighbours. Occupying the highest and most central position in the Kimbu symbolic scheme is the sun at its zenith. Below it is the sacred hill of the chiefdom. These are images of God associated with successive theological emphases, a sky-centred theology and an older earth-centred one. The hill rises from the earth, the womb of humanity, and the rivers which symbolize the stream of life flow down the hill to water the fields and homesteads at its foot.

On either side of these central images can be ranged the two categories of symbols associated with the fulfilment and the diminution of life. At the top of the former are the high-flying birds which are symbols of transcendence. Next in order come the great carnivores which stand for animal beauty and power. It is not surprising that eagles' feathers and the skins of lions and leopards are prominent in the chief's regalia. Below these creatures in symbolic importance are the birds and beasts of the forest which are hunted or snared, the fish, the fruit-bearing trees and the trees with nectar-bearing flowers, and finally the friendly python which lurks among the rocks, a symbol of ancestral spirits whose graves are its home.

On the other side are the night-flying owls and the hyenas and other scavenging birds and beasts which are the familiars of witches, the spirits which are called 'masters of the animals' and other ambivalent 'bush-spirits', the witches themselves, the zombies or resurrected dead who are the witches' servants, the snakes and all the horrid creatures that live in stagnant pools and water-holes. In the centre, at the foot of the hill is envisaged the human race, caught between the two polarities, and all the animals and plants that are assimilated to humanity. These include the elephant renowed for its oracular powers, the pangolin and chameleon with their 'human' modesty, domestic animals and vermin, domesticated crops and plants, and trees which have a sap like blood. In this familiar, human world, the chief is God's plenipotentiary, wearing his conus-shell sun-disc and honoured with the reverberating notes of a ghost-horn fashioned from the wood of a 'tree-with-blood'. The chief rules on behalf of his ancestors, the territorial spirits, who mediate every blessing that comes from God, while ordinary householders look to the ancestral spirits of their own family to provide for their immediate needs.

Such an organic universe is a satisfying scheme which takes care of every department of experience and clothes it with meaning. It is a reduced model for any and every religion which owes its primary symbols to a natural environment. Secularism is essentially a distancing from nature, a preoccupation with man and his works, man, not as the priest of creation, but as its interpreting principle—its God. Shielded by artificial things and lulled by their own mental inferences and abstractions, human beings find their sensibility diminished. Worse, they find themselves at war with their environment, polluting natural resources, upsetting the balance of nature, causing whole species of wildlife to become extinct, encouraging desertification, dumping toxic wastes, bringing new diseases into existence, the so-called 'diseases of civilization'. In the depths of their cities, they become alienated from their real nature, frustrated, aggressive, fed on a diet of surrogate experiences, while over all looms the terrible shadow of nuclear war and the possible extinction of the human race itself.

The yearning for direct contact with the world of nature, for a healing of the rift with nature, repeatedly surfaces in modern urban and industrial societies. In an earlier generation it was a romantic back-to-nature movement that tried unsuccessfully to counterbalance the complexities of modern living. Perhaps it is more pragmatic today, setting up conservation societies and health food shops and demonstrating against pollution and nuclear armaments. For some it means erecting an alternative society with a more simple, communal life. Some observers are pessimistic. For them there is no corner of the world which remains uncontaminated. Others look forward wistfully to a global return to the simplicity of the wilderness after the catastrophe of Armageddon. One remembers the dialogue between Percival and Hargreaves in Graham Greene's *The Human Factor*, subject: 'the old Africa'.

> 'It's gone forever.'
> 'I'm not so sure. Perhaps if we destroy the rest of the world, the roads will become overgrown and all the new luxury hotels will crumble, the forest will come back, the chiefs, the witchdoctors. . . .'[5]

Assuming, of course, that the chiefs and witchdoctors are not just hiding around the next corner, operating out of sight of the luxury hotels.

It is not a question of rushing to extremes, but one of real healing where there is a conflict between human technology and the world of nature, and that healing must take place first of all in the human mind itself. The value of the traditional ethnic religion in the Third World consists in the fact that a proximity to nature forces one to inhabit a larger world than that of a suburban dormitory, that it drives the individual to ask bigger questions of life. Human beings in such a situation see themselves more clearly at an intersection between a material world and a world of the spirit. They find themselves affirming and denying themselves in a single breath. They become, as Zahan says for African religion, 'a synthesis of the universe'.[6] The human race must rid itself of the illusion or the dream of total control. People must have the ability to discern a power exterior and superior to themselves.

The Kimbu who have already featured in this chapter have a number of stories which are designed to inculcate a respect for nature. One of these concerns a youth called Miyunga who was exceedingly skilled in snaring birds. In every snare he laid in the forest birds were always found. Never did he have a failure. Miyunga enjoyed a great reputation in all the villages round about. One day, however, when Miyunga went to the forest he did not find a single bird in any of his snares. He walked on and on, going from one trap to another. At length in the two furthest snares he found two beautiful birds. They were so beautiful that Miyunga did not kill them. He tied them carefully and carried them home. At this juncture, the two birds began singing a prophetical song, using human voices. The song accused Miyunga of killing too many birds and of wanting to make all the birds extinct. When the birds started to sing, Miyunga was so afraid that he released them, and then birds came from all sides. Even birds which had been killed and cooked rose to life, flocking together around Miyunga. On reaching his home, all the birds set upon Miyunga and pecked him to death. Miyunga's success was an abuse of nature and nature took revenge. Miyunga was blind to the beauty he was destroying until the very last moment. When he spared the last two birds it was too late.

A grim story with an obvious moral. We need to have a healthy, balanced relationship with nature. Miyunga is not typical of Kimbu hunters, but he represents a temptation that afflicts all successful people, the temptation of not knowing when to stop, the temptation of placing oneself in the centre of the picture as the arbiter and exploiter of creation.

Created nature is our *milieu*, our life-context. We cannot do without it. More than this, it is the sacred zone, the elementary cathedral in which we enter the presence of God. The world of nature speaks to us of divine reality. It is not enough to be a nature poet, one must know how to listen to God's voice, and see his presence in nature. The Jesuit poet Gerard Manley Hopkins once wrote:

All things therefore are charged with God, and if we know how to touch them, give off sparks and take fire, yield drops and flow, ring and tell of him. . . . God's utterance of himself in himself is God the Word. Outside himself is this world. This world then is word, expression, news of God. Therefore its end, its purport, its meaning is God and its life or work to name and praise him.[7]

What is needed is this wonder-working 'touch' which can make created things give off 'sparks' of God. That touch is religious faith and, particularly, a religious faith that discerns God's action in sacramental forms. Ultimately, it is a faith in world health and in final world restoration or renewal.

Sacramentality is an attitude of mind which discovers the interrelatedness of things, and particularly the relevance of certain images and symbols for the inner reality which underlies the whole of existence. Third World peoples tend to take a sacramental approach to life. Their love of ritual demonstrates this. Much ritual is concerned with creating spatio-temporal models of, and for, this inner reality. One example is animal sacrifice. The cattle-keeping, Luo-speaking peoples of southern Sudan make their sacrificial cows into a kind of social map, assigning the different parts of the beast to different relatives at the moment of communion and thus strengthening the spiritual bonds that unite them. Another example is that of the Iraqw of central Tanzania who cut up the sacrificial animal and send its various organs and quarters by runner to different landmarks on the borders of their country, thus affirming their right to a specific territory, a right that is divinely sanctioned. Christian liturgical symbols also have a spatio-temporal function, and one of the most graphic is the Easter Candle, with its five grains of incense recalling the wounds of Christ, the alpha and omega and the current year of Our Lord inscribed on its surface.

Christ yesterday and today
the beginning and the end
Alpha
and Omega
all time belongs to him
and all the ages.[8]

The words of the priest, as he traces the symbols in the wax, transform a candle into a spatio-temporal model of the cosmic Christ.

The sacramental approach to the world of nature is one basic reason why people in the Third World seek an integrated approach to healing. It is not only that all our pharmacopoeia is produce of the earth, that the diet of a sick person, the climate and surroundings which are conducive to healing and convalescence are all part of the natural world that heals us. Much more important is the concept of being at rights with that world and, through this relationship, at rights with the world of spirit, the world of ultimate and paramount reality. This concept demands a sacramental approach to nature and a conviction that created things are 'news of God'.

In 1981, during a visit to the Holy Land, I sat on a slab of rock near the top of the Mount of the Beatitudes and gazed down over the Sea of Galilee. From my vantage point I could see nearly all the places associated with the Galilean ministry of Jesus, Capharnaum, Chorozain, Bethsaida, the place where the loaves and fishes were multiplied, and behind me in the hills, Nazareth, Cana, Naim. Many countless pilgrims must have shared that experience of peace and beauty. Flocks of sheep were grazing on the grassy slopes below, and wild flowers coloured the folded landscape. The live blue waters of the lake shimmered in the sun. The whole landscape could scarcely have changed since the time of Jesus.

Jesus was a countryman, brought up in a tiny country town with scarcely two hundred inhabitants. His audiences were farmers and fisherfolk and he spoke to them about their daily occupations, sowing and reaping, threshing and winnowing, casting nets and dragging in the catch of fish, about baking bread and lighting lamps, about vines and vine-dressing, about day-labourers and farm tenants, about sheep and sheep farming. The whole panorama of Galilean country life is there in the parables and aphorisms of Jesus' teaching. Jesus was an observer and lover of nature and he turned the whole of created nature into a parable of salvation. He watched the birds in the sky and he noticed the brilliant colours of the flowers on the Galilean hillside, more splendid—he thought—than Solomon in all his glory. He appreciated and spoke about the basic things of life, salt and yeast, fruit and seed, wine, oil and water, fire and earth. These were some of the images he used when he spoke about the kingdom, the inauguration of God's reign of goodness that was slowly being realized in our world. In God's kingdom there would be no more tears or sorrow, no more sickness and death. The kingdom would be a source of final health and wholeness. The kingdom was a transcendent reality available already to those with faith, available to those who could read the signs in the book of the world and of human life in that world. The elements of created nature speak to us of the divine order, of the plan of salvation, of the hope of wholeness. As in the theologies of traditional ethnic religions, the primary symbols of Christian teaching are drawn from the world of nature.

The material world is not only not evil, but it shares in the same destiny of goodness as the human race itself. The salvation of humanity entails the re-creation of the material world—a new heaven and a new earth, and human beings have the privilege of co-operating in this renewal. Humanity was created in the image of God and told to multiply and fill the earth and dominate it.

Be masters of the fish of the sea, the birds of heaven and all living animals on the earth.[9]

The whole of creation is in travail—in one great act of giving birth to a new order. The world, like the resurrected human body, awaits its transformation.

The whole creation is eagerly waiting for God to reveal his sons. It was not for any fault on the part of creation that it was made unable to attain its purpose, it was made so by God; but creation still retains the hope of being freed, like us, from its slavery to decadence, to enjoy the same freedom and glory as the children of God. From the beginning till now the entire creation, as we know, has been groaning in one great act of giving birth; and not only creation, but all of us who possess the first-fruits of the Spirit, we too groan inwardly as we wait for our bodies to be set free.[10]

For we know that when the tent that we live in on earth is folded up, there is a house built by God for us, an everlasting home not made by human hands, in the heavens. In this present state, it is true, we groan as we wait with longing to put on our heavenly home over the other; we should like to be found wearing clothes and not without them. Yes, we groan and find it a burden being still in this tent, not that we want to strip it off, but to put the second garment over it and to have what must die taken up into life. This is the purpose for which God made us, and he has given us the pledge of the Spirit.[11]

The images and mixed metaphors tumble out of St Paul's fertile thinking—giving birth, slavery and freedom, first-fruits, houses, tents and garments, but the clear meaning emerges. A new creation is coming into being, brought about by the Spirit of God, and humanity itself is part of the process, groaning and straining towards the revelation of this new order. Created nature is not simply a flat mirror or reflection of transcendent reality. It is an 'eschatology in process of realization'.[12] The material world we see is subordinated to, and being transformed by, the transcendental reality which it signifies.

This whole process is basically the work of God's Spirit. It is the Spirit who constitutes the interrelatedness of created things, their harmony or consonance. The Spirit is the constructor of personality, bringing about the revelation of the sons of God, the ultimate freedom to be our true selves. The person is the very subject of freedom and awareness and our personality develops as we become aware of the material world and discern the patterns which make it intelligible to us. To an even greater extent it develops as we relate to other self-aware beings. In all of this the Spirit draws us ever further beyond ourselves. He represents, as John V. Taylor has written, a principle of 'beyondness', drawing us through the visible world and the experience of tangible human relationships to another deeper relationship, another more harmonious world.[13] Humanity is at the summit of an evolutionary process which has witnessed an ever-increasing growth in consciousness. The Spirit is the pledge that this process will continue—endlessly in God.

The evolutionary process was carried forward in nature through periodic choices which ensured adaptation to changed circumstances and consequently survival. The Spirit, also, calls

us to ever more subtle choices in the light of our faith in God's
providence and his will to conserve and to renew. It is through
such choices that we exercise our freedom as human persons and
that we grow in moral and spiritual stature into the freedom and
glory of God's sons. Such choices involve self-sacrifice. If this is
true—as it is—of the created world in evolution, how much
more true must it be of human progress? Every great forward
leap towards the consolidation of God's Kingdom is based on
sacrifice, on the denial of self and on the longing to be dissolved
into the God who loves us. This is the essential energy of the
universe, the love 'that makes the world go round', that reverses
our possessive instincts and makes us want to belong to another,
to others, to God.

The Christian believes that Jesus Christ exercised this awareness, this freedom, this sovereign ability to choose and this
readiness to sacrifice himself in the highest degree possible for a
human being. His passage from death to life released the Spirit
for us and it is in the strength of this Spirit that we are able to
follow in Christ's footsteps as his followers and co-heirs. It is this
attitude which enables us to make sense of the world, that helps
us break through into the real world of which the present is a
shadow, and which finally makes it possible for us to redeem this
world of the present, assisting in its transformation into the
transcendental reality. At a more sublime level of understanding,
and in the light of God's self-revelation in human history
through Jesus Christ, what the Christian does is not so very far
removed from the organic involvement of the Australian Aborigine or the Tanzanian Kimbu with their natural environment.

An integrated approach to healing demands a degree of organic involvement with the world of nature and a preoccupation
with the health of the world. Industrialized and suburbanized
westerners find the 'cosmobiology' of the Third World attractive. Inhabitants of the Third World find themselves bewildered
by western technology and the spread of an urban consciousness.
Both are affected by environmental pollution, the squandering of
resources and the onset of desertification. If we are 'flesh of the
flesh of the world', then it is no use our being restored to bodily
health in order to inhabit a sick world. A balanced relationship
with the world of nature is a precondition for helping it to
achieve its destiny and ours with it.

Later in this book we shall attempt a revaluation of the
Church's sacraments in terms of healing. The sacramental out-

look in all forms of healing is vital. It is not enough simply to recite 'grace' over a medicine one is about to take, though that is a laudable practice and one which helps fit our own medical treatments into the human life-context, reminding us that the therapeutic properties of our pharmacopoeia are given to us by the Creator. But we must go further. Like the traditional witchdoctor we must be concerned to restore harmony on several levels and especially, through the level of our rapport with created things, to align ourselves with the world's destiny. Healing involves a re-appraisal of the world of nature. We need to experience that world to the full, to open our eyes to its diversity, and experience its events in their uniqueness so that we can inhabit a larger and more real world.

Above all, we need to adopt the approach to nature which Jesus demonstrated in his Galilean ministry, the ability to appreciate and care for simple, basic things which put us into direct contact with our mother, the Earth, and which tell us again and again about the Kingdom. Those primary symbols of the Gospel are not an optional extra. We have to experience them, if we are to understand the teaching of Jesus. If we have no inkling of the life and life-style of Jesus of Nazareth, if it cannot enter into our imagination, then there may be something amiss with our own way of life. We need a world we can relate to, a world which speaks to us of the ultimate reality. Degrading material conditions do not do this. Physical slums *and* spiritual slums are a barrier to this revelation. The concrete jungle and the suburban dormitory hold us captive. Somehow, we have to find the real experiences, our own, not those of other people. We have to resist becoming 'cassette-ized', locked up in secondary, vicarious living.

The sacraments and the healing ministry must unlock doors and windows on to a real world, creating in us that sacramental attitude of mind which is either lost or endangered. Recently, I was in a discussion group in Nairobi, planning the details of a parish Easter Liturgy. 'People do not understand the Easter Candle and its symbolism', volunteered one of the participants. 'Let's scrap all that stuff about grains of incense and alpha and omega. Let's just light a candle and get on with the readings.' Diminished sensibility? An inability to appreciate spatio-temporal models? Could not a door be unlocked when someone used to electricity experiences a candle and a living flame? A flame to set the whole earth and all the ages on fire?

3

The scandal and scope of sickness

He had jumped from a second-floor window in the university and had been taken up alive—an unsuccessful suicide, if suicide can ever be associated with success. It was ten years ago when I was working in Uganda at the height of Idi Amin's bloodstained régime. As he was the brother of our library assistant at the Institute where I was teaching, I was called to his bedside. He was a graduate student in the law faculty and it was already several hours since his bid for death had failed. His brother and I searched for him in the maze of wards and corridors in the huge hospital which had been Britain's 'golden handshake' to Uganda at independence. We waited for lifts, we ran breathlessly up staircases. Eventually we found Eric, as they had carried him in.

He lay on the bed in the vast hospital ward, naked under the single sheet that was his only covering, a tall, good-looking youth, with the finely sculpted features of the Hima people of Ankole. There was no nurse or doctor in attendance, no clipboard at the foot of the bed. Occupants of the ward said he had been brought in earlier in the day, but no examination had been carried out. We examined him ourselves. Both ankles and the right wrist appeared to be broken and there were other bruises on the body.

As we stooped over him, he looked up at us with unseeing eyes. I could not penetrate the mist in those eyes. Was he still in the toils of depressive illness, or had his suicidal leap shocked him out of his melancholia? He began to speak incoherently. It was clear that he was in pain and that he still clung to life. Perhaps, in the strange paradox of suicide, his desire to live was now stronger than his earlier wish to die. Stoicism seemed to have replaced surrender. We sat by him in silence until I heard a peal of careless, gullish laughter from the nurses' room in a distant corridor. There was a shortage of drugs in Uganda at that time, and fewer doctors than ever. Government hospitals were demoralized and little could be done for the patients. I found the giggling nurses and read them 'the riot act'. They agreed sullenly to give Eric something to ease his pain until the doctor came. Who was this white man with his misplaced concern for a youth who did not deserve to be helped? Eric's brother and I prayed a little at the bedside and then departed. A doctor eventually saw him 24 hours after he had been admitted.

What had caused this attempted suicide? I thought about it as I drove home. Here was a young man with the best education available in the country jumping from a second-floor window in the graduate school of law development. Was his the frustration of seeing the world for which he was being educated crumble around him? Summary executions, military tribunals handing down death sentences, students arrested for torture and interrogation, even the Chief Justice seized at gun-point during a session of the Court of Appeal. What is the prospect for an idealistic young lawyer in a land without law? Or was it a personal problem, his own anti-social aggression taking suicidal form?

Whatever it was, he had been cheated of that solution to his problems and his despair of life had been turned into a new reason for living and a new reason for flirtation with death. After the overthrow of Idi Amin Dada and the restoration of his unpopular predecessor, Eric joined the guerrilla army of one of the Ugandan rebel leaders. Instead of a motive for escape from life, he now had a cause for which to die, and his death-wish in its new form was granted. In an ambush on a main road south-west of Kampala City he and his fellow guerrillas mowed down twenty soldiers of the Uganda Army. Two guerrillas only were killed and Eric was one of them. No doubt he died with the same stoicism I had witnessed in the hospital six years earlier.

There is a great deal of stoicism in Third World countries. Perhaps these people also have a higher threshold of pain. However, it is also true—in Africa at any rate—that the initiation of young men at puberty includes as one of its objectives the sublimation of pain. This is one of the ascetical traditions of Africa. Boys who reach the age of puberty are prepared for adult and conjugal life. In a series of harsh lessons and rituals they are taught the manly virtue of self-control in the face of pain and the threat of suffering. To signify a mutation of personality their physical body is marked by an operation, circumcision or a visible scarification such as that of the Nuer of Sudan—the cutting of six parallel lines on the forehead. The candidate is expected to show not the slightest squeak of fear or the slightest hint of flinching under the knife. Otherwise his prospects of finding a marriage partner are diminished. In these tribes no girl wants to be married to a coward. The sight of these young boys, lying trance-like during the operation, or even singing loudly as the circumciser performs his task, is unearthly for a westerner. Yet it is clear that the suffering which serves society and the life of society is bearable.

It is the suffering that saps life that is intolerable, the suffering that serves no cause. Such suffering reduces the will to live. People even will themselves to die in such circumstances. Missionaries and doctors working among the traditional societies of the Third World frequently report cases of 'witchcraft illness', people dying with no apparent scientific medical cause, people who have just decided to die. Anthropologists and medical scholars have speculated about the physical effects of grave fear and auto-suggestion, but such theories by no means account for all the phenomena. The state of mind of the patient undoubtedly affects the chances of recovering or not recovering. In Europe and America most doctors fear to speak frankly to patients about a terminal condition, and although many such people may be adversely affected by the conspiracy of silence that surrounds them, it is true that there will always be some, perhaps the majority, who surrender more quickly to death when sentence is frankly pronounced. For them, there may be no reason to continue the struggle for life and a very good reason for embracing death. It is a fact that suicide and suicidal acts are by no means rare among those who have contracted a fatal illness. Stoicism or surrender, the release or the embrace of death. This may be the difference between Eric's suicide attempt and his actual death in a guerrilla ambush.

Suffering that is unrelated to a cause, suffering that is apparently meaningless, is the hardest to bear when it persists. The human attitude to sickness is almost always one of seeking a cure at all costs. Westerners go from treatment to treatment, even on occasion from doctor to doctor. They want to be satisfied that every possible treatment has been tried and that no avenue has been left unexplored in the search for a cure. Africans also ring the changes on all the possibilities, the possible sources of their sickness. In this they are assisted by the diviner's 'switchboard'. With the diviner's help they identify the cause of their suffering and remove it if they can, particularly if it is due to some occult agency in a preternatural or religious sphere. But when all these methods fail, sickness becomes a scandal, a stumbling-block because it serves no constructive purpose. It is purely and simply destructive of life.

In 1965, during fieldwork in Tanzania, I visited a village that has now ceased to exist, having become a casualty of the government's village re-grouping programme. I was taken to see a disabled man. He was a young man, as it turned out, in his early twenties, and both his legs were paralysed. He sat huddled in the corner of his hut as if ashamed that the world should see him. The village was extremely remote, accessible only by Land Rover in the dry season. The chances of getting callipers, crutches or other appliances were slim. A wheelchair would have been useless. The young man grasped me by the hand and poured out his story with a flood of tears. He had lost interest in life. He could do practically nothing for himself. His marriage prospects were nil, which is to say in Africa that a person is already virtually dead. I do not remember what I said to comfort the man, but whatever words I used must have been less than adequate in the situation. Perhaps the concern I showed by being there and the gesture of holding his hand was a comfort to him, I do not know.

A disability like that is the hardest to understand, the hardest to live with. It is enduring and incurable. It is plainly life-diminishing, robbing sufferers of any normal social role, cutting them off from their own community, their own family. In the preceding chapter we spoke—perhaps too easily—of material creation revealing a transcendental reality, being transformed even by the reality it reveals. We spoke of the sacramental view of life, about the beauty and uniqueness of created things. Where is the truth and beauty in such suffering as I witnessed in that Tanzanian village? What kind of transcendental reality could be revealed by such disability? These are hard questions. Perhaps an answer is to be sought in the very nature of revelation itself, in its very symbolical quality, of both saying and unsaying, affirming and denying at one and the same moment. Suffering definitely belongs to human transcendence, to the 'beyondness' which gives meaning to existence, but it has no permanent place in the scheme of things. Suffering is destined to disappear. It is a limitation that has to be removed if creation is to be renewed and liberated. It exists only to point towards that fulfilment. Like the affliction of the blind beggar whom Jesus cured at the Pool of Siloam, its purpose is 'so that the works of God might be displayed'.[1]

This saying of Jesus sounds quite cynical until one realizes that he was leaving aside the causes of sickness and was speaking only about its purpose in the plan of God. It is really an answer to the question: 'What does God do with sickness?' rather than 'Why does it happen in the first place?' The answer to the first is of course: 'God takes it up and cures it'. Suffering is a denial of the ultimate wholeness which God reveals, but it also plainly yearns for that wholeness through its very absence. This is the ambivalence of the human condition so acutely realized in the traditional societies of the Third World. The human being in continuity with his 'organic universe' is the synthesis of a material and a spiritual world, and a synthesis of good and evil. He stands at the intersection between the fulfilment and the diminution of life. Confronted with sickness and disability, we should not have to choose between stoicism or surrender. Surrender is an agnostic, fatalistic act. It is an act of despair that embraces the scandal but denies the scope of suffering. When we speak of stoicism, we do not refer merely to the classical philosophy of remaining indifferent to the pleasures or sufferings of the moment, but to the ideal of fidelity to one's own nature. Here again, it is insufficient to reduce the ideal to the 'ethic of reason' or to the medieval conception of 'natural law'. It is faith, implicit or explicit, which ultimately determines our understanding of reality and which offers meaning and therefore scope to sickness.

But there remains that nagging, second question: 'Why does suffering happen in the first place?' Evil cannot be justified by the good which is drawn out of it. Surely, prevention is better than cure? Why therefore does a good God permit suffering? How does one reconcile the violent death of a single child with the infinite goodness of God? When we try to answer these questions we tend to think only, or mainly, of instances of suffering which are dramatic or which evoke extremes of fear and compassion, and yet our whole human existence is permeated with suffering in one degree or another. Even when we narrow the concept of suffering down to sickness or disability it is far from easy to equate these concepts with the total experience of a lack of wholeness or a want of health. Creaturely existence necessarily includes the experience of growth and decay. As we grow older we not only experience a failure of bodily and mental powers, but we also become more susceptible to disease. It may be theoretically possible for us to die of old age, but in practice for most of us it is simply that, as we become older and weaker, the tide of illness cannot be held back. In the end, it is some latent or unexpected sickness that carries us off. Suffering is written into our human constitution.

The Buddhist position on suffering is eminently logical. At the root of suffering is craving or desire, therefore to eliminate suffering one must be released from all desire, whether for good or for evil. One must pass beyond joy and pain, good and evil, to the realm of no desire. Christians, on the contrary, do not, at all times and in all circumstances, seek to avoid suffering, because they discern a meaning and a purpose in suffering, as we have seen. In any case the Buddhist teaching does not, any more than the Christian, offer an explanation for the existence of suffering. Why not begin with, and remain in, *nirvana*? However, it has the merit of showing how deeply rooted in human nature suffering is.

Rationally, one can speculate about suffering and about sickness being inexorably bound up with the kind of world God wanted. A world of organic, sentient beings, possessing free will and the ability to determine their own destiny, perhaps cannot exist without the risk of natural disasters, disease, ageing and death, let alone the possibility of human wickedness. To that extent, we may probably inhabit 'the best of all possible worlds'. But there is no ultimate explanation of why God permits suffering and evil. Jesus, as we have already said, certainly did not offer one. At the level of explanations we cannot go beyond God's answer to Job which could be summed up un-Scripturally as: 'Who do you think you are anyway to ask the question?'[2] The suffering of the innocent is simply a mystery to be accepted, a fact which leaves the mind swinging, as it were.

We have already offered some partial answers to the question: 'How does the suffering caused by sickness and disability reveal the goodness of God?', or to use the words of Jesus, 'How does the suffering caused by sickness and disability allow the works of God to be displayed?' It does so by its yearning for wholeness. It does so by the faith which offers scope and meaning to sickness. It does so by the free offer of a final cure by God for all our ills and the installation of a new Earth or Kingdom in which suffering has no place. The definitive evil is the rejection of God's offer and the definitive suffering this causes is exclusion from the Kingdom, loss of eternal life. This is the true meaning of suffering. Sickness and disability are signs and symptoms of a sick world, a world heading for definitive suffering from which Jesus alone can save us. Careful, as always, not to say that the disease was the result of sin, Jesus told the cripple of Bethesda: 'Now you are well again, be sure not to sin any more, or something worse may happen to you'.[3]

It is obvious that the disability suffered by the young man in the Tanzanian village was a form of alienation, particularly a social alienation. Sickness is always in some sense an alienation. Alone in the big hospital, even on a sick-bed at home, one is removed from many or most of one's daily occupations and contacts. Social intercourse is rationed and there is a dramatic change of life-style. Unfamiliar surroundings, unpleasant medical tests and procedures, being placed in the hands of others, of strangers—these are all part of the alienation caused by sickness. The sick-bed, the hospital, is a prison. In the hospital there may be the further stress caused by the proximity of other sick people and the interplay of emotions within the hospital ward. Finally there is the anxiety which a serious illness causes in a patient and the diminished consciousness as a result of illness and/or drugs. When one is sick one is not oneself. One is alienated from oneself.

To be removed from the world of everyday life, from the normal structures and expectations that make up that world, is comparable to being in what Victor Turner has called 'the liminal situation'.[4] The concept of liminality is an elaboration by Turner of the middle phase in the initiation rite or rite of passage, as described by Arnold van Gennep.[5] We have already referred in this chapter to African initiation rites. It is a characteristic of these, as of all rites of passage, to display three steps or phases. The first is that of separation from a previous state or status, the last is that of incorporation in the new state or status, while the second or central step consists in being suspended in a 'limbo' of statuslessness. One pauses, as it were, on the threshold (*limen*) of the new status, belonging neither to the old nor to the new, experiencing a destitution and yet also a deep bond of inter-relatedness with one's fellow initiants. In this liminal condition which Turner compares to both tomb and womb, the initiant is moulded and formed by society. Through ascetical rituals and trials, through isolation and specialized instruction, society helps the individual to pass through a particular life-crisis, puberty, marriage itself, election to office, or passage into the ranks of elders or title-bearers. Turner sees the threshold period as one of great creative potency, even at times a deeply felt spiritual experience which has a continual function as regards the health and progress of society. So much so, that human beings re-create this experience of liminality artificially in other institutionalized ways.

The experience of sickness may have much in common with the liminal experience. To be removed from the world of everyday life may in fact help a person to stand back and view it better. For many people a long bout of sickness may be a positive experience. There have been scholars who have written their best works from a sick-bed. Forced to eschew all the detailed apparatus of scholarship and to concentrate on major insights and interpretations, they have produced works of synthesis which are more readable and more influential than their normal output. A lengthy sickness has also been the occasion of a moral conversion. The story of St Ignatius of Loyola is well known: his reading of the lives of the saints, the only reading matter at hand, and his personal reflection and self-examination arising from them. The wound he received at the siege of Pamplona was the start of his spiritual journey and of the history of the Society of Jesus. Some sick people, even people who are terminally ill, manage to accept their suffering with unbelievable sweetness and gentleness. Heroically, they try to conceal their sufferings from those who love them and do all in their power to make things easier for those who nurse them and care for them. For many older people in their last illness it seems that they have already glimpsed another world and that their sick-room is an antechamber to heaven itself. They feel that God is slowly taking them to himself. Very often a terminally ill person, especially a cancer patient, becomes not only a focus for prayer and concern in a given community, but also a point of reconciliation and a source of moral strength. People who go to visit such people in their illness find that it is they who are being consoled, they who are being helped, rather than the sick person.

Reaction to the experience of sickness and disability, therefore, is ambivalent. Sickness is the symptom of a world that is sick and 'the whole earth is our hospital'. Recognition of this fact through faith, implicit or explicit, allows some people to turn sickness to

advantage and to make it the basis for socially and morally
constructive action, regardless of whether a cure is likely to
follow. Often in the healing ministry it is noticed that a turning-
point comes for a sick person when he or she asks: 'Why do I need
this illness?' It is the acceptance of the fact of illness and of the
good that can come from illness which often places sick people
on the path to recovery. Anger, denial, rebellion, depression—
these are not helps but hindrances to healing.

All of which is not to say that God is responsible for illness. If
God were responsible for illness, then it would be sinful to try
and get better. In Old Testament times pestilence was thought to
be directly caused by God. In that curiously unsympathetic
picture of God conveyed by the story of David's census, the king
chose pestilence for his people, rather than famine or military
defeat, precisely because it was thought to be directly sent by
God and therefore more easily mitigated by an appeal to his
mercy.[6] Everything in David's day was attributed to God as
ultimate cause, even the crime which David himself had committed, that of holding the census in the first place and so usurping God's prerogative of giving increase to the nation. This idea
is an early form of the 'act of God'. Famine might be mitigated by
storing and sharing food supplies. Military defeat might be
avoided by military prowess, but there was nothing one could do
in the time of King David about pestilence.

We have already discussed the mystery of physical evil in the
world and its relation to faith in an infinitely good Creator. The
problem here is more perhaps that of sickness permitted by God
as a punishment for a specific sin. We have seen that Jesus did not
make a specific causal link between a given sickness or misfortune and the personal sin of the sufferer. However, he was also
careful not to deny the possibility of some kind of link. In Jesus'
teaching and in his healing ministry, sickness was seen as a
symptom of the world's sin and as a basis for further action,
especially for faith and moral conversion. Such a view includes
the invitation to examine one's conscience and to ask the question
already suggested above: 'Why did I need that sickness?' One
answer that may suggest itself is precisely that the sickness
was needed as a remedy for sin, as a warning perhaps or as a
requital.

There are also, of course, ways in which sin is directly related
to illness. Illness can be brought about by dissipation, by self-
indulgence, by addiction, by excesses of one kind or another, by

culpable negligence or imprudence, by neglect of oneself, by suicidal and self-destructive tendencies where these are morally culpable. Anger and the consciousness of guilt are known to trigger illness, and a frequent cause of sickness is a life-style that is characterized by impatience, superficiality and disorientation. Sin certainly plays its part in the havoc wrought by sickness, one's own sins and the sins of others. Congenital diseases may also be linked with human culpability, for example where sexually transmitted diseases are related to sexual promiscuity and affect the children that are born. Finally, there is the limitless area of mutilation, sickness and disability that is caused by human wickedness and collective selfishness, by war, pollution, radiation, risks taken by drivers of vehicles and other means of transport, reluctance to guarantee safety at work and so on. When Jesus told the paralytic: 'Your sins are forgiven', before healing him of his paralysis, it may have been more than a didactic purpose which prompted him to deal with the man's afflictions in this order.[7] Perhaps, he sensed that moral conversion was crucial to the man's physical recovery as well as being logically more important.

Jesus has called the world to a wholeness that is the pure positiveness of God. He is on our side, fighting against evil, relieving suffering, curing illness, reconciling people. His image of the good Samaritan is a self-portrait. This was the love he proclaimed. However, when it came to his own Passion, he embraced suffering without reserve. 'He saved others', said the priests and scribes, 'he cannot save himself. He is the King of Israel; let him come down from the cross now. . . .'[8] It was his ultimate power, the power of his kingship, that caused him to stay on the cross and not to attempt to save himself. It was his power-through-weakness that saved both himself and others. In the most literal sense possible the passion, death and resurrection of Jesus was a rite of passage, a test or trial that preceded his status-elevation as Christ and Lord. Jesus suffers with us. In him God draws near to the world of suffering to assume it and to transform it through a share in his own transformation. This is suffering's redemptive power.

Christ endured his passion in silence. The silence of the suffering Christ is strident in the Gospels, speaking volumes about his attitude to pain and humiliation. No complaint, no cringing plea for mercy, no recrimination, no threat of revenge—just silence. In him there was no surrender, either to bodily weakness or to mental despair. He did not surrender to death as a release from his sufferings, even though Pilate was surprised he had died so soon and the Passion accounts suggest that his actual death took place with a loud cry and with the voluntary offering of himself to his Father. In Christ's attitude to pain we see the true stoicism which gives it infinite scope, the entrusting of his life to God, the faith in, and obedience to, his Father's will. This is the ultimate generosity of God which makes human suffering creative and even redemptive.

The mystery of suffering is the mystery of a suffering God. If sickness is already a scandal, then this is a greater scandal by far, God suffering in the cause of humanity. Such an idea is repugnant, incomprehensible to the great monotheistic religions of Judaism and Islam with their emphasis on the omnipotence, the sublimity and the inaccessibility of God. The God who suffered would not be God. In deistic religious systems where the concept of God is deprived of religious reality, and in the religious philosophies which are based on the flight from suffering, the suffering God is also a scandal. The idea that God should freely subordinate himself to the law of suffering inherent in his own creation is an idea that is pre-eminently Christian, that is to say, deriving from God's self-revelation in Christ, and it is only in grasping this Christian paradox that scope for redemption can be discerned in suffering.

In the last chapter we noted that the spirituality of traditional ethnic religions in the Third World was essentially the feeling that human beings are at once the image or model, and an integral part, of the organic universe in whose rhythms and cycles they participate. In such religions, the transcendent enables humanity to understand itself as the synthesis of the organic universe, as portraying its ultimate meaning or wholeness by affirmation and denial. Humanity lives out this affirmation and this denial in its own experience. The created world communicates its meaning and holds out its hope of wholeness by this same means, this saying and unsaying. Such a spiritual attitude is relevant to a Christian understanding of sickness and disability.

On the one hand, the hope of wholeness is communicated by both growth and health as well as by the experience of alienation and diminution of life. On the other hand, God has entered into this process of communication through the life and person of his Son Jesus Christ. In assuming human nature and in accepting to live a human life and to die a human death, he has also taken upon himself the human synthesis of joy and pain, affirmation and denial, and has made it his own.

We began this chapter with the real-life story of a would-be suicide who found a cause for which to die. It was the difference between death conceived as an escape or a surrender and death seen as a sacrificial act—between death as a form of tempting God and death as a voluntary self-offering to God and to one's fellow human beings; between surrender and stoicism. This ambivalence towards death extends to all forms of pain, sickness or disability. The 'failed suicide' on the anonymous hospital bed in Kampala had a context of culture, a whole store of cultural resources in fact, upon which to draw. No doubt, he did draw upon them consciously or unconsciously in his discovery of a new rationale of life and death.

Christian healing in the Third World must also draw on these cultural resources if it is to be readily available. As this chapter has attempted to demonstrate, there is a parallel between the sublimation of pain and the practice of asceticism in the non-Christian societies of the Third World on the one hand, and the 'beyondness' which gives meaning to suffering in Christianity. Illness is a prelude to dying and the approach to dying has been included in this chapter's discussion. From dying, we now turn to the inexorable fact of death itself.

4

Sickness unto death

Imagine a vast and limitless cathedral, with dark columns and a vault of green. Such is the rain forest of Cameroun. I had been attending an ecumenical conference in Yaoundé, the capital, and now I and my fellow participants were setting out in a hired bus to visit a training college some sixty miles away. The road was an earth road, badly corrugated, and there was rain forest all the way. The road twisted through the trees, round deep ravines and gorges filled with foliage, climbing all the time. The whole journey took nearly three hours. Most of the way, the road was lined on either side by small houses, built without exception out of mud and wattle. A few of the houses had corrugated iron roofs, but most of the roofs were made of palm leaves.

In front of nearly every house, outside its front door in fact, stood a grave or group of graves. The opulence of their funerary architecture and sculpture was in marked contrast to the poverty of the owners' houses. Most of them were of white painted cement. There were crosses or headstones on each. Some had a small roof. Others had brightly coloured statues, vases of flowers or bottles and containers with offerings in them, placed on the grave itself. In several places, there was quite an extensive roadside graveyard and every now and then there was a wayside Madonna or cross. I had the impression of travelling through a vast cemetery. The graves continued endlessly until we were out of the forest and into the clearing occupied by the college which was the goal of our journey.

It was evident that in the forest the road was the only focus of life—and of death. I was reminded of Wole Soyinka's play *The Road* where it is both a symbol of on-going progress and a theatre of death.[1] The world, too, as a whole has this ambivalence. Earth is both a womb and a tomb for us. If it is true that the whole earth is our hospital, it is equally true that the whole earth is our cemetery. Physical life begins and ends in this world of ours, but the funerary art of the Cameroun people was evidence of faith in a life lived at another level. There was something both naïve and attractive about the ostentation of their graves and the simple offerings of food. There was no 'lumber-room' atmosphere about these graves, as there is in the great bric-à-brac cemeteries of the industrial west. These were effective memorials— sacramental links with the departed. People were proud of their dead and were at home with them. Living and dead shared the same compound.

Death being the ineluctable fact that it is, it is not surprising that cultural attitudes towards it are the slowest to change. What I saw in Cameroun was only a more striking example of an atti- tude common to every corner of the African continent. Every African newspaper I know contains memorial notices of the dead, and not only of the recently dead. Often these notices are commemorations of remote anniversaries. Nearly always there is a photograph and a caption such as: 'We can never forget you' or 'You are always in our hearts'. Sometimes the newspaper devotes two or more pages to these memorials. Memorials of the dead take different forms but they are an everyday fact of life in Africa. Graves, for example, play an important part in mourning rites, for anniversary celebrations and for the important rituals of 'calling the departed home', accommodating the spirit and rein- stating the deceased in a new role. Such rituals are an aid to emotional restitution of the bereaved, and they nourish a well- founded hope. Although, in Africa, the dead are a burden carried by the living, they are also a continuing consolation. Sometimes the metaphor of planting is borrowed from the practice of agri- culture to express this hope. The dead are 'planted'.

Mourning acts as a socially approved catharsis of grief and it is usually quite elaborate in the cultures of the Third World. In western, industrialized countries it is often felt that reference to death adds to the emotional distress of the bereaved. This playing down of the fact of death may help to encourage delusions in those who are grieving, particularly the numbness that refuses to accept the fact that a loved person has gone. Mourning rituals emphasize the fact of death and help the bereaved to assimilate the painful fact. Public recognition of death affirms the loss. Above all, religious beliefs and practices ensure a role for the mourner in the continued existence of the deceased. Even though the dead are believed to enjoy an entirely new kind of existence, religion establishes a bond between them and the living. The emphasis which one finds in the cultures of the Third World on a vital communion between living and dead certainly contributes to the restoration of emotional balance in the bereaved, to an extent that western uncertainties about death do not.

Death, however, poses the problem of cosmic ambivalence in its acutest form, whatever forms of self-deception we may practise in order to circumvent the thought of it. We asked, in the preceding chapter, how sickness could be a vehicle of wholeness. The paradox is even greater where death is concerned. Death is felt to be unjust, an unwarranted interference with individual development. How can death be a vehicle of life? The explanatory question is dealt with up to a point in the various mythologies. Death is attributed to a primeval fault, as it is in the Book of Genesis, or to a chance mistake of failing to recognize, for example, God's messenger of life and refusing to entertain him. But such aetiologies are in reality parables to enable the living to cope with the unexpected and to make the right moral choices, rather than offering satisfying explanations of death.

Death is a fact of experience to be confronted, rather than analysed and explained. In the western world there is much fear of death. Some would say fear of dying, rather than fear of death, and undoubtedly, for some people, dying is accompanied by considerable mental and physical pain. On the other hand, death may also be welcomed as the end of all sensation and as a release from suffering. Moreover, some of the dying appear to suffer hardly at all. Pain-killing drugs may ensure that suffering is reduced to a minimum and often in the ordinary course of events the dying person's diminished state of consciousness is the kindest drug possible. A human being, however, cannot conceive what it is like to be dead. Such a conception is a psychological impossibility and this dilemma may cause considerable emotional and mental anguish. The approaching dissolution of the human person as a subject of consciousness can be a distressing thought. Equally, anticipation of an afterlife described in terms of the presuppositions and experiences of the life one has known may be helpful. Doctors and psychologists seem to agree that religious believers derive great psychological benefit from the ministrations of a priest when they are on their deathbed, and such people are among the least anguished at the prospect of approaching death.

How can death be associated with wholeness? One approach is to conceive of death as a consummation of life. It is certainly the end of individual physical life, but it is also a summation or summing-up of that life. It is an important principle of individuation. In the early stages of the evolution of species, there was no death. Living cells simply coalesced into one another in the most elementary form of life possible. Obviously, if the amoeba is the only form of life, there can be no individuality. It was only when death intervened to distinguish one life from another that the individual living creature was born. There has to be a term to human life in order to evaluate it, even in order to comprehend it. Death and judgement are necessary concomitants of human individuality and autonomy. Among the recollections of people who have been resuscitated after 'clinical death' or who have been involved in near-fatal accidents, is that of seeing countless pictures of their past, sometimes a rapid survey of their whole life. This would seem to confirm the view of death as a summation.

On 5 August 1977 I myself had a reasonably close encounter with death. I was flying by an African airline from Nairobi to Dar-es-Salaam, a journey that normally takes about 50 minutes in a jet plane. My plane—which I learned afterwards had been requisitioned for troop carrying in one of Africa's petty wars— was six hours late. I was assigned to a front-row seat on the right-hand side of the plane with two young German volunteers beside me. Across the aisle sat an Italian who ran a bakery somewhere in Tanzania. There were several Chinese and East Germans on board, but few women and even fewer children. As we took off there was an audible hissing noise from the forward door which could not be closed because the rubber surrounding it had perished. One of the cabin staff plugged the cracks with a blanket and pillows. This was alarming enough but nothing compared with what was to follow. As we rose into the air there was the sound of a loud explosion and almost immediately a red warning-light in the ceiling began to flash ominously. The cabin staff were called into the cockpit and emerged a little while later with long faces. The plane gained no further altitude and the 'Fasten Seat-Belt' sign remained switched on.

The cabin crew then began taking away any hand-luggage that was on the floor between the seats and asking us to remove our shoes and spectacles. The Italian baker asked the reason for all these precautions and was told: 'We may have a landing problem'. (No public announcement had been made.) Shortly after this, a steward approached me and asked me to follow him up to one of the forward emergency doors. 'When we come down', he said impassively, 'I want you to slide down the chute and then hold it for the other passengers.' Without any reflection, I agreed. On regaining my seat, I was given a pillow against which to brace myself for impact.

In this position, I began to compose my thoughts. It was then that my 'review of life' occurred. I must have prayed for about ten minutes or a quarter of an hour, reviewing my past life, and trying to make a calm act of contrition in the face of death. I was amazed at my own calmness. We were not allowed to leave our seats, so I half-turned in order to give general absolution. 'If you have the dispositions, I absolve you from all your sins and censures in the name of. . . .' Then I turned to try and calm my neighbours. The Germans beside me were quite composed. The Italian baker, however, was becoming hysterical, crossing himself a thousand times and every now and then joining his hands like a child at prayer, mumbling incoherently. Behind me some Chinese in high-collared blue suits glared at everyone, especially the cabin crew. They seemed to represent a stolid insensibility bred of materialism freely chosen. Was mine an over-confident faith? Was the Italian's attitude a nervous post-Christian reflex and that of the Chinese a heroic atheism? Whatever the reaction, the value—the worth—of our lives was being tested at that moment.

Survival stories are always an anti-climax. Shortly afterwards, the pilot spoke to us, saying that he did not know the cause of the explosion, but that he intended to get rid of extra fuel, reduce speed and attempt a normal landing. The landing, when it came, was perfect and the passengers broke into spontaneous applause. We taxied towards the huge crowd of nurses, ambulance-men, first-aid men, stretcher-bearers, firemen, soldiers, police . . . whose presence was rendered unnecessary. As we emerged, there was more applause, and we were greeted like people snatched from the jaws of death, as indeed we were.

Experiences of this kind have a chastening effect. I had been given longer time to prepare for possible death than someone involved in an accidental fall or a split-second car crash. But my life up to that moment had been summed up. In my case there had been no emotional distress, no struggle, no anger or denial. My one overriding impression is one of amazement at my own calm acceptance of the prospect of death, a death which at the time seemed probable enough and which I could do nothing to avoid.

To view death as somehow appropriate and to approach it without fear is characteristic of traditional ethnic cultures in the Third World, particularly when the death in question is that of elderly people. In the traditional societies of Africa elders have high social status. Whether this state of things will endure may well be questioned in the light of present population trends. At the time of writing only some 30 per cent of the population of the continent is over the age of thirty. Perhaps it will continue, if only because old people will have a rarity value. The respect shown to old people in Africa is associated with the concept of social growth. These elders are people who have sired or borne many descendants. If they are polygamous, they have multiple marriage connections. The range of their social relationships is extensive and they may wield a far-ranging moral influence, if they do not actually enjoy political, administrative or judicial power.

When such successful people die their social growth takes a qualitative leap and, as spirits, they are credited with immediate knowledge of the thoughts, words and actions of their living descendants and relatives, and a power to bless or punish them in hidden and mysterious ways. There is little speculation about the present state of the spirits of the dead beyond a reference to the 'spirit-place' which usually carries overtones of aversion for their disembodied condition, although it recognizes very often that they are somehow 'at home' with God. On earth they are associated with their own place of burial and with living things, such as trees and streams which symbolize immortality. Apart from concepts of reincarnation which we shall consider later in this chapter, the spirits of the dead may enter permanently or temporarily into living human beings through spirit-possession. It is a popular inaccuracy to refer to these African spirits as 'ancestors', although they may not literally be ancestral to those who revere them, and although the vernacular terms by which they are known cannot, in fact, be translated as 'ancestor'.

Where these spirits enjoyed territorial power during their lives, they may be thought to occupy a special position in traditional theologies. Sometimes they appear as plenipotentiaries of God himself. Sometimes their role is more in the nature of intercessors, like the saints of the Catholic Church. In certain religious systems they rival God as virtually autonomous divinities, holding sway over particular aspects of human experience. In such cases they cease altogether to be 'ancestors' or family-spirits and enjoy a cult from worshippers in free association.

When death is viewed as inappropriate and untimely, spirits are placed in a category of unfortunates. Their ancestral character is irrelevant to the misfortune they have suffered. They may have died unmarried or childless, or they may have died in tragic circumstances such as murder or suicide or have been struck by lightning. They may include the spirits of deformed persons or of babies whose top teeth grow first. Or they may simply include any individual identified as such by a diviner who has examined the circumstances of death and consulted the oracle. These spirits of the dead may be regarded as wholly malevolent, revenging themselves on society for their own misfortune.

The concept of social growth goes much of the way towards seeing death in a positive light, but it is not proof against all possibilities. As it is worked out in Africa, it is not a primarily moral concept, although the elders may be credited with moral riches along with mental wisdom and an accumulation of relationships and experiences. It cannot cater for those whose deaths—by these criteria—are held to be untimely, the unfortunates whose case we have just been considering. Nor does it cope with senile dementia and with the physical and emotional distress of the elderly. Perhaps this is because the elderly are so few in Africa and the expectation of life so relatively low. A positive view of death must see it as timely and appropriate in every case, according to the will of an infinitely good God, even if we ourselves cannot comprehend a particular death.

One way of realizing a positive view of death is survival in one's descendants. Death is transcended, according to this idea, through human generation, and such a notion is common in the traditional societies of the Third World. Such societies are labour-intensive and social and economic importance is attached to having a large progeny. Children are wealth, and failure to have children of one's own is the greatest misfortune possible. It may be for that reason that death is sometimes seen as a form of rebirth. The Kimbu people of south-western Tanzania have this idea. The grave is orientated in such a way that the feet of the corpse point in the direction of his or her birthplace. In this way the dead person finds it easier to walk back there as a spirit. Death is a return to the origin of life and that origin is identified by the Kimbu as God, the Life-Giver. For them, God is the ultimate ancestral spirit, the ultimate parent or begetter. The idea of death as birth-in-reverse may owe something to the concepts which characterize initiation rituals. Certainly death is usually viewed as a rite of passage. Without any clear doctrine of resurrection, death can be seen as a rebirth to a new state of life, even if ideas about this state are shadowy. At any rate, the idea of death as rebirth is linked in many minds with the actual birth of descendants. Immortality is somehow conditional on the continuation of one's line.

Not everybody can have children and it is obvious that a more spiritual understanding of fecundity is necessary if death is to be wholly transcended in this manner. Immortality cannot be simply a vital power, a commodity to be augmented by subsequent births, nor can it crudely depend on 'feeding' through offerings made by interested descendants. At least, such ideas prove unsatisfying in practice. This may be why reincarnation in one form or another is attractive to many people and plays such an important part in the beliefs of non-western religious traditions. There are many varieties and gradations in reincarnation beliefs. There is the Hindu-Buddhist belief in a literal reincarnation, in which people when they die take on the life of another human being or even of a non-human living creature, according to their deserts in life. The Buddhist pursuit of enlightenment is, at least in part, an attempt to escape from the endless cycle of rebirths.

In the African continent, reincarnation is usually human reincarnation, although evil people such as sorcerers and witches may be thought to be able to enter into other living creatures and take their forms permanently or temporarily in order to harass or molest their enemies. The expectation of those who believe in literal reincarnation is usually that the circumstances of life will improve with rebirth. This is expressed in a prayer from the Edo people of Nigeria:

When you come back, may you once again bring a good body with you.
Money, health, all the things that are used in living, you must bring with you.
. . .
When you come again may sickness not send you back.
May you not suffer the diseases of this world in your next incarnation.
Great Man, you will come back![2]

Further along the spectrum lies the concept found among the Akan peoples of Ghana, that of a life-soul or essence of the soul, the *kra*, which is successively reborn in different generations, and which has the opportunity of being purified and re-purified.

However, most African peoples seem content with a more or less nominal reincarnation or pro-existence. According to this belief, ancestral spirits and the members of their families still alive in this world exist for and on behalf of each other. The spirits guard and protect their offspring. They ensure that they receive their full share of the good things of this life. They remove sickness and danger of death. The living, for their part, ensure that the work of the spirits continues. They imitate their way of life. They invoke them as guardians and companions. They recognize their ultimate authority and ownership, by offering them first-fruits of harvest and hunt, offerings and libations at meal-times or in formal prayer at gravesides and shrines. The spirits of the dead are somehow in need. They need to be remembered and their names perpetuated. They are especially interested in vital events, such as the birth or marriage of their descendants. Choosing the right name, therefore, and commemorating the right spirit can be very important. The spirits, too, must be given their share in the ritual feasts. They are also on hand to receive into their company the newly deceased members of the family. In this way living and dead help each other and cater for each other's socio-spiritual needs. The world is seen to be a theatre of action for both living and dead.

There is no doubt whatever that such ideas may appeal to the secularized Christian of the western, North Atlantic world. They may also stimulate faith in a real reciprocity between living and dead so long as it is compatible with Christian doctrine, and they may also assist the bereaved to adjust to life without the loved person who has died. But there are also limitations and pitfalls. Literal reincarnation is definitely incompatible with Christian tradition. It also appears to establish an endless reign of death. One is reborn in order to die once more. The Buddhist dissatisfaction with the doctrine is understandable. The idea of pro-existence or living on behalf of the dead can also establish a universal reign of death, to the extent that interest in the dead is focused on life in this world, and the dead remain a burden to the living. There is no prayer for the salvation of the dead and no belief in a definitive liberation from suffering and death. There is always the tendency to appease the departed spirits and to fear their anger and ill-will. One does not attribute to them the joyful and everlasting companionship of the saints in the glory of the Risen Christ. Nevertheless, the healing of bereavement, as we have seen, may depend on the bereaved having a role to play in

the continued existence of the departed. The African contribution is perhaps the assurance that the departed also have a role to
play in the present existence of the living.

The healing of bereavement and of human fears about death,
which is certainly an important area of healing and a necessary
part of an integrated approach to healing, depends on this positive view of death that we have been seeking. It is sometimes
assumed that a positive view of death entails a negative view of
life. Of course, this may be true of the suicide who, to some
extent, is in love with death. John Hinton quotes from the final
letter of a Japanese kamikaze pilot:

I have been given a splendid opportunity to die. This is my last day. The destiny
of our homeland hinges on the decisive battle in the seas to the south where I
shall fall like a blossom from a radiant cherry tree.[3]

Such ecstatic faith based on uncritical nationalism can perhaps
only be achieved under special conditions of enthusiasm for a
cause deemed to be greater than the worth of a human life. In the
war between Iran and Iraq which began in 1980, we have witnessed a similar enthusiasm for martyrdom on the Iranian side.
Christians are under the obligation of choosing death rather than
to deny their faith, and—apart from the Crusades of medieval
Europe which were not uninfluenced by the Islamic *jihad*—
Christian martyrdom is, as it were, 'pacifist'. One is not allowed
to court death presumptuously by aggressive provocation or
attempted suicide. But even Christian martyrdom only
flourishes in ages and situations where people are mistakenly
prepared to take human life for religious reasons and where that
life is—in any case—held cheap, where religious faith is not only
important enough to die for, but also important enough to kill
for. A positive view of death does not depend today on expectations of martyrdom, even though religious intolerance is still
with us on this earth.

The positive view of death depends basically on a faith that
death is somehow transcended in this life. It cannot rely on a
mere postponement of rewards and punishments, a relegation to
the Last Judgement of the solutions to all our problems of living
and dying. Fear of the Judgement, in any case, may encourage a
very negative attitude to death in highly religious people. The
Christian view is that eternal life begins already here and now,
that we are already enjoying a life that is impervious to physical
death. We are already beginning to experience something of that

future wholeness, that ultimate reality which is to be revealed. If we can live this new life to the full, death will only be an advantage, the removal of an obstacle to complete fulfilment. St Paul was unable to choose between life and death. His continued life would be of service to others, but his death would bring him the goal he was seeking.

Life to me, of course, is Christ, but then death would bring me something more; but then again, if living in this body means doing work which is having good results—I do not know what I should choose. I am caught in this dilemma: I want to be gone and be with Christ, which would be very much the better, but for me to stay alive is a more urgent need for your sake.[4]

We are full of confidence, I say, and actually want to be exiled from the body and make our home with the Lord.[5]

Paul did not think he was perfect. He knew he was being judged in this life already, and he did not speak as if there would be any temporal gap between his death and his making his home with the Lord.

The source of such confident faith is the resurrection of Jesus Christ. This is an eschatological event, at one with his death, but revealed through real experiences, eschatological encounters of the apostles with the Risen Christ, and experienced again in the act of faith of every Christian. The resurrection was the transformation of Christ's humanity that allowed him to transcend the limits of his own lifetime, his own culture, his own nationality and homeland—his own death, and to share his new existence with others. The resurrection is experienced as a power in people's lives. As such, it not only removes the fear of death for ourselves and the grief at the death of others, it permits us to welcome death as a means of sharing in Christ's victory and of bringing salvation to the world.

All I want is to know Christ and the power of his resurrection and to share his sufferings by reproducing the pattern of his death. That is the way I can hope to take my place in the resurrection of the dead. Not that I have become perfect yet: I have not yet won, but I am still running, trying to capture the prize for which Christ Jesus captured me.[6]

The Christian act of faith enables us to know this power, because it is a response to God's self-disclosure in the Risen Christ. It is a personal relationship in which we place ourselves in total submission to God's self-gift. This gift activates our own self-realization, our own liberation.

The resurrection of Christ also explains and articulates our relationship to the departed. Any view of ultimate wholeness, any vision of the future, must offer a place to those who have already suffered, those who have already died. Otherwise, the dead will, in the words of Abraham Lincoln at Gettysburg, have 'died in vain'. While, on our side, we can help the dead achieve their purification-in-death, their judgement and requital, through prayer, they, through the communion of saints and through their place in the resurrection, can plead for us as companions of the risen Christ. This is the true reciprocity of living and dead.

Death remains, however, the darkest of mysteries, even if it is not to be called the 'last and the worst insult' done to a human being. Like all suffering, the prospect of death is to be accepted in the humility of repentance for sin. There is no doubt that our death is deserved as punishment, while being timely and appropriate in God's plan for our salvation. Death is a darkness we cannot escape.

O dark, dark, dark. They all go into the dark,
The vacant interstellar spaces, the vacant into the vacant,
The captains, merchant bankers, eminent men of letters,
The generous patrons of art, the statesmen and the rulers,
. . . all go into the dark.[7]

But the poet accepts the dark, as ultimately we all have to:

I said to my soul, be still, and let the dark come upon you
Which shall be the darkness of God.[8]

Death is dark, but it is the darkness of God. Our approach to death is one of risk, but it is the risk born of faith, hope and love.

5

Sickness and society

During the course of some twenty years' experience as a missionary I have had contact with thirteen large hospitals run by missions or governments, and I have been admitted as a patient to
four of them. In one case I spent two full months on an African
hospital bed. There are both similarities and differences between
the western hospital and the hospital in the Third World. On the
one hand, the latter often has beautiful modern buildings and
equipment and the familiar antiseptic smell in the wards and
corridors, white-uniformed staff and quite often pleasant
grounds and surroundings. On the other hand, one soon notices
that facilities are inadequate. If there is not actually more than one
patient in a bed, one may find patients for whom there is no bed,
sleeping on mats and mattresses on the floor of the ward. Then
there is a group of relatives surrounding the bedside, camping in
the ward and probably more relatives on the grass outside the
window with a cooking-stove and some baskets of food. In
many of these hospitals the staff do not provide meals for most of
the patients and it is up to the patients' families to cook their food
for them. The sick are usually far from lonely in their illness.
Embarrassing though their presence may sometimes be to the
hospital staff, the relatives help to care for the sick and to offer
them moral support in alien surroundings.

When Africans are sick, they usually do not want to be left
alone. Sickness is a social concern and the sick are a focus of
solicitude on the part of their family and immediate community.
In 1978, when I was on the staff of a large theological seminary in
Tanzania, I fell ill with a bad attack of malaria lasting a full eight
days. During that time all the African staff and virtually all two
hundred students called on me in my sick-room, hanging around
and murmuring the Swahili condolence *ugua pole*—'sympathy in
your sickness'. The room was continually full of people, with
people even sitting on the bed, although I was in no condition to
be social. It was touching but it was tiring.

Often in the cultures of the Third World it is implied that sickness has both social causes and social consequences. The disorder of the body has implications for social order and disorder. In this it resembles bereavement. Sick people are temporarily removed from their ordinary social life, from their family and their work. Obviously, these implications vary according to different social levels and different stages of what we have called social growth. A mother may be very much affected by the sickness of her baby, especially if the condition is difficult to diagnose or if it persists. However, fewer people are affected socially by the illness of a baby than by the illness, say, of the family breadwinner, or the illness of a teacher or business director. Other people are socially diminished by the absence of such a person. Workmates, husband, wife, mother, all may be affected, and their anxiety may have repercussions on the sick people themselves.

Physical sickness may also be aggravated or alleviated by social factors. Quite apart from accusations of sorcery, witchcraft or poisoning, with which we shall deal in later chapters, quarrels and unhappy relationships, failure and lack of fulfilment, all of these situations can affect physical health. We have already spoken in Chapter 3 about the possibility of people willing themselves to die, especially when their social personality has been destroyed and they believe themselves to be the object of occult and malevolent influences.

Scientific medicine has achieved a great deal in the treatment of acute conditions and sudden infections, in surgical emergencies requiring immediate operations and in the dangerous diseases of infancy and childhood. In the western world very few diseases, as Dr Una Maclean observes, are allowed to run their 'natural course'.[1] But severe conditions are only a tiny minority of the cases brought before a doctor in day-to-day practice. Western doctors rely mainly on drugs to alleviate minor infections, digestive disturbances or seasonal symptoms of pain, such as rheumatism. They display a scientifically detached and objective attitude to the patient's problem. Such an attitude has been encouraged by their own training in clinical medicine and surgery. Until fairly recently they were not interested in the social dynamics of the patient's family or basic community. Living as they do in a pluralistic society, they do not always feel professionally competent to answer the interpretative questions which the patient may be asking. In the cultures of the Third

World the dynamics of social relationships have always been considered to play an important part in a sick person's recovery. Not only are relatives and friends gathered around the bedside to reassure the patient, but final recovery from, or continuous resistance to, disease may be thought to depend upon the patient's joining a therapeutic community or community of affliction.

For the witchdoctor, or traditional healer-diviner, the illness behaviour of patients and the social implications of their condition are of paramount importance. The traditional doctor carries out a diagnostic interview in which actual physical examination plays a quite insignificant part. Much more important are the questions put to the sufferers.[2] These may concern their relationships with their family and business associates. Has the illness followed upon a quarrel? What are the patients' expectations and future plans? Were they preparing to go on a journey? Did they have a new business venture in the pipeline? How has their illness affected these plans and future relationships? Maybe the patients' social relationships and anxieties are reflected in the subconscious, so questions are asked about dreams. If patients have had no apparently relevant dreams, they may be given a drug to help them have dreams. Although herbal cures and remedies may be prescribed, an equally important therapeutic role may be given to forgiveness and reconciliation, or to the right performance of duties in family or society.

This is rather different from the procedure of western doctors with their concentration on the physical body and their scientific approach to illness. It is easy to understand how alien and frightening a hospital can be for someone who is used to the homely surroundings of a diviner's homestead. Teaching hospitals can be especially frightening, when doctors and their white-coated pupils are gathered round the sick-bed to discuss a 'case'. In the countries of Europe the figure of the 'family doctor' and even that of the rural, general practitioner is disappearing, replaced by the less homely but more efficient medical centre. Family doctors were social figures, involved in the public discussion of social issues and carrying other responsibilities in their community which were not directly connected with their profession. Their social accomplishments went considerably further than that of a successful bedside manner. Advanced medical treatment and specialization seems now to preclude such homeliness and social involvement.

Scientific medical practice in the Third World has perhaps gone further in the direction of social medicine than in the countries of Europe and North America. Very often a large regional hospital is the pivot upon which turns a whole programme of preventive medicine and health care. The churches are often heavily committed to primary health care projects, to the running of clinics, teaching child-care, setting up nutrition programmes, educating people in basic hygiene, ensuring a safe water supply and so on. Much of this work entails educating or re-educating society, getting people to take collective decisions and to take part in the projects. Basic community-building which is an ecclesial policy in many parts of the Third World is playing an increasing role in stabilizing relationships, giving support to the sick and helping them to get to hospital in emergencies.

Social deprivation is not only a cause of emotional distress and of physical disorders, it can also be said to *be* a sickness in itself. In a strongly communitarian village community, with clearly defined bounds for who is, and who is not of the community, competition for leadership or for a specific status-role may be acute. The inability to obey social norms and expectations in a village community and the situation of having an ill-defined social status are conditions which cry out for healing. Equally so, in the urban situation, are the inability to achieve, the frustrations of endless and unsuccessful job-seeking, of failing to set up one's own survival-network, being an outcast or a member of the unwanted, 'surplus' population of the shanty-towns, having a disability which renders employment impossible—all these factors are causes of social deprivation in which people need to restore or renew their social personality. School-leavers in Third World countries, like their counterparts elsewhere, are one class of people who frequently suffer from social deprivation. Their anxieties about getting employment and the shame they feel in their enforced idleness give them headaches and cause them sleeplessness. In fact, the psycho-somatic problems of young people, particularly in Africa where as many as 70 per cent are under the age of thirty, are certainly associated with their social disorientation and instability. There is a crying need to help all these people come to terms with their social situation, as well as to help society come to terms with them. Such people need to define their social status at a time of change and uncertainty, and they deserve a great measure of support from those who undertake the ministry of healing.

If the physical body is constrained up to a point by the categories and imperatives of social life, it is equally true that human society is very frequently conceived and described in terms derived from the human body.[3] The human body offers humanity a residual symbolism that is universally employed in every culture known to history. Society is said to be a 'body', or to have numerous 'bodies'. Or it is compared to an animal 'organism'. It is said to have a 'head' and 'members'. It is described in terms of age and health. There are 'young' and 'vigorous' nations, as well as 'old' and 'declining' ones. Society speaks with a 'voice', and it may even be credited with a 'mind' or a 'soul' and very often—in sociological parlance—with 'social sentiments'. There are limitations in the usefulness of this metaphor, as the late Sir E. Evans-Pritchard pointed out.[4] Organic changes in animals, for example, are nothing like as drastic as the structural and organizational changes of society. Moreover, there is the illusion of what J. H. M. Beattie has called 'misplaced concreteness', of alluding to society as if it really was an autonomous subject of activity in its own right.[5]

However, there is sufficient interchange of symbolism between human body and body politic to suppose a real interaction of fact. In the rites of passage which we have already mentioned several times, symbols borrowed from the experience of death and of childbirth are used to express the separation from one social status and the entry into another. Everywhere in the traditional societies of the Third World, the symbolism of family relationships is used in order to express socio-political leadership or the relationship of social groups to one another. It is not surprising, therefore, that periods of extensive social change or disorientation should be compared, and even related, to human bodily sickness.

One of the earliest novels written by an African in the English language described the state of shock and alienation experienced by a West African village society at the time of the white man's coming. Chinua Achebe chose as title for his tragedy a phrase from W. B. Yeats: *Things Fall Apart.*[6]

Things fall apart; the centre cannot hold;
Mere anarchy is loosed upon the world.

This phrase has entered into the vocabulary of anglophone Africa. It represents the social disorientation and moral breakdown which is the legacy of the colonial experience, the sense of hurt and bewilderment, of anger with an unjust world. Africa is experiencing the effects of sweeping organizational change and its people are finding it difficult to comprehend, let alone to cope with this experience. 'Things fall apart' is recognizable as the theme, or at least the background, of much recent creative writing from Africa.

Victor Turner has suggested that human societies, like human individuals, also have their life-crises and that there are 'liminal' periods of history, as there are liminal moments in the lives of individuals, moments which are made explicit in the rites of passage.[7] Society is emerging from one well-defined, traditional form into an altogether new and unfamiliar form. In the meantime, during the period of incipient change, there is a great deal of tension and frustration. People are searching for ways to cope with a new experience. They borrow ideas from their cultural tradition and give them modern application. They turn to neighbouring cultures for extraneous images to express the unfamiliar. They are innovative and syncretist, bringing forth 'treasures old and new'. This is the liminal period of social history, when new redressive and liminal rituals come into existence, and society celebrates not the rites of passage of its own members, but a rite of passage for itself.

In such a situation of baffling social upheaval, society itself appears to be sick and the sick member of society becomes a social paradigm. It may even be that new diseases—the diseases of civilization perhaps—are also seen to typify the unintelligible social experience. Certainly in the communities of affliction, or clubs for sick people, in which alien spirits are manipulated as part of the cure, people are ready to admit the existence of hitherto unknown diseases, symptoms of body pain, hysteria, mental dissociation and other phenomena which express the state of social disintegration. Perhaps these are symptoms of understandable neuroses. Perhaps they are indicative of a deeper social malaise, a more implacable sickness of society, an experience of mass paranoia. The sick individual is burdened with this disease of society, and becomes the scapegoat or carrier. This is an ancient African concept and one which Wole Soyinka made the theme of his inspiring play *The Strong Breed*.[8] In the modern community of affliction, sick people are not usually sacrificed or punished, but their sickness is viewed as being inseparable from a condition afflicting society as a whole, and in treating them, the community is carrying out a social therapy. The community becomes a therapeutic one in which the members act as healers to each other. The restoration of social harmony and wholeness is an object of communal concern and the rituals that are used are a celebration of social healing.

Traditional healing in Africa includes the social dimension, and the restoration of social harmony is the goal of a great deal of social medicine. There are many rituals of redress in which the sickness of an individual is linked with a communal experience of misfortune, a famine, a drought, a crop or cattle disease. Quite apart from cases associated with physical sickness, there are also mechanisms of social reconciliation operating at every social level. During my fieldwork in south-west Tanzania I witnessed a reconciliation between neighbours. I was staying with the local chief who, on a given day, attended a village beer party, along with a life-long friend and right-hand man of almost the same advanced age. The chief's younger son was also at the party and, after becoming drunk, allowed one of his host's dogs to lap some beer from his beer-bowl. The boy angrily cursed his host *and* the dog and entered into a hot dispute with his father's friend. At the height of this dispute, he cursed the friend obscenely, to the horror of all those present. This was the height of impropriety for a young man, and two days later when everyone had recovered from the effects of the party, the incident was coolly discussed by all the persons concerned. The hearing took place at the chief's homestead, and injured feelings were soothed when the youth apologized and agreed to pay a chicken in compensation.

Later in that same year, 1970, I witnessed another reconciliation at a higher, territorial level. This was in Ghana on the other side of the continent, where I was visiting the new Bishop of Kumasi, Mgr Peter Akwasi Sarpong. The Bishop was in the midst of a congratulatory progress through his diocese and I had caught up with him at the gold-mining town of Obuasi. The Bishop wished to go to a small, neighbouring town called Fomena where there had been a dispute between the Chief and his Queen Mother. I travelled with the Bishop, who was in choir dress, in the episcopal Mercedes. At the outskirts of the town men were waiting with shotguns ready to fire off joyful, warning volleys. The car stopped and the procession formed. I walked with the Bishop under his immense umbrella of blue and gold silk. This was carried in relays by men who twirled it and made it go up and down as we walked. A huge crowd swarmed around singing a joyful song with a 'hosanna' refrain. Children were carrying baskets of loaves and fruit on their heads. In fact there was a Palm Sunday atmosphere as the procession flowed like a gentle tidal wave down the main street of the town.

The Chief and his retinue (though not the Queen Mother) were drawn up in the main square, outside the government offices. They were handsome men, clad in their colourful *kente* togas, and seated under a variety of colourful umbrellas. Our party first queued up to shake hands with the seated elders. We then sat down under our umbrella on the other side of the square and the Chief and his retinue came in file to shake our hands. After they had returned to their umbrellas, an exchange of greetings took place through linguists or spokesmen who carried gold-plated staves. The Bishop whispered messages to his spokesman who shouted them across the square, while the Chief did the same through his spokesman. It is the custom to communicate indirectly with great persons in Africa, hence the complication of two great men communicating on a public occasion such as this. When the exchange was over, Bishop and Chief each half rose from his seat with right hand raised in salute. Once more there was a mutual shaking of hands and then the Chief and his retinue joined the Bishop's procession to the field where an altar had been erected for Mass and thatched shelters for the congregation. The Queen Mother was waiting with attendant ladies under one of the shelters, and the Bishop went up and shook hands with her.

After Mass, there were speeches and songs. Great stress was laid on Mgr Sarpong being the first Ashanti Bishop and he was asked several times to arbitrate in the dispute between the Chief and the Queen Mother. At length the Bishop responded. He said that he would undertake the arbitration of the dispute. He was of their very clan, he said. The Queen Mother was his 'mother' and the Chief was his 'brother'. The applause was deafening and more singing accompanied the Bishop to the rest-house where he was to spend the night, while gifts in their hundreds continued to arrive, a goat, chickens, eggs, yams, crates of beer and Coca-Cola and many other assorted things. This had been reconciliation on a grand scale, appropriate, too, in that the setting had been a Eucharistic celebration by a new Ashanti Bishop. It is significant that the traditional conciliatory assembly and communion feast was made the model for the inculturated Cameroun

Mass at Ndzon Melen by Fathers P.-C. Ngumu and P. Abega.[9] We shall refer to these precedents later in the book, when we consider the aspect of social healing which is inherent in the celebration of the Christian sacraments.

In the rural societies of the Third World disputes end, not in the punishment of convicted offenders, but in social reconciliation. Apart from cases where the culprit is caught red-handed and punished violently on the spot, it is usual to settle a case by compensation when tempers have cooled. Customs, such as the blood-feud, may of course reinforce the demand for compensation, especially in cases of murder or bloodshed. Nobody wants war, and usually compensation is agreed upon and the guilty person is allowed to settle down again to a normal life as if nothing had happened. It is easy to see why such a method of dealing with offenders should be favoured. Prisons and imprisonment were unknown in these traditional societies, being an idea that developed in the western world and one which was imposed on Third World countries during the colonial period. Traditional societies could not have maintained a prison system, even if they had wished to do so, since it belongs to a different economic level of living. However, although prison food and lodging may be superior to local standards, it is often felt that to deprive people of their freedom is intolerable, quite apart from the mental cruelty of prison anonymity, lack of privacy, random body searches and so on. Coupled with the fact that prisons are very often 'schools of crime', rather than places of remedial education, one can see the advantages of a public acknowledgement of guilt, followed by compensation and the integration of offenders into normal life without any stigma attaching to them. Odd though it may also sound to our western, humanitarian ears, one can sympathize even with the opinion that a punishment of the body, such as a brief flogging or a heavy, but limited, manual task, is preferable to the harm which a long term of imprisonment can do to the mind and morals of a criminal. These are some of the reasons why social reconciliation is preferred in the traditional world of the rural village to relentless or retributive punishment, and why mechanisms of social reconciliation exist at the different levels of society. Whether it is a quarrel between neighbours at a beer-party or a deep-seated dispute among chiefs, or even if it is a violent anti-social act by a criminal, society must be healed, rather than the offenders punished.

It is characteristic of religious systems to introduce a unifying dimension into life, a sense of divine order or, as Clifford Geertz called it in a famous definition, 'a general order of existence'.[10] It is this perspective that underlies the concept of what we have referred to as the 'organic universe', the idea that the material world in which we live shares in our human destiny and vice versa, and that this destiny is ultimately divine. This is why people of every culture have felt that there has to be a religious dimension to the restoration of social harmony and wholeness, whether it is caused or exemplified by either sickness or crime. The religious reconciliation ritual, and especially the communion sacrifice, accompanies the re-establishment of harmony at the ordinary human level of relationships. It sets a divine seal, as it were, on human peace-making and it also brings about a reconciliation between the human and the divine levels.

The notion of sacrifice certainly cannot be exhausted through explanatory comparisons with human gift-giving, but there are many types of sacrifice, particularly gift-oblations, which are analogous to the human institution of the gift. The gift is a remarkable social phenomenon, found in every human culture, which not only symbolizes a relationship between individuals and groups, but actually helps to bring such relationships into existence or to consolidate those already existing. A gift signifies the giver. It is a part of the giver as it were, placed in the hands of the receiver. The receiver, conversely, is obligated by the gift, placed in the giver's debt. Gifts have the peculiar power of creating what they signify. Refusal of a gift is the refusal of a relationship, perhaps a declaration of war. The symbolism of the gift is especially powerful when it concerns food and drink, the ritual feast, by which giver and receiver nourish their life-processes by the same means.

The transposition of such human customs on to the religious plane, as a sign of relationship between divine reality and humanity, poses a number of problems. One cannot, in fact, give gifts to God, if everything is first of all his gift. What we give him is therefore a 'giving back', a recognition that he is the creator and master of all things. Everything is his and we also are his as we try to express it through our gift-oblation. Where parties to a dispute share in the same sacrifice, or offer alternate sacrifice, the element of mutual human belonging or reconciliation also enters in. The following example given by Evans-Pritchard in his account of the religion of the Nuer of Sudan contains elements both of social and of bodily healing.

A youth had been injured by a spear-thrust in a fight with a man of the next village. This man and his fellows who had been the attackers offered sacrifice first of all to be reconciled with their neighbours whose son had been injured. It was then the turn of the home party to immolate a castrated ram. This was consecrated by rubbing ashes on its back and then a libation was poured over its tethering peg before the invocation and sacrifice. In the prayer which Evans-Pritchard quotes, the sacrificial ram is referred to as a ransom.

Friend, God, who is in this village
As you are very great,
We tell you about this wound,
For you are God of our home in very truth.
We tell you about the fight of this lad,
Let the wound heal,
Let it be ransomed. [11]

Human disharmony yearns to be ransomed, in a final, total reconciliation or redemption. Even human social healing requires divine intervention and this experience of human inadequacy makes us yearn for the definitive redemption. The redemption which Christians believe was achieved for the human race by Jesus Christ is far from being merely a pardoning of individual sin. It is a reconciliation with one another in God. That is why fraternal love was Christ's new commandment and why mutual forgiveness plays such an important part in his teaching. We must love one another 'as I have loved you'[12] and forgive each brother from the heart as our heavenly Father forgives us.[13] 'If you forgive others their failings, your heavenly Father will forgive you yours.'[14]

In the Pauline writings there is no social barrier, no hostility, which is impervious to the reconciliation brought by Christ. Many times St Paul announces that in Christ there are no more invidious distinctions between Jew and Gentile, between the various nations themselves, between slave and free or between male and female. Christ is the ransom. He is the peace. Speaking of Jews and pagans, Paul says:

But now in Christ Jesus, you that used to be so far apart from us have been brought very close, by the blood of Christ. For he is the peace between us, and has made the two into one and broken down the barrier which used to keep them apart, actually destroying in his own person the hostility caused by the rules and decrees of the Law. This was to create one single New Man in himself out of the two of them and by restoring peace through the cross, to unite them both in a single Body and reconcile them with God. In his own person he killed the hostility.[15]

The Christian, according to Paul's teaching, is called upon to continue Christ's work of reconciliation and to be an 'ambassador' of that reconciliation, a fellow worker with Christ in God's work of world restoration.

It is all God's work. It was God who reconciled us to himself through Christ and gave us the work of handing on this reconciliation. In other words, God in Christ was reconciling the world to himself, not holding men's faults against them, and he has entrusted to us the news that they are reconciled. So we are ambassadors for Christ; it is as though God were appealing through us, and the appeal that we make in Christ's name is: be reconciled to God.[16]

Social healing takes several forms, as we have seen. There is the social dimension of physical sickness, its social causes and consequences. There is the healing of social deprivation. There is the problem of a sick society, a society unable to comprehend the changes of structure and scale to which it is being subjected; and there is the need for reconciliation after anti-social activity. There is also the need for social reconciliation in situations of class conflict. We shall deal with the concepts of liberation and social sin in Chapter 7, but inevitably anti-social activity raises questions of morality as well as of practical disharmony. In and beyond all these levels of social healing lies the social healing wrought by Christ and the reconciliation between humanity and God which is the indispensable basis for any and every restoration of social harmony.

6

Psychiatric and emotional disorders

Emmanuele was an athletic youth just out of his teens. In 1971 I was teaching in Uganda and my office faced an inlet of Lake Victoria known as Murchison Gulf. Between my windows and the lake were lawns, flower-beds and a football pitch on which Emmanuele was frequently to be seen practising in a bright red tracksuit. Sometimes, driving back from Kampala, I would pass him jogging on the road. Although he lived in the village in which our institute was situated, I had hardly talked with Emmanuele. On one occasion, when we did exchange a few words outside my office, he told me he had been offered a scholarship to study in the United States by the Greek Orthodox Church. He seemed the usual frustrated African youth, dreaming the impossible dream of throwing off the straitjacket of his birth, nationality and social position. I also began to see him kneeling silently in church for long periods, but did not see anything untoward in this development.

Then, on a day in early January shortly before Idi Amin's *coup d'état*, Emmanuele burst into my room, shouting and raging. He was a terrible sight, half-naked, with cuts on his head and face, back and buttocks, from which blood was streaming. He was clutching the Bible and book-rest and some scraps of Christmas decorations from our chapel. He flung himself on his knees before me and begged for my blessing. I gave it and then got him to sit down and talk calmly. He said that 'horns of witchcraft' were being used against him and that he was possessed by Kiganda hero-spirits whose names were Wamala, Kibuka and Jesus. He also added that I myself had appeared to him in a vision, that he had escaped from the mental hospital and that the man at whose house he was staying had beaten him with a stick.

He clearly seemed to be suffering from a psychiatric disorder, caused, it may be, by some febrile illness, cerebral malaria perhaps. His explanations were syncretist. Not only had he named Jesus among the Kiganda hero-spirits but he had offered two conflicting, traditional explanations for his 'spoiled brain'—witchcraft horns *and* hero-spirits. The local people were generally very afraid of violent madmen and used violence themselves against them in order to pinion or confine them, and if possible take them to the mental hospital.

Emmanuele had meanwhile calmed down completely, allowing me to dress his wounds and find him some clothes which he put on. As he departed, he said he was not going home because they would beat him again if he went there. I heard afterwards that he had had another attack after the *coup d'état* and had gone raving to the soldiers' barracks asking to join the army. The soldiers had beaten him badly. Later, his brother told me he was in the hands of a witchdoctor in Bugerere.

I did not see Emmanuele again for two years. In December 1972 he came into my office looking hale and well. He told me he had left the witchdoctor's a few months back and that he had spent a total of eight months there. He had been given medicine to drink every day and had stayed on another three months to work for his benefactor in lieu of payment. He was playing bass in a band at a local social centre and hoped to continue with his education. From what he had told me, it seemed the witchdoctor had accepted the horns-of-witchcraft diagnosis. They are thought to produce sudden and disturbing illnesses. Probably the spirits of the 'horns' had been made to identify themselves in a process of mental dissociation, after which the appropriate medicines could be prepared and administered. No doubt also, there was a strong element of social medicine in the treatment given to Emmanuele. At any rate, he was himself again and the credit went to the witchdoctor.

Psychic disorders induce fear in those who witness them, for many reasons. Apart from the fear of not knowing what the disordered person might do or say, there is the further embarrassment of not knowing how to help, of appearing foolish oneself if one tries to enter the disordered mental world. Above all there is the scandal of a human being, a 'rational animal', ceasing to be rational. Madness is a mystery which, by its very nature, defies understanding. Africans react with violence, as happened in the case of poor Emmanuele. Perhaps this can have the side-effect of being a crude form of shock treatment, though beating a madman is more likely to be a self-interested act. Westerners prefer to pretend the problem does not exist. Their attitude is similar to the response they make to death, that of attempting to ignore it. People with such disorders, they feel, must be removed from public sight. I remember the embarrassment caused by a madman who entered a church in Nairobi, the capital of Kenya, during a celebration of the sacrament of Anointing. Sick and disabled people had been given places of honour and the service was being led by a European hospital chaplain. The priest was just beginning his homily as the man created a loud disturbance. Presence of mind is not always easy on such occasions and the preacher ignored the man completely. Even after he had been hustled out, shouting and protesting that he had a right to be at the healing service, the preacher made no comment on what had happened. And yet I felt that the man had been correct. He had a right to be there, and he had a right to the healing love of Jesus Christ. It was just that his condition was too disturbing for the priest to know how to deal with it.

Psychic disorders are nevertheless far more common than we may like to admit. Studies made in general practices in England have revealed that as many as 40 per cent of the cases presented to ordinary doctors may have a psychiatric basis.[1] Emotional stress and instability are common and are at the core of the neuroses, though, as Anthony Storr has remarked, the neuroses themselves may be attempts to restore equilibrium.[2] From time to time one hears it said that neurosis and depressive illness are 'diseases of civilization' and that their incidence in the countries of the Third World is rare. It is very difficult to substantiate such a claim. If one takes a country like Uganda where my encounter with Emmanuele took place, it is perfectly true that the mental hospital contains mainly excited, manic patients, but this, John Orley argues, is because depressed people who are unduly slow and quiet are never sent for treatment.[3] It is only the excited and violent ones who are taken to the hospital. It is possibly true that westerners tend to bury their emotions more, but emotional stress is certainly encountered and suicide rates in Third World countries are not noticeably more favourable than in the western countries, even though reliable figures are hard to come by.[4]

One comes across aggressive psychoses and the delusions of paranoid psychoses—the states of mind of people who bear a grudge against society and those who are unable to doubt their own ideas or to admit any dependence on others. Psychotic persons are unable to relate to others, while schizophrenics feel so completely self-sufficient that they are totally isolated and their personality—to use Anthony Storr's phrase—fails 'to cohere as a whole'.[5] Perhaps the social and economic conditions of Third World countries contribute to such disorders of the mind. Perhaps racial discrimination and the disparity between rich and poor, between haves and have-nots, can fuel the aggressive psychoses. Perhaps rapid decolonization and the sudden access of power and responsibility can nourish immaturity, over-confidence and the delusions and paranoia of the psychoses. Psychiatric disorders are by no means always 'illnesses', though they may relate to illness. The emotions of anxiety, fear, anger and guilt may not only cause headaches and ulcers, they may even affect the course of more serious illnesses, such as cancer or heart disease. Emotions must be considered along with other factors such as infection, climate, diet, in the treatment of a sick person. The link between depressive illness and suicide and between terminal illness and emotional stress is already well established. Once again we come up against the relevance of an integrated approach in healing. We are not treating 'illnesses', but people who have illnesses and disorders. Much has still to be done, and Dr Una Maclean has this to say about the present situation:

Although awareness of psychological and social factors in disease is slowly growing, most doctors, both by virtue of their training, which has been predominantly in clinical medicine and surgery, and by inclination, still pay scant attention to the state of mind which accompanies or precedes their patients' complaints.[6]

We tend to fear madness because of its unreality. Schizophre-nics inhabit a totally private world that is unrelated to everyone and everything about them. That is their tragedy. Yet, how many of us are living—to one extent or another—in an unreal world. Shiva Naipaul remarked in 1978 on the air of unreality he encountered during his African journey.[7] It was a kind of millenarian dreaming that afflicts people from Third World countries. I thought I had identified it in Emmanuele before his crisis—his dreaming of foreign travel and studies abroad as the key to happiness and success in life. Naipaul was sharply critical, but the attitude emerges in a world ruled by a white 'minority régime', a world in which power and wealth are controlled by a fraction of the population. 'Why are blacks poor and whites rich?' is one of the hardest questions to answer, and one which is put again and again by the younger generation. Perhaps it is the attractive unreality that should be feared more, the dreamworld or 'never-never land' to which poor nations often aspire in vain and which induces lethargy and despair, or else corruption and violence. People found the madness of Hitler and Mussolini attractive because it flattered their national ego and made them a chosen race. The Jingoism of the New Imperialism in Britain was a similar fantasy. In Africa, ordinary people often evince an exceptional fear of violence, yet group violence is greatly en-joyed. 'There is no sign of fear', writes John Orley, 'in the faces of a crowd beating a thief. In fact, everyone joins in even though they may know the circumstances do not justify such action.'[8] Mob-justice is yet another form of madness and unreality.

'Fantasies', says Anthony Storr, 'are compensatory strivings towards normality',[9] and when we are deprived we cannot avoid having them. The danger is, however, when private fantasies become contagious, when situations of deprivation and social disintegration induce delusions and paranoid systems on a mas-sive scale. Norman Cohn has studied this phenomenon and we shall return to it in Chapter 13 when we consider 'Yearning for the Millennium'.[10] If there is an interaction between private and public fantasy, then there is a clear need for mental hygiene and for the discipline of a return to reality. This does not mean that we should not dream, or that we should not harbour ambitions, but it does mean self-discipline, mature and satisfactory rela-tionships and a readiness to be conditioned by others.

Madness may be unreality; it is also essentially linked to prophecy, which is a revelation of inner reality. We fear the mad for much the same reason as we fear the child. They may sudden-ly blurt out the truth when everyone else is too polite to do so. So, in Shakespeare's greatest achievement, King Lear's irretriev-able insanity becomes a prophetic vehicle for human incompre-hension before the mystery of human wickedness. At the height of the storm Lear's own mental powers disintegrate, as he chides the heavens for conniving with the injustice of his own children, and sees his whole world in ruins.

Blow winds and crack your cheeks! Rage! Blow!
You cataracts and hurricanoes, spout
Till you have drench'd the steeples, drown'd the cocks!
. . . And thou, all-shaking thunder,

Smite flat the thick rotundity o' the world,
Crack nature's mould, all germins spill at once
That make ingrateful man![11]

I came across a modern Lear in the Tanzanian village where I was staying at the end of 1982. The country had been going through the trauma of economic recession. Commodities were scarce and violence was running high in the rural areas. People were persistent but circumspect in their criticism of government. One could lament the shortages and cast the blame on local officials, but nobody dared to say in public the thought that was in everyone's minds, that perhaps the national policy of socialism was misguided or the President just plain wrong. These certainties could never be questioned. They were like the heavens in *King Lear*, the gods whom no one but the mad king could accuse of injustice. It was left to the village madman, a young man called Herman, to ring the church bells in one of his frenzies and shout to the assembled people: 'Down with socialism! Down with Nyerere!' Like the infant in the story of the Emperor who had no clothes, he alone could state the obvious with impunity. In a land of stereotyped slogans and fearful patriotism, it was the madman alone who could express what people saw as the truth of the situation.

Old Testament prophecy began its history with the humble diviner or seer who would help you track down a lost animal, and with the group hysteria of the 'sons of the prophets'. These had a bad name. They were derived from Canaanite prototypes who induced their contagious ecstasy by means of narcotics and self-inflicted torture. Even when they entered into Jewish tradition and became associated with the service of such Yahwistic shrines as the one at Bethel, they were regarded with a certain measure of disdain by ordinary Israelites who thought them irrational and mentally deranged. When Saul, after his anointing by the 'seer' Samuel, fell into ecstasy in the midst of a troop of prophets he became the object of unfavourable criticism.

From there they came to Gibeah, and there was a group of prophets coming to meet him; the spirit of God seized on him and he fell into ecstasy in their midst. When all who knew him previously saw him prophesying with the prophets, the people said to each other, 'What has happened to the son of Kish? Is Saul one of the prophets too?'[12]

People were surprised that a man of Saul's birth and standing should mix with these low-class enthusiasts and their stimulated ecstasy.

Pursuing his idea of liminality, Victor Turner has reminded us of the liminal or marginal character of prophets, their low status and their power-through-weakness.[13] Like their European medieval forebears, African monarchs employed court jesters who were often dwarfs or deformed people and who were given licence to gibe at the ruler. The drummers of the Barotse royal barge in Zambia enjoyed the same function, and literature in every culture and continent abounds with marginal figures of this kind. In *King Lear* the Fool provides added pathos to the tragic figure of the mad king. Turner writes:

In closed or structured societies, it is the marginal or 'inferior' person or the 'outsider' who often comes to symbolize what David Hume has called 'the sentiment for humanity' . . . .[14]

The prophet must act like a madman and the madman play the prophet. Prophets have to be professional misfits, living paradoxes, if they are to draw attention to their message. Even Jesus of Nazareth was thought by members of his own family to have lost his reason.

He went home again, and once more such a crowd collected that they could not even have a meal. When his relatives heard of this, they set out to take charge of him, convinced he was out of his mind.[15]

Madness and paradox help us to experience more fully the generic human condition and perhaps also to reaffirm the attributes of wholeness. Turner again:

Thus, humility reinforces a just pride in position, poverty affirms wealth, and penance sustains virility and health.[16]

Liminality implies power-through-weakness and this is the principle which we have identified from the beginning of our discussion as the means by which healing takes place and definitive wholeness is restored.

People with severe psychiatric disorders need expert, professional help, but everyone afflicted in this way to a greater or lesser degree needs the support of a community. Tolerance and even acceptance has to be shown towards them. In the African village, barring the occasional beating when they become violent, such people seem to be given a place, and even a social role. They may even be regarded as people with a message for society, a revelation of an unadmitted part of the human self, perhaps even people with a message from divine reality. This idea is frequently shown in traditional societies through their linking of madness and the world of the spirit. Emmanuele, being a devout Christian and a man of his own Kiganda culture, understood his crisis in religious, syncretist terms: Christ, hero-spirits and horns of witchcraft or *mayembe*, themselves deemed to be spirits that dwell in horns or gourds and are thought to be manufactured and 'sent' by evilly disposed persons.

There is a comparable ambivalence about our experience of the emotions. If they are buried, they can lead to instability, but if they are worked through and admitted they can help us to build up right ideas – about ourselves and about God. Fears and anxieties can become sources of frustration which lead to anger or feelings of guilt. They can even trigger physical illness, quite apart from depressive illness. We need to heal the painful memories as well as the painful expectations of the future that cause such fears and anxieties. Healing a memory, say Matthew and Dennis Linn, is like dying.[17] The sufferer has to go beyond denial, anger, bargaining and self-reproach to a state of acceptance, the recognition that in every experience there is something positive. One is not trying to kill the memory, to forget it. Rather one accepts it and, at the same time, discovers a new dimension in it. Any moment, however painful, can be a gift or a curse. It is we who make that decision. It is for me to decide why I need this illness or why this painful experience was nevertheless good for me. It is only then that I can also decide what my prayer can obtain for me from the healing love of Christ.

Ultimately the healing of life's hurts involves reaching out to other people. It is just this that the schizophrenic or the one who suffers from a paranoid psychosis cannot do without professional therapy. For many depressed and emotionally stressed people help is more easily obtained from a sympathetic listener who can help them bring to light the hidden hurts. Simply talking about them is a healing process in itself. As Anthony Storr remarks: 'What cannot be fully admitted to another person, cannot be fully accepted by the person himself'.[18] Here the stress must be placed on the word 'fully'. The process takes time. One must go right back to the beginning, to the real roots of the problem, to the real underlying causes of the hurt. Sufferers must go beyond repentance and the exercise of will-power (under grace) to keep a good resolution. There must also be a readiness to forgive those who have wronged them. In the Christian context there has to be real faith in the power-through-weakness of Christ to heal the hurtful memories and to unloose the fetters constituted by these memories. As Matthew and Dennis Linn point out, Christ heals when he removes all the blocks to our reaching out to others.[19] Psychic and social healing are closely related, for to be normal, to be ourselves, we need others. We need a mature dependence on others. We have to overcome our own isolation which is the real cause of our hurt.

Depressive illness and other abnormal depressions are frequently associated with suicide attempts. In these attempts there is what Erwin Stengel calls the appeal effect.[20] Those who attempt suicide are making an appeal for friendship and love through their dramatic self-aggression. In different parts of the world suicide prevention centres have been set up as a kind of short-term emergency clinic which people who contemplate suicide can get in touch with, usually by telephone. The best-known suicide prevention organization is probably that of the Samaritans, founded in 1953 by Chad Varah in the City of London. The majority of suicides present social and spiritual problems more than medical problems. At least, this is the assumption of the Samaritans and similar organizations, and the assumption seems to be borne out by the evidence. The existence of these centres has certainly helped to reduce the suicide rate in the areas where they operate.[21]

Samaritans try to help people with suicidal intentions and people in despair just as a member of the sufferer's own family would do. They try to befriend the sufferer and to offer love and friendship, be a source of strength and refuge in a time of crisis. They are equipped by their own inclination, gifts and training to receive and to respond to the various messages they receive from people in despair. Using their experience and their common sense, they have to recognize those who are suffering from abnormal depressions and refer them to a doctor for professional therapy. As Erwin Stengel points out, this is what a concerned member of the sufferer's own family would do.[22] Again, we can appreciate the role of human relationships in the healing of such people's emotions.

We have already noted that dying people often experience emotional distress and even depression.[23] Sometimes the emotion is one of anxiety. All seriously ill people experience some degree of anxiety and certainly the prospect of death is an added cause of anxiety in sick people. There are many other causes. One is separation from the people one loves. Another cause, especially in younger people, is the disappointment of hopes and expectations. Also, in a gravely sick person, any minor discomfort or irritation may aggravate anxiety. Hinton reports that it is especially when breathing is affected that dying people appear anxious.[24] Dying people are only too ready to talk about their fears if they can find anyone to listen. Sympathetic listening to such an outpouring of anxiety is clearly a form of healing emotions and allaying fears.

Dying people are frequently overcome by deep melancholy and sadness. Part of their depression is due to the withdrawal of people they love. The living are separated from them. They cannot share the experience of dying. They have to get on with their own lives, and they may even be embarrassed or resentful when they see someone they love dying. Such isolation of a dying person can be very cruel, and once again there is a need for loving relationships to sustain the dying person. Hospices for the dying, if they are well-run places, can create a loving environment in which death is accepted with calmness and dignity and emotions are controlled. Associated with such places for the dying, very often, are teams of people who go out to sit up at night with the dying in their homes, to talk to them and to hold their hand as they make their last lonely journey. All the evidence shows that such assistance is extremely comforting and reassuring.

There is a danger in burying one's emotions and this danger must be circumvented by giving adequate expression to emotions. They are, after all, the normal vehicles for expressing our relationships with others, our concern for them, our affection, friendship and understanding. The danger reappears at the other extreme when we lose emotional balance and control and when the emotions block our reaching out to other people. In the recent tradition of Catholic Christianity, considerable emphasis has been placed on reason and on a rational attitude towards religious practice. Theology borrowed its systematic method from rational philosophy and such theological 'rationalism' was even introduced into the formularies of the liturgy and of ordinary prayer. In the spiritual life one was taught to distrust one's emotions. 'Consolations' in prayer, as they were called, were suspect. In many ways, there was good sense in this approach, for it helped those who made progress in the spiritual life to cope with aridity and religious insensibility. Yet the emphasis seems to have been unbalanced and the Catholic Church tended to cater for religious emotion outside its official formularies through popular devotional art, through side-altars, shrines and candle-sconces. The exuberance of private and popular devotions has to be pruned from time to time and artistic good taste must also be maintained and taught. However, there is a place for popular religion, as there is for popular art, and there is a danger that, in a time of renewal, a new rationalistic spirit and even a higher-class aesthetic might be imposed from above.

Inevitably, being a Church of the People means putting up with much that a highly educated clergy might consider to be 'bad taste'. It also means tolerating a measure of emotional display. Certainly, if faith and prayer are to be genuine, formulation must not be limited to what people think they *ought* to say. Shakespeare's tragedy of *King Lear* ends with a couplet which sums up the prophetic role of the mad king. Albany concludes:

The weight of this sad time we must obey,
Speak what we feel, not what we ought to say.[25]

To be genuine, there is a need to speak what we feel in church. It is our loving relationship with God in faith which must speak.

As we have the same spirit of faith that is mentioned in scripture—I believed, and therefore I spoke—we too believe and therefore we too speak.[26]

The emotions themselves are not, of course, prayer, any more than discursive theological reasoning is prayer, but they can be vehicles of prayer. In many parishes of the western world charismatic prayer groups are giving people a real experience of prayer and are teaching them to give free rein to their emotions in prayer, even in the inchoate or non-rational prayer of speaking in tongues. All of this can be very positive so long as the 'enthusiasm' of such groups does not become an end itself and powers of dissociation are not manipulated. Prayer should lead to commitment and not to withdrawal. Such groups can also become a favoured context for the exercise of the ministry of healing.

There is a whole spectrum of attitudes towards the display of emotions in the cultural traditions of Third World countries. In the cultures of the Far East, the public display of emotions is often strongly disapproved, while in African, Oceanian and Latin American countries there is an exuberant display of emotions in public. In 1983 I travelled from East Africa to Singapore and having been used to the warm, lingering handshakes of Africa at the 'Kiss of Peace', I was struck by the distant nods of the head given by the Singaporeans at Mass when I said: 'Let us now give one another the sign of peace'. It was a dramatic change of culture.

There is a problem when official liturgy is rigid and the normal popular expression of feeling is exuberant. A compromise has to be found so that Christians can express their faith in song, gesture, movement, cries of joy—even tears when necessary. A parish liturgy must try to cater for every taste, without letting any one form become dominant or any individual emotional tendency be given a monopoly. In the prayer group there is greater room for the emotions and a better opportunity for therapy and healing, perhaps, than in the Sunday crowd. Jesus was not afraid of his emotions. He wept before the tomb of his friend Lazarus. He displayed a righteous anger when he drove the money-changers from the Temple. He was overcome by deep sadness and melancholy at his approaching death, when he was in the garden of Gethsemane. He showed a special affection for the disciple whom he loved. He had a yearning and protective instinct towards Jerusalem and its inhabitants. Jesus appears in the Gospels as emotionally balanced, but capable of giving play to his emotions in a controlled way.

Jesus also appeared to us as tender, gentle, forgiving with the sinner, the weak and broken-hearted, and the bereaved, as well as compassionate towards the sick, the poor and the outcast. One thinks of the woman taken in adultery, of the widow at Naim, of the father of the epileptic boy.

Come to me, all you who labour and are overburdened, and I will give you rest. Shoulder my yoke and learn from me, for I am gentle and humble in heart, and you will find rest for your souls. Yes, my yoke is easy and my burden light. [27]

After laying bare all the deeply rooted hurts from which we suffer, and their causes, after prayer for their healing and for grace to forgive those who have hurt us, we turn to Jesus to fill us with his healing love. To be healed we need to feel loved by God, even in the midst of our weaknesses and failures, in the midst of the burdens which we feel are too much for us. We need to be convinced that God-in-Christ really loves us, to learn from Scripture how to live out in our own lives Christ's reactions, and then, at the end of all, to be able to thank God even for the deepest hurts.

7

Sickness of the soul

During a brief visit to New Zealand in 1983, I had the pleasure of meeting groups of Maoris and Samoans and hearing something at first hand of their social concepts and customs. It was a Maori student who explained the concept of *tapu* to me. A thing, or a place or a person is *tapu* when he, she or it is 'tied up' or 'marked off', as it were, by prohibitions. It was clear from the way he spoke that *tapu* was associated with ritual power, a sort of veto power which could be wielded by influential people. I was interested in the Maori idea of *tapu* because it is the original form of our word 'taboo', a word that has a long history as an analytical category in modern psychology and social anthropology. In common ethnographic usage the word 'taboo' has come to mean any form of ritual or symbolic prohibition to which is attached a mysterious automatic sanction.[1]

In Eastern Africa one certainly comes across the taboo in this latter sense. It is usually called *mwiko* in Swahili and related languages, and it owes its power to the mysterious sanction, rather than to the social prestige of a leader exercising a veto power. Whether that sanction is provided by a retaliation on the part of preternatural forces, spirits, divinities, God himself, or whether it is so automatic as to be merely magical, it is essentially mysterious and universally feared. If you do such and such, such and such will follow. It is rather like Conrad Suck-a-Thumb in Struwwelpeter. If you suck your thumbs, the great long red-legged scissors-man will come and snip them off! The taboo appeals to something elemental in our make-up, something that goes right back to the fears of early childhood. That is why the psychologist, in turn, is interested in taboo and sees it in Freud's terms as a kind of 'holy dread', an irrational or unintelligible fear.[2]

Whatever the psychological factors in the genesis of taboo, in Eastern Africa the concept has a wide application. Taboos proliferate especially in the area which concerns the transmission of human life: marriage, sexual activity, pregnancy, childbirth. Clusters of taboos are to be found in every traditional ritual—particularly in the rites of passage. For example, an initiation rite very frequently contains a taboo against looking backwards towards a place associated with ritual action. One is reminded of Orpheus and Eurydice or of Lot and his wife. The mysterious sanction attached to this taboo ensures that the candidate makes a complete break with the past and looks only forwards to the new status that he is acquiring in the rite of passage.

Pregnancy taboos are very numerous. The pregnant woman is forbidden to eat eggs, or kidneys, or liver, or to cast eyes on a baboon. All of these things symbolize a pregnancy that goes wrong, a miscarriage, a premature or malformed baby. The pregnant woman's husband is also surrounded by taboos. For example, he must be careful, when chopping trees, not to allow the falling timber to lodge in the branches of a neighbouring tree. Anything that gets stuck symbolizes a difficult childbirth. The husband, in some tribes, must practise what anthropologists have called the *couvade*. This is a simulated pregnancy. The husband must pretend that he is pregnant! And all the taboos that apply to his wife apply to him.

Taboos have their purpose in human cultures. They are a kind of teaching-aid. They are, if you like, 'screaming headlines'—a highly colourful and exaggerated way of making a point or inculcating an attitude. In the case of the pregnancy taboos, they highlight the possible dangers to the future mother and her baby, and they inculcate an attitude of caution and solicitude on the part of those involved. Taboos, being didactic, are laws of life. They do not generally have any conscious moral basis. They are simply there and to break a taboo is the height of foolishness. The breaker of the taboo is the one who gets punished and has only himself or herself to blame. Taboos have an obvious purpose. If there is anything irrational about them, it is the fear of the mysterious sanction which is attached to their infringement. This fear diminishes with the growth of education, or perhaps one should say more correctly that it tends to be transferred on to other objects and experiences. A woman may no longer believe there is a connection between eating kidneys and having a miscarriage, but she may have transferred her 'taboo mentality' to the commandments of God, or of the Church, or even to the laws of the state.

If taboos were essentially amoral in traditional ethnic cultures, there was always another level of fault which was seen to have a moral relevance. This was a fault which was destructive of relationships, both the human relationships of family and society and the relationships of human beings with the guardians of family and society, the ancestral and territorial spirits and the supreme being himself. Although public and private offences were distinguished, both could be a spiritual danger to the whole community. What made such faults so pernicious was that they offended the spiritual sources of life and invited retaliation from them. Many anti-social acts fell into this category. They could include murder, theft, rape, incest, adultery, injury, violent anger, as well as ritual faults and omissions which were considered to be a direct affront to divine reality in its various forms.

When divine reality is affected by the perverse behaviour of human beings, we usually employ the term 'sin'. Following Durkheim's extrinsic definition of crime as 'the acts which society punishes', some functionalist anthropologists have tried to define sin as an action to which a divine punishment is attached. According to this definition, consciousness of sin would be reduced to the simple fear of divine punishment. Such, in fact, is far from the case, even when the state or consciousness of sin is referred to in terms of the punishment feared as, for example, destruction, annihilation, wasting-sickness, death. In any case, the symbolism of sin often goes to the heart of the matter in referring to broken family relationships. The prayer for salvation from sin and its effects often pictures the offended spiritual being as a 'father' or 'parent' offended by the actions of a child. Sin is essentially an attack on the divine order—a disorder in the ultimate sense. The rituals by which people are purified from sin demonstrate very clearly that it is conceived as a lasting spiritual state. When people blow water from their mouths, or let blood, or throw a stick or stone on to a heap, or even simply 'confess' by word of mouth, they symbolize their desire to be rid of an inner state, and often also their desire to be reconciled to the community.

In African traditions, sin is very often closely associated with the concept of shame before others. This may be why private sins were not treated seriously until they came to light. Guilt feelings followed society's judgement on the presence of guilt. Inner states, such as guilt feelings, shame before others, and the consciousness of sin, could be expressed on occasion through extrapolation on to external agents. This in no way undermined the character of such phenomena as 'inner' states. It was simply a manner of imaging the human self as 'scattered' or as receptive of experience, rather than as an independent agent. Many African languages cater for this view of reality through their modes of speech and their passive verb forms. Such a manner of speaking can, but does not necessarily, imply a desire for exculpation. People who say: 'A mistake came to me', rather than 'I made a mistake' are not necessarily trying to exonerate themselves.

Such a notion of sin has much in common with traditional Judeo-Christian ideas. Although much of what is said about sin in the Old Testament is couched in terms of 'law', 'transgression', 'treason', 'infidelity' towards Yahweh, it becomes progressively clear that the real malice of sin consists in desiring to be morally independent from God, in attempting a religious autonomy or 'auto-salvation'. This was the meaning of Israel's apostasy in the desert and of Adam and Eve's disobedience in the garden. The sense of sin develops in the prophetical writings as a senseless rejection of God's tender love for humanity and of a refusal to imitate that love in human relationships. This concept of sin reaches its fullest application in the rejection of Jesus Christ in the New Testament, God's loving-kindness in person. And yet God's love so far triumphs over human infidelity that this very rejection becomes the means of human salvation. Christ becomes himself 'an offering for sin'. St Paul goes so far as to say: 'For our sake God made the sinless one into sin'. Christ identified himself with sin, so as to take away the curse which sin incurred.

In recent centuries religion in the western world has tended to become privatized. This is partly because of a situation of religious pluralism and moral relativity. Sin is also popularly regarded as a purely private affair, a matter for the individual's conscience and stemming from a person's private religious faith. This is an altogether misguided understanding of sin. Our moral choices, our perverse actions do affect others. So also does the way in which we understand those choices and actions. In our turn, we are affected by the choices and actions of other people and their understanding of what they do. If sin is a denial in practice of the divine order, it can never be a purely private affair. It always has an anti-social dimension. Ideas of collective guilt and social sin are certainly present in African tradition and such ideas are not necessarily incompatible with the safeguarding of individual responsibility. A balance has, of course, to be held between the social and individual aspects of sin, but there is a sense in which sin or moral evil is something outside ourselves, something that is over and against us, as it were. It is a progressive build-up of wickedness in the world, a growing reign of iniquity, to which our individual acts contribute.

In traditional societies collective responsibility for the perverse actions of an individual member of a family, clan or village was common. The group was responsible, after all, for the moral formation of the individual, for moral support and restraint. To punish, or demand compensation from, a whole group when one individual had erred was certainly an effective way of ensuring that the peace was kept, but the collective responsibility was accepted as a matter of course. We *do* share in one another's guilt. The Lebanese poet, Kahlil Gibran, expresses this very beautifully:

... as a single leaf turns not yellow but with the silent knowledge of the whole tree,
So the wrong-doer cannot do wrong without the hidden will of you all.[3]

The Bible traces the development of social sin, as well as the growth of individual moral responsibility. The first sin had portentous consequences for subsequent generations. Sin and the disposition to sin were bequeathed and inherited. The reign of sin took hold upon the world. Sinful actions grew in number and in gravity, and sin became a cumulative experience for humanity, a well-nigh overpowering one. The Biblical picture corresponds to our own circumstances in the last quarter of the twentieth century. We continue to experience the 'reign of sin', the 'sin of the world', the world's moral sickness. We experience countless situations of collective selfishness, of rich people in solidarity against the poor, of minority régimes oppressing those of another race or religion, of militant nationalism, of conspiracies of silence in the face of rank injustice, of corruption and graft because 'everybody does it'. This is social sin, the sin that is shared.

Social sin brings into existence flawed social structures and institutions which are objectively wrong in themselves and which encourage immoral attitudes and actions by those who subscribe to them and who operate their systems. For too long teachers of ethics and moral theology have assumed that the social *status quo* is inherently just and that injustice consists in hampering the working of the *status quo* or in its violent over-throw. It is now increasingly recognized that the *status quo* can itself be unjust and even violent and that to refuse to co-operate with it, perhaps in the last resort to contemplate its violent overthrow, is not necessarily wrong, as long as such a course of action is the lesser of the two evils, the final option, and stands a good chance of succeeding in creating an order that is more just.

The difference between sin and crime is certainly not the difference between perverse actions that are private and those that are public. Durkheim said that crimes are 'the acts which society punishes'. This is true so far as it goes and it helps to provide a rough and ready description, but it is certainly not a satisfying definition. Why does society punish some acts and not others? To the extent that society defines crime, it may be said to 'create' it. Crimes are actions which are ascertainable and susceptible to punishment under law, and laws must be drawn up and passed by a legislative authority. Not every anti-social action is defined as a crime. For example, in Nairobi City a number of ragged street-boys who varied in age from seven to seventeen years found an ingenious way of raising money. Since finding parking space is extremely difficult in the city, the boys started showing motorists where the empty spaces were, for a small financial consideration. This was considered to be a nuisance by the city council and the Kenya authorities enacted a new law in the 1970s declaring it to be an offence to guide a motorist to an empty car space in return for money. A new crime had thus been created overnight by the legislator.

Suicide and attempted suicide are actions which have, and which are often intended to have, repercussions on others. Yet many would hold that a lonely individual who takes his life by, say, swallowing an overdose of sleeping tablets, or putting his head in the gas oven, is committing a private action. Governments in different countries have taken different views of suicide. In the past it was very often considered to be a crime and there are still countries which regard it as such. That is society's decision whether or not the action is private or public. Privacy itself is a relative concept. There is less privacy in an African or Indian village than in a vast conurbation in Europe, America or Australia.

There is a tendency in the western world to define crime in terms other than those of moral responsibility.[4] It is difficult to know why some people commit crime and others do not. Questions of publicity and detection apart, there are those who would place the emphasis on hereditary and biological factors. Yet this line of explanation has not been satisfactorily established. Others would place the onus on social factors, on poverty, on degrading conditions of living, on unemployment, on overcrowding in urban areas. All these may be factors that encourage the committing of crimes, but they do not explain why the majority of people who put up with these conditions remain law-abiding, nor why crimes occur, as they do, in conditions of affluence. Still another line of argument stresses the psychological side, the upbringing of children, the influence of 'broken homes', the lack of mental balance. Yet once again, the arguments are not completely satisfying. How does one define a 'broken home' in Asia or Africa where children are traditionally distributed among the members of an extended family community for their education and upbringing? And certainly crimes cannot be satisfactorily explained in terms of emotional disorders.

However reluctant we may be to admit it, we cannot ultimately set aside human responsibility as a factor in crime. Human beings are naturally perverse and they exercise some degree of autonomy over their actions, or they would not be human beings. Crimes are the result of an interplay of many factors, one of which is the responsible choice of the criminals themselves. That being said, it can be more easily appreciated that the concepts of crime and sin overlap. Even if we did not experience the moral relativity of the twentieth century, there would be innumerable sins which by their nature could not become the subject of criminal legislation. There would also continue to be oppressive laws, creating crimes in order to eliminate an embarrassment for a rich, law-making minority—the law against 'parking-boys' perhaps? Sins are by definition anti-social, and, although all that is anti-social is not by any means sin, crime in general terms derives its meaning from ideas of morality. Sin depends on subjective factors, such as full knowledge and full consent, while ignorance of the law does not exonerate the criminal. Moreover, objectively, society does not declare an action to be anti-social out of pure caprice. What is 'anti-social' is usually unjust, harmful or inconsiderate to others and such things are incompatible with the love of God. People sometimes speak of a 'traffic-law morality', meaning a morality which has no higher goal than that of preventing accidents, yet I would submit that even the Highway Code has a spiritual side to it.

Irresponsible drivers may end up maiming themselves or other people for life, possibly causing complete loss of life through their own criminal negligence. In my submission, such careless-ness transgresses the commandment: 'Thou shalt not kill'. A traffic law which is pro-life is on God's side.

The criminal stands in need of healing and healing may be one of the motives of punishment. Other motives, however, deserve to be considered. One is deterrence, though this is difficult to establish, even in the case of capital punishment for murder. Most murders are committed in circumstances which do not permit reflection on the possible consequences. Where they do, reflection can encourage desperation and even greater danger to life. Another motive is the protection of society, though here again there may be scant relationship between how safe society feels (having its criminals behind bars, or buried six feet under) and how secure it actually is. Finally, there is also the motive of retribution, of making the criminal suffer for a crime, and this motive clearly presupposes a measure of personal responsibility. Once again, there is room for endless discussion as to which punishment fits which particular crime. Punishment as a reme-dial, healing or educative action is very problematical. Although enlightened penal systems provide opportunities for convicted criminals to learn trades, read and even write books and to improve themselves in a hundred ways, prisons are still 'schools of crime' and on leaving prison the criminal is still at an almost insuperable disadvantage when it comes to starting to live a normal life. One should add to that the possible effects of the prison régime on the mental and emotional state of the prisoner. Needless to say, capital punishment leaves no room for re-education in this world, and it also leaves no room for redress in the all too frequent cases of judicial error.

In many Third World countries it was a colonial power that invented the penal system now operated by politically indepen-dent governments. Colonial powers used their prisons in various ways. Prisoners were cheap labour for communal projects, road construction, state farms and so on. Prisons were also places in which elements considered dangerous to the régime could be incarcerated. By and large, these traditions have been continued after political independence. Prisons, however, are increasingly inadequate as the population expands and the problem is com-pounded by more lengthy sentences, by bottlenecks in the hear-ing of cases and by new policies with regard to capital punishment. In some cases the sentence of death has been attached to a broader variety of crimes, armed robbery for example, or stock-theft, even if no homicide was involved. On the other hand, there is a greater reluctance to carry out sentence of death in some countries, and prisoners in death row may have to wait for several years before knowing the outcome of their appeal for clemency to the highest authority. A number, however, are not reprieved, and this makes the state of anguish suffered by the condemned more acute.

The care and welfare of convicted prisoners crosses the border between social and moral healing. There is no doubt that categories such as young offenders and those in death row need special attention. In my own limited mission experience I have seen admirable examples of regular visiting and weekly liturgical celebrations in prisons, often in the hands of a local parish or seminary. There are noteworthy examples of centres and clubs for the rehabilitation of young offenders. In some countries, for example Kenya, the Catholic Church has organized a prison chaplaincy service on a national scale, run by local Kenyan priests who even go so far as to allow themselves to be locked in with the prisoners and to share their life at certain times of year, such as Christmas. Attempts are also made to help the prison staff and to make them more conscious of all the implications of their work.

There is no doubt that a sense of sin is closely related to a sense of God. A true sense of God necessarily entails a sense of sin. 'God, be merciful to me, a sinner' is the reaction of the man who knows himself to be in the presence of God.[5] It is a truism to say that the sense of God is in doubt in the western world, and that this has had an effect on the sense of sin. Probably the two 'senses' interact, and there are also reasons why a sense of sin should become diminished independently of a lack of faith in God. In many Third World countries a sense of God would seem to be still strongly present, yet the sense of sin is wanting. One reason why this should be is our old friend the taboo. The great age of Christian missionary expansion was the nineteenth century, an era of considerable individualism and legalism in popular religious practice. Sin was very often taught as a transgression of a law, rather than as an infidelity towards a person or a refusal of love. Moreover, the social aspects of sin were largely ignored in the Church's ministry of forgiveness and the sacrament of Penance was concentrated upon particular confession by an individual to the priest.

Many nineteenth- and early twentieth-century Catholics, perhaps a large proportion even today, had a 'taboo mentality' towards sin. This was heightened by local taboo attitudes when Christianity came to the countries and cultures of the Third World. Valid local concepts of sin as an offence against God and society tended to be swallowed up by the taboo mentality. The 'tabooed' actions were not necessarily viewed as immoral in themselves. Nor did personal guilt or responsibility, let alone a relationship with God, play a part in the confession of sins as taboos. The effect of much Christian moralizing has been simply to lengthen the taboo list. Penitents very often are confessing their own irrational fears, rather than their misguided choices. Laws of the Church, such as attendance at Mass on Sundays or Friday abstinence, are particularly susceptible to taboo treatment, and they often figure prominently in the confessional, whether or not the infringement was due to forgetfulness or to a perfectly acceptable excuse such as sickness or absence on a journey. In one African parish I know, the confessions of many people became suddenly concentrated on Friday abstinence, when the Bishop reintroduced the rule during Lent after a lapse of many years. A Durkheimian definition of sin: acts that must be confessed?

Generally speaking, a renewed catechesis of sin has gone far towards correcting the taboo mentality. Moreover the new Order for the celebration of the sacrament of Penance in the Catholic Church has restored the social aspects, particularly that of reconciliation with the community. This is achieved very largely by communal penitential celebrations. However, it remains true that a sense of sin depends on a heightened sense of God. The closer to God we come, the more we lose our sense of complacency, the more we realize our own spiritual poverty, our self-inflicted wounds and those we inflict on others. The more we know God, the more we realize his forgiveness of us in Christ. Salvation from sin is the ultimate level of healing, the ultimate application of God's healing and reconciling love.

We have already discussed in Chapter 3 the possibility of a direct relationship between physical sickness and sin. We noted that sin plays its part in the havoc wrought by sickness and disability. Often the anxiety and uncertainty caused by sickness is complicated by a consciousness of guilt and the physical and moral conditions of the patient are interrelated. Jesus, as we saw, forgave the sins of the paralytic who was lowered down to him through the roof, before he tackled the paralysis. Only God can forgive sins. Healing from sin relies on the penitent's faith that God has exercised his forgiving love in his or her particular case. For Christians who accept the sacramental system, Baptism, Penance, Anointing are all channels of God's forgiveness. When the priest says: 'I absolve you', he lends his lips and voice to God. For the Evangelical Christian the sense of forgiveness is necessarily more subjective, depending on periodic revivals and conversion experiences. Testimonies delivered at revival gatherings tend not to be very specific about present states of sin, and to stress rather the fact that the sinner is now restored by God's love and in a state of grace. We can have a moral certainty about our fundamental option of God, but we can never become complacent. St Paul gives us a fine example:

I can assure you my brothers, I am far from thinking that I have already won. All I can say is that I forget the past and I strain ahead for what is still to come; I am racing for the finish, for the prize to which God calls us upwards to receive in Christ Jesus. We who are called 'perfect' must all think in this way.[6]

As Christians, we may reach a certain level of spiritual maturity in this world, but perfection belongs to nobody. There is always further to go.

The message of Jesus Christ is a message of salvation—but of salvation from what? From all the evils we have considered so far. From our abuse of the world's resources, from sickness of body, from mental anguish and psychic disorder, from social inadequacy and disharmony, from death and the fear of death, from the hurtful memories that make us angry, fearful, anxious or guilt-ridden, from all that constitutes a barrier in our relationships with others, from an inability to discern between sin and taboo, or between sin and shame, or between real consciousness of sin and mere guilt-feelings. We pray to be saved from our own moral failures and limitations, as well as from the oppression of sin outside ourselves, the sinful structures of society, the sin of the world. Prayer for salvation from sin is the deepest level we can reach in our hunger for salvation. Sin is the final evil from which we beg to be set free when we pray: 'Deliver us from evil'.

We are so used to the idea of human responsibility that we tend to be more scandalized by the so-called 'acts of God'—earthquakes, hurricanes, droughts, volcanic eruptions and plagues—than by acts of human wickedness. Yet, as we suggested earlier, probably all these physical contingencies underpin the nature of man as an organic, sentient being, possessed of reason and free will. The extraordinary paradox is not that God created volcanoes or hurricanes, but that he created reasonable beings capable of refusing the love that had brought themselves into existence. Was this the price he had to pay to share his love, not with robots and automata, but with creatures capable of exercising a creative freedom that participated in his own? We can only ask the question, for it is ultimately a mystery beyond our comprehension. To create a being in his own image and likeness with the capacity to disfigure that image is paradoxically the height of God's creative achievement. Human wickedness has resulted in our nature becoming permanently flawed, in our having a capacity for perversity that is ever present. Human beings are capable of the highest courage and selflessness and they are also capable of surrendering to their lowest instincts. A sense of sin connotes an acute awareness of inner conflict.

I cannot understand my own behaviour. I fail to carry out the things I want to do, and I find myself doing the very things I hate. . . . The fact is I know of nothing good living in me—living, that is, in my unspiritual self—for though the will to do what is good is in me, the performance is not, with the result that instead of doing the good things I want to do, I carry out the sinful things I do not want. . . .

What a wretched man I am! Who will rescue me from this body doomed to death? Thanks be to God through Jesus Christ Our Lord![7]

Paul's words of gratitude seem to answer his agonized question. It is Jesus Christ who rescues us from the captivity of our unspiritual selves. God in his infinite capacity for drawing good out of evil has, in Jesus Christ, identified with human sin so as to take away its curse and free us from the body doomed to death. God's re-creation of humanity is more unexpected and more stupendous than his first creation. In its own improbable and unaccountable way, sin becomes a pointer to divine transcendence and a field for the exercise of an infinite mercy.

8

Human sources of evil

On a day in mid-January 1966, when I was living in the small Tanzanian village of Maziinbo, during my anthropological field research, my friend Angelo Manyanza told me the story of the witch Mpanda Goye.[1] He had the account from Pesa Mbili, one of the principals in the story. Some years before, Pesa Mbili went hunting in the forest with two companions, Mageta and Hela Tatu. They slept the first night in a stockaded forest camp and continued their hunting the following day. Hela Tatu went off by himself and before long came face to face with an elephant; he wounded the beast with a shot from his muzzle-loader and the animal made off. After this he returned to camp for another night. Next day, Hela Tatu, who was an experienced hunter, persuaded his two companions to help him track the wounded elephant and they followed the blood trails all day until late afternoon. At the very moment they set eyes on it, the infuriated animal charged them, scattering them in different directions. The elephant went for Hela Tatu and gained on him quickly, for he was tired with the day's exertions. The exhausted hunter ran up over a large anthill in order to deceive the elephant, but with terrifying speed the beast uprooted a tree and brought it down in front of the running man, who tripped and fell. His two companions, afraid to shoot as the elephant closed with the man, watched in horror as the beast gored him with one of his tusks and made off.

Pesa Mbili and Mageta carried the wounded hunter back to camp and Mageta went for help. Shortly afterwards, Hela Tatu died and Pesa Mbili, having fired his muzzle-loader as a signal of death, washed the corpse and bound it to a pole ready for transport. Sitting in the dark stockade beside the corpse, Pesa Mbili heard the sinister hooting of the screech-owl, whose very name in the Kimbu language means 'witchcraft'. He wondered who it was who had sent the bird of ill omen and began to reflect on the occult causes of the day's sad events. His reveries were disturbed by a new and fearful noise, the sound of a lion pawing at the door of the stockade. He took aim in the dark with his muzzle-loader, pointing the barrel through a crack in the wall of logs. The gun misfired no fewer than three times and the lion returned. In desperation, Pesa Mbili seized the dead man's weapon, fired and heard no more.

By this time, in the early hours of the morning, people were on their way to the camp from the neighbouring village of Kipembawe. They heard the sound of the shooting and were afraid they would find Pesa Mbili dead as well. Wailing and lamenting, they arrived to find the carcass of the lion at the door of the camp. On examination it was found to be no ordinary lion. Its body was emaciated and its claws were thin like human fingers. It was definitely an instrument of witchcraft.

Shortly after Hela Tatu's burial in the village, his family decided to consult a diviner to identify the witch. The diviner named another family member called Mpanda Goye, a man with an evil reputation who lived in the same village. The diviner-witchdoctor said he did not have medicines strong enough to kill Mpanda Goye, but that he must not be suffered to live. The bereaved relatives of Hela Tatu travelled many hundreds of miles north to Mwanza where they consulted a well-known diviner of the Sukuma tribe. The latter explained to his credulous clients that Mpanda Goye was immune to retaliatory medicine because he took his heart out and buried it in a pot in a hole dug in a section of the main road that passed through Kipembawe village.

Hela Tatu's relatives returned from Mwanza and not long afterwards Mpanda Goye fell ill on his return from a beer party. It was said that the relatives had used a medicine to locate the pot with the disembodied heart. However, Mpanda Goye mysteriously recovered, and this, in its turn, was popularly attributed to the witch's recovery of the pot. Another visit to Mwanza brought the Sukuma witchdoctor himself to Kipembawe and this time the pot definitely ended up in the possession of Hela Tatu's relatives. In his death agony, Mpanda Goye trumpeted like an elephant, roared like a lion, hooted like a screech-owl, in fact made all the noises of the different animals whose shapes he had assumed in life. With a cry like that of the elephant that had killed Hela Tatu, Mpanda Goye yielded up the ghost. But even in death Mpanda Goye resisted to the last. When digging his grave they struck rock after only a foot or so of earth. They tried digging in several other places, and each time they struck rock near the surface. Eventually the celebrated witch was buried in a shallow grave, under a foot of topsoil. And that was the last of Mpanda Goye.

This story has never before appeared in print, but it is similar to many other witchcraft stories. It contains the whole fantasy, the whole collective nightmare or mass paranoia that afflicts certain types of society. A concatenation of disasters and terrifying experiences are taken as evidence of a cosmic conspiracy of implacable evil. Fact mingles with fantastic interpretation. Mpanda Goye is one of the 'fifth column' concealed in the midst of the human community acting in a reverse way to the manner in which a human being acts. He is the epitome of all wild beasts. Witchcraft is a kind of penumbra of human wickedness, an inborn preternatural power to harm and kill, enjoyed for its own sake.

To see all misfortune, especially the more dramatic disasters, as eventually traceable to human causes is intellectually satisfying. It also creates an illusion of control over evil forces, but ultimately it is not credible and, worse than that, it entails unjust judgements and the rendering of real for imagined evil. Suspected witches may have an evil reputation (which is presumably why the oracle is able to identify them), but, as we have seen many times already, in the mind of Jesus human sin does not directly provoke specific physical misfortune as a divine punishment, let alone as an overflow of human wickedness itself, in a wholly unmerited punishment of the innocent. Nor is suffering an evil that is to be avoided and/or revenged at all costs. Suffering is deeply rooted in the human condition and it is even a revelation of saving power that must be acknowledged and accepted. The intellectual fabric of witchcraft belief is so persuasive that the diviner is never doubted, the link between wickedness and natural disaster never questioned and the alleged evil will of the witch never disbelieved.

For witchcraft beliefs and accusations to flourish, more is needed than a theory. There must also be certain social conditions which make the theory practically impregnable. Social analysis reveals that witchcraft accusation serves mechanisms of competition in enclosed communities. Such communities have clear external boundaries but vague internal structures. In such a situation conformity is the yardstick of who is, or who is not, 'with us'. The misfit, the innovator, the eccentric, the outsider, the rival quickly becomes the outcast, the threat to the system. In a period of socio-economic change such as affects large areas of the Third World today, new factors and new roles are appearing in traditional human life which fuel social tensions and competition. Social change is not, however, sweeping enough to offer an effective choice of explanations. Tension and competition are sharpened, but traditional explanations go unchallenged. That is why witchcraft explanations are applicable to urban situations where job competition and inter-ethnic rivalry is at its most acute. Witchcraft beliefs constitute in any case a theory that is crying out for constant verification and the right set of social conditions ensures that the verification takes place.

Witchcraft theory is basically a form of dualism. It is the belief that the whole world can be divided into the wholly good and the irredeemably bad. The knack of survival consists in unmasking the bad. The conflict between good and evil is a desperate one and the wicked appear always to have the edge over the good. Evil is always on the verge of victory and must be constantly held at bay. Witchcraft accusation enables individuals to exculpate themselves and to receive public acknowledgement that they are 'on the side of the angels', that misfortune is not due to their own incompetence or even their own sin, but to an enemy who is the enemy of the whole community. Witchcraft accusation is a form of auto-salvation or self-justification.

Belief in witches is a belief that some people actually rejoice in doing evil and have gone so far as to say: 'Evil, be thou my good'. This is expressed in the whole topsy-turvy nightmare world which is a distorting-mirror reflection of the real world. It is a world in which people are born with top teeth growing first, with red eyes and unnaturally coloured skin, with ugly or deformed features, who are cannibals who eat babies or dig up the dead to feast on corpses or else resurrect them to work as zombies, who turn into wild animals or fly through the air on their backs, who make themselves invisible, who dance naked on graves, who cause crops to wither with one glance of an evil eye. Above all, it concerns people who frustrate the life-processes, causing death itself, making people sexually impotent or sterile.

To make a pact with evil is not in itself impossible, or even perhaps improbable. To believe in a cosmic conspiracy of evil— a 'Mystical Body of Anti-Christ'—is not beyond the powers of reasonable belief. The problem arises when one is asked to point an accusing finger at the members of this Satanic Mystical Body and to reveal their secret. It is then that the witchfinder usurps the place of God who is the sole judge of people's good and bad actions; it is then that the accusers turn themselves into both judge and executioner, while the suspects have no ultimate line of self-defence other than to accept the imputation and to utter venomous threats against their accusers, thus tightening the noose around their own necks. To accuse people of witchcraft practices is to destroy their social personality, if not to condemn them to a more merciful death. Witchcraft theory is backed by authority and authority derives its power from the fact that it shares in the theory of the community. In recent years witchcraft has often been felt to be increasingly dangerous and oppressive and millenarian expedients such as witchcraft cleansing or witch-eradication have developed. These phenomena will be dealt with in a later chapter. Suffice it to say here that a kind of witch pest-control service (which is what these movements are) always results in strengthening people's fear of witches and consequently their acceptance of the theory. If they give a temporary respite from fear, they leave the intellectual fabric of witchcraft beliefs untouched.

In a differentiated society, such an idea as witchcraft is no longer plausible as an explanation for overwhelming misfortune. For one thing, there are other levels of explanation and, for another, authority no longer backs it. Social sin we can accept, so long as we realize that we ourselves are a part of it and that it is not simply an external conspiracy. We who set out to redeem the times do not justify ourselves by this same token. We stand in need of redemption also, for nobody is free of original sin and its consequences. The innocent continue to suffer—in the mysterious plan of God which permits such suffering as the by-product of the world he has created—but who can decide which of their neighbours is innocent and which guilty? Too many witchcraft confessions can be sociologically explained for comfort and this means that society is making innocent people the victims of its own paranoia in a situation of socio-economic misery and disintegration.

Towards the end of August 1975,[2] when I was teaching in Uganda, there was a knock at my office door. On the threshold was a religious brother in a white cassock who introduced a well-dressed Ugandan lady. She was a tutor in a Kampala College of Education and she owned a beautiful house and garden on a hill which I could see from my window. She told me that her husband had found 'bad things' in the garden. 'What bad things?', I asked. The lady was reluctant to say more, but after a little more conversation, it transpired that they were bundles of leaves and certain instruments of sorcery. Her request was that I should come to bless the garden and so neutralize the evil spell. I was struck by the incongruity of the situation. Here was a highly educated, smart and westernized lady, a Catholic who was the mother of a beautiful family, who seemed to have everything that one could desire—husband, children, job, house—but for one thing: she was under an evil spell. And here was I, a missionary priest, being drawn into this world of sorcery by a religious brother in a white cassock!

A fierce debate began in my much-battered conscience. Could I offer to help without strengthening her belief in sorcery? 'No', said my good angel, 'you will be pandering to those beliefs if you go up there and bless her garden.' 'Rubbish', said my bad angel, 'even if you don't go and bless it, her fear of sorcery will remain, perhaps be even stronger.' 'It's ambiguous', spluttered my good angel. 'Just a blessing', said the bad angel, 'what's wrong with that?' 'She will misinterpret it', fired the good angel. 'Yes, but you can explain what a blessing means', retorted the bad angel. 'Will she believe it?', asked the good angel cynically. 'Maybe not', confessed the bad angel, 'but you can only do your best, and she needs help, that's obvious.' It was my bad angel who had the last word.

I drove to her house with the brother in the evening. The air was flower-scented and a gentle breeze wafted up from Lake Victoria towards the house. There was nothing remotely redolent of sorcery or evil magic. The husband was not yet back from work, so the lady took me to the garden. It was enclosed by a stout wooden fence and was very much overgrown with weeds and rank grass. Nobody had ventured into the garden since the discovery of the 'bad things' two months before. Such is the power of sorcery! The gate was stiff with disuse, but I managed to force it open and slip in among the weeds and briars. Neither the lady nor the religious brother had the slightest intention of entering the garden with me. I was left to carry out my own priestly mumbo-jumbo by myself. Yet I felt I had to talk to her and make some attempt at explanation. That, after all, was my only justification for coming.

I told her that the blessing was not magic, that my holy water had no preternatural fertilizing power. It was simply an effective sign of the garden's owner putting her property into God's hands and trusting him to protect her and provide for her and her family. She listened respectfully and then I turned towards the centre of the plot. I blessed the garden as thoroughly as I could, and sprinkled the holy water around until the bottle was empty. Then I emerged unscathed but for a few burrs and grass-seeds sticking to the bottoms of my trousers. She led the way into the house where I hoped to get down to brass tacks on the subject of superstition. On the verandah she served me fresh orange-juice in a cut-glass goblet and peanuts from a china bowl. My attempts to moralize any further were drowned in hospitality and small-talk, and I came away with a bad conscience. 'Guilty!', said my good angel. 'You were no better than a witchdoctor.' It was a few days later when I remembered the way Jesus had dealt with the woman who had a haemorrhage. He had cured her when she touched his clothes, but he had made her acknowledge her faith openly afterwards. Jesus's pedagogy would not allow any hole-in-the-corner mumbo-jumbo. Had I, in my stumbling way, attempted something similar? And failed!

One may doubt the exaggerated fancies of witchcraft beliefs and wonder whether anyone actually claims to be a witch before being accused, but people *do* practise sorcery, or evil magic. What is more, they may even justify it in their own eyes, as a means of getting even with a tiresome neighbour or relative. Although sorcery is a technique and not an inborn power like witchcraft, the issue of its distinction from the latter is complicated by the fact that many African languages use a single word for both sorcerer and witch. This is not merely a semantic problem, for quite often people in Africa consider that only a witch would be wicked enough to practise sorcery. Can evil magic really harm, hinder or kill? We shall deal with magic in general—good magic mainly—in Chapter 11, but in answer to the question now I would confess that I have few illusions about sorcery. We have already mentioned so-called 'witch-illnesses', when people languish and even die as a result of an evil spell. The destruction of the social personality, parapsychological powers we do not yet understand, auto-suggestion, the power of the collective unconscious, simple coincidence or chance—all of these may explain how, in fact, magic does work, quite apart from the use of poisons which may be feared for their symbolic, rather than their toxic, qualities. However, the belief that an actual rite contains an automatic power of its own, without reference to any other agency physical or psychical, is mistaken. Evil magic works, if it does, for reasons other than those assumed by its practitioner. And there are, of course, built-in reasons for failure: the spell was incorrect, taboos were not observed, the victim's protective or retaliatory magic was stronger and so on. More important, however, than how sorcerers harm their victims is the fact that they inevitably harm themselves. Even if the means taken to harm another are objectively groundless, they *are* intended to harm and, furthermore, they may have chance effects, social effects, psychical or even physical effects on the victim. The intention to harm and actions taken to realize that intention are seriously culpable and contrary to charity.

The main difficulty with beliefs about witchcraft and sorcery is that they assume the only effective answer is to retaliate in kind. That is how the witchdoctor got a bad name and how witch and witch-finder became confused. Even though the traditional doctor in ethnic cultures such as those of sub-Saharan Africa is regarded as a great blessing to society and a benefactor to his clients, he dabbles in rituals and medicines which are known to be objectively harmful, even lethal. We saw this in the case of the witchdoctors consulted by Hela Tatu's relatives in their anxiety to be revenged against Mpanda Goye. Set a witch to catch a witch! There is more than just a grain of truth in it. Beliefs about witchcraft and sorcery tend to reduce those who hold them to the level of witches and sorcerers themselves. The cosmic conspiracy of evil is so successful that one can only beat it by playing its own game.

Nothing could be further from the true spirit of religion than pandering to beliefs of witchcraft and sorcery. No account is taken of God's providence or omnipotence. There is no trust in God or in fellow human beings. The belief feeds on popular fears and rumours. It is a despair of ultimate goodness and encourages the very attitudes which are the props of witchcraft theory: enmity and envy, secrecy and revenge. This is the reverse of the teaching of Christ.

You have learnt how it was said: Eye for eye and tooth for tooth. But I say this to you: offer the wicked man no resistance. On the contrary, if anyone hits you on the right cheek, offer him the other as well.[3]

By giving examples of injustice of which we ourselves are the victim, Christ showed that he did not forbid his followers to resist unjust attack in order to defend themselves and others, still less to struggle to eliminate wickedness from the world at large. What we are strictly commanded to do is to desist from returning evil for evil, revenging, getting even, paying off scores. The Mahatma Gandhi echoed Christ's teaching in his own way: 'If everyone took an eye for an eye, the whole world would become blind'.[4] Eye for eye—this is the peculiar blindness of witchcraft theory and the fears it generates. True religion calls for repentance as far as the past is concerned and amendment for the future, but witchcraft theory has no faith in the convertibility of man. Once a witch, always a witch. True religion calls for healing, reconciliation, mutual service, not a preoccupation with searching out and exterminating (or at least ostracizing) the alleged human causes of misfortune.

How does one heal a society suffering from its own self-inflicted wounds of witchcraft and sorcery? How does one eliminate a paranoid system of such magnitude? Anthropologists and missiologists have been debating this question for many years. It is a constant preoccupation of pastors in missionary regions of the Third World. To answer the question, we cannot do better than to turn to the historical example of Europe's own witch-craze, and even to examples old and recent in the new world of North America.

Professor Norman Cohn has studied the evolution of European witchcraft theory and practice.[5] In pre-Christian Europe there was a fairly generalized belief in witches and also in evil spirits that copulated with human beings. Up to the tenth century, the teaching of the Church was clear (cf. the *canon episcopi* in the collection of Abbot Regino of Prüm) that one who believes in witches is a pagan or infidel and that witchcraft belief is incompatible with Catholic faith. However, in the eleventh and twelfth centuries economic and social conflicts began to multiply while competition for leadership within and between the emerging nationalisms began to be intensified. At the same time Islam posed a serious threat to the survival of Christian Europe. Fears of divisions within Christendom grew, as did popular anxiety about individuals and groups who failed to conform to the accepted norms of religious and social practice. The ancient beliefs about witches and demons now assumed a fearful relevance and were linked in people's minds with heterodox groups such as the Waldensians. Heresy, and any other misfortune which seemed to strike at human survival, particularly crop blights, livestock plagues and human sexual impotence, were laid at the door of witches and copulating devils.

At the same time the practice of ritual magic developed among some learned clerics who believed that devils could be conjured in God's name to reveal secret knowledge which would benefit humanity. Although the Church condemned such intentions, the practice of exorcism survived as a means of identifying demons and their human agents, the witches. As a result, the obsessive fears of the age gave rise to a belief in a secret sect of demon-worshippers or witches who made a pact with Satan and who held secret meetings known as covens, sabbaths or synagogues, at which they adored Satan and practised infanticide and cannibalism.

By the thirteenth and fourteenth centuries, the popular fantasies linking demons, witches and heretics had come to be accepted by the highest authorities in Church and State alike and justified the persecution of Jews and Christian sects, as well as any and every social misfit or innovator. Learned and saintly theologians like St Thomas Aquinas devoted their wisdom to explaining and rationalizing the fantasy that witches were actually 'children of the devil'.[6] Popes Gregory IX and Innocent VIII published Bulls which showed that Rome had completely accepted the witchcraft theory and which gave full credence to the popular fantasies.[7] Perhaps the most horrifying document of all was the book called *The Hammer of Witches* (*Malleus Maleficarum*), compiled by two Inquisitors, Sprenger and Kramer, in 1486.[8] This was a manual of witchcraft beliefs which detailed all the fantastic activities ascribed to witches: flying through the air, infanticide, changing people into wild animals, destruction of crops and domestic animals and above all impeding the power of procreation. The book's second part details all the tortures to be inflicted upon the accused as part of the judicial proceedings in cases of witchcraft accusation. The book fanned the flame of judicial fanaticism and sent thousands of men and women to a horrifying death.

From the fourteenth to the seventeenth centuries an organized campaign took place on the part of the authorities against suspected witches. Mass trials were held and the combination of exorcism and torture resulted in hundreds of people being put to death as allies of Satan. The witch-craze was subscribed to by both Catholics and Protestants and it has been estimated that as many as a third of the population of Europe were at one time regarded as 'secret witches'. The craze gradually flickered out at the end of the seventeenth century with the Essex witch trials in 1645 in England and the Salem witch-scare in America as late as 1692. However, it must be said that many modern social phobias operate on exactly the same lines as classic witchcraft. Joseph McCarthy, the Senator from Wisconsin, was responsible for a famous 'witch-hunt' after the Second World War, in a climate of mass paranoia against secret Reds. Popular fear and authoritative investigation were combined in the classic pattern until McCarthy was discredited. In many countries, politicians inveigh against unnamed 'enemies', 'opponents', 'traitors' who are subverting the country. There are often widespread fears in Third World countries of 'imperialists', 'Zionists', 'CIA' etc. who may not be a real threat but who are symbols of the invisible enemy in one's midst on whom all misfortunes are blamed. Such blanket explanations can easily develop into a 'witch-hunt', given the right social conditions, even though traditional popular fantasies may not be involved.

By and large, however, witchcraft (in the sense we have given to the term) is a thing of the past in Europe and North America. Social change brought about a measure of pluralism and individualism that destroyed not only the theoretical fabric of witchcraft but also the social structure that supported it. Church and State were able at last to break free of the popular fantasy and once authority ceased to support the beliefs and practices, they could not survive. Christians awoke from a long nightmare, determined never to allow themselves to become enmeshed in a similar craze.

In many Third World countries today health and health behaviour are linked to fears about witchcraft and sorcery. One even encounters Church leaders who privately support such explanations of misfortune. An African Bishop once told me that he attributed the deaths of three of his priests to witchcraft. Another Bishop asked me to investigate a witchcraft case concerning a prominent member of the diocese, who sincerely believed he was under a spell. There is, of course, much to be said about bringing fears out into the open, since witchcraft beliefs and practices thrive on secrecy. Yet there is but a small step between airing one's private fears and seeking support for one's sinister interpretation of events. The private fear may rapidly become a popular fantasy or social paranoia, especially if authority gives approval. The Church burnt its fingers during the European witch-craze and has no desire to repeat those five hundred years of misery. Yet, on the other hand, convinced believers in witchcraft can become even more firmly assured when they encounter a dismissive attitude that refuses to take their explanations seriously. The foreign missionary, for example, who pooh-poohs witchcraft is often treated as an ignoramus.

My own inclination in these matters is to refuse to enter into any discussion of the objectivity of the beliefs, for that is what they are, beliefs which do not rest on empirical, scientific evidence. As Evans-Pritchard discovered among the Azande people of Sudan, convinced believers in witchcraft are not impressed by scientific arguments.[9] Equally, nothing should be said or done which gives the slightest official or authoritative credence to the beliefs. If people bring secret fears of this kind out into the open, one must be very careful indeed not to enter into their mental world. Instead, they must be encouraged to take positive action in other directions.

Witchcraft fears can be endemic to a whole situation. That social world must be transformed, if the fears are to disappear. Socio-economic development and Christian community-building are certainly helpful in bringing about the transformation that is required. What is needed is to abandon the dualistic philosophy. People must be convinced that they can win the battle of life. They must discover self-confidence through a greater trust in God and in each other. This they can only achieve if there is communication with both God and neighbour and with God-in-neighbour, and when a person's preoccupation is shifted away from self to a concern for the neighbour. Believers in witchcraft see their neighbour as a threat. They also see suffering as something to be avoided at the expense of their neighbour. Such attitudes nourish witchcraft fears. What is it that prevents people from loving their neighbour? It is their own sin and their own selfishness. If practical attitudes can be changed, then witchcraft theory and the social institutions through which it operates will be discredited. In fact, they will no longer be relevant, because God's victory over evil will generate greater trust and confidence.

9

Non-human sources of evil

Spring sunshine dappled the tall white buildings that lined Bota-
fogo Bay and in the distance wispy clouds swirled around Rio de
Janeiro's famous Sugar Loaf Mountain. Corcovado, with its
giant statue of Christ, was invisible on that September morning.
This visit to Brazil in 1983 was my first and the enjoyable
stay with the Brazilian branch of my family was ending all too
rapidly. I had wanted to leave with a few souvenirs and I had been
fascinated by Brazil's African religions and the lighted candles or
offerings which I was continually seeing on rocks or roadsides.
My brother guided me down a crowded narrow street to a 'cult
shop'. The shop was a mixture of store and sanctuary. There was
a counter all right, and a shopkeeper, but all around were gods
and goddesses, brightly painted, many with lamps or candles
burning in front of them and some with small bottles or plates
containing food and drink. It was not like a Catholic repository
where statues are just so much merchandise until they have been
blessed and installed on their altar or destined pedestal. Here
everything was already sanctified and statues, as soon as they left
their mould or had their last lick of shiny paint, were already
vehicles of mysterious power. There must have been many
among the poor of Rio who could not afford to buy a statue of
Oxala, Shango or Ogun, but who could still pay their respects to
the gods in the shop.

I was mainly interested in the god Exu. Originally one of the
pantheon of the Nigerian Yoruba, he was, like most African
divinities, morally ambivalent. He was the god of paths, door-
ways and openings. He also possessed phallic importance, presiding over the sexual act. He was a mischievous god and a god of
vengeance whose power to harm could be turned against the

worshipper's enemies. In the syncretist religious traditions of Brazil, he was most frequently identified with the Devil, but because one of his functions had been that of divine spokesman or messenger, he could also be identified with St Anthony of Padua or with the angel Gabriel.[1] These are the peculiar problems of religious syncretism but there are many devout people in the world who feel more comfortable with a devil who is not too devilish.

The shopkeeper took several plaster Exus off the shelf and dusted them down. They came in all sizes. In each case the god was represented in Mephistophelean scarlet, but he wore an ordinary jacket, trousers and bowler hat. He was clearly a god of dissipation and good-living and I thought of the libations of brandy that people in Rio made to him. I had wanted a really diabolical-looking statue to take with me, but Exu was a disappointment. He was too genteel and there was no real harm in him, I thought. Somehow he epitomized the whole problem of evil and its relationship to a Deity that is good. He was too disturbing for me and I left him behind in the cult-shop with the disappointed shopkeeper.

The Brazilian Exu was a devil with a likeable streak in him. Akuj was a 'good' deity with an ugly habit of making his worshippers die of hunger. I met Akuj in the Karamoja district of Uganda, an area of endemic famine. Karamoja is a triangle of country where the frontiers of Uganda, Sudan, Ethiopia and Kenya all meet. Its gateway is formed by two grand mountains, Akisim and Napak, the former having an impressive free-standing pillar of rock in front of it, called Alekilek, 'the thing which totters'. Once through the gateway, the road takes you into another world, a flat lunar landscape dotted with conical volcanic hills and browny-blue thorn-scrub. The men wear elaborate headdresses of painted mud, stuck with feathers, but apart from a black cloak blowing in the warm wind are otherwise entirely naked. Karimojong women, on the other hand, are heavily clad from the waist with bunches of skins and ornaments of metal chains. They also have innumerable copper rings around their necks, lined with grease for ease of movement. The Karimojong are semi-nomadic pastoralists, keepers and tireless raiders of cattle.

1969 was another year of famine for the people of Karamoja and I was taken by a friend to a small village called Nawanatau to distribute famine relief in the shape of sacks of maize. It was April

and the rains, expected in March, still showed no signs of mater-
ializing. Making up the party was a priest whose name in the
local language meant 'meat'. This turned out to be a good omen,
for at Nawanatau we walked straight into a bloody sacrifice
being offered to Akuj. The Karimojong have no other god beside
Akuj. His name means 'sky' and his principal function is to send
rain to provide the cattle with pasture. A black bull, the colour of
the expected rain-clouds, had been slaughtered and was being
divided and roasted in a communion rite. Only men could participate and we were welcomed, not least because of our friend
whose name was 'meat'. Naked worshippers were squatting
around camp-fires, cooking the meat on the end of their razor-
sharp spears. Under a large tree, where immolation had taken
place, the hindquarters of the beast had been set aside as a
portion for Akuj. A young man advanced towards me with two
pieces of meat on a spear. I took the first piece, a well-cooked
fillet, and thought I had escaped lightly enough. However, the
man had kept the second piece of meat for me also. It was a large
steak, burnt black on the outside but raw and bloody inside.
Without knife, fork, or plate, I struggled to tear at the meat with
my hands and teeth, getting my shirt front stained with the blood
of sacrifice in the process. It was late afternoon when we left the
hospitable people of Nawanatau and I continued my stay in the
area till the end of April, but there was still no sign of Akuj's rain.
'Maybe', said the priest whose name was 'meat', 'Akuj is sending
famine this year, instead of rain.' It would not have been the first
time.

Praying to a God who 'sends' famine put me in mind of King
David's idea of Yahweh. David had carried out a census, thus
usurping God's prerogative of caring for the increase of the
nation. For his punishment, he had to choose between three years
of famine, three months of military defeat and three days of
pestilence. As we saw in Chapter 3, David chose pestilence
because it seemed to come more directly from God and to be
more amenable to his mercy. It seems particularly hard when
even David's sin was also regarded by the author of the Second
Book of Samuel as the work of Yahweh:

The anger of Yahweh once again blazed out against the Israelites and he incited
David against them. 'Go', he said, 'take a census of Israel and Judah.''

The parallel passage in the First Book of Chronicles gives a
different identity to David's tempter:

Satan rose against Israel and incited David to take a census of the Israelites.[3]

A cynical Satan, or an angry Yahweh? We are back at the problem of Exu and the origin of the Devil in a good Deity. In the three hundred years or so between the Books of Samuel and Chronicles, Satan had been dissociated from Yahweh.

The question of God's ambivalence is, in fact, never very far away. After all, even Christians in Europe and North America pray for rain, or for fine weather, without apparently wondering why God allowed the drought or the flood in the first place. We are not likely to push the discussion about God as absolute cause of everything, including evil, much further than we did in Chapter 2. God permits evil in the present order of things. Are the various non-human causes of evil simply an alibi for God, or do they correspond to genuine human experience? Let us consider some of the suppositions and alternatives.

It is clear that human beings cannot, in the ordinary course of events, be held responsible for natural disasters such as earthquakes, hurricanes or droughts. The concept of the divine king is nevertheless a kind of halfway notion. It is believed that his own physical well-being is mysteriously bound up with the well-being of the material universe. The Emperor of China had to sit motionless for a period of time every day so that his country would remain at peace. The Mogo Naba of Burkina Faso (formerly Upper Volta)'s Mossi tribe still comes out of his palace before dawn in order to make the sun rise and the Mukama of Bunyoro in Uganda was supposed not to turn over in bed in case there should be an earthquake. One poor divine king of the Bungu in southern Tanzania was deposed because he allowed Lake Rukwa (which is subject to intense evaporation) to dry up.

However, the divine king remained a human being, even though he constituted in himself a kind of sacrament for his people. He was simply part of a pre-existing divine order for which he was not ultimately responsible. These rulers were 'vicars' of God whose own lives were bound up more closely with the rhythms and cataclysms of the natural world than were the lives of their people. They were the most 'tabooed' human beings imaginable and their responsibility really went no further than the avoidance of super-taboos. The taboos were not of their making.

Generally speaking, apart from the concept of witchcraft which was discussed in Chapter 8, physical evil is attributed to

non-human sources in the various religious systems of humanity. Even so, it is usual to personalize such non-human sources.
In the small-scale village world of rural societies, where social
differentiation is minimal and personal relationships are maxi-
mized, it is understandable that clear distinctions are wanting,
that natural events, whether good or bad, should be treated as if
they were persons, or at any rate ascribed to personal, though
non-human, causes. Such a tendency to personalize experience
can be very satisfying, both in terms of explanation and in terms
of human control. It helps people to come to grips with the
unfamiliar or fear-inspiring in their experience. It helps to clas-
sify that experience and, to some extent, even to humanize it. A
person can be spoken to, can be bargained with. One can enter
into a relationship with a person, even a non-human one.

A problem that arises, however, is whether such personalizations of experience have an objective reality and, if so, what kind
of objectivity. Are they mere metaphors or modes of speech in
the minds of those who invoke them? In many parts of eastern
and central Africa, for example, people speak of 'Mother Earth'
without imputing objective personality to the Earth. Over much
of western Africa, however, when people speak of 'Mother
Earth', they refer to an objective and personal Earth Goddess. If
such personalizations are not autonomous beings with an independent existence, they might be psychic realities—a kind of
socio-psychiatric reaction to shared experiences, although the
people who have these reactions may not worry very much
about the kind of reality they possess. They are real enough for
them and, in seeing them as persons, they tend to treat them
accordingly. Such personalizations which are more than
metaphors are by no means necessarily objects of religious
worship. Usually, this is very far from being the case. They are
neutral spirits or talking 'germs', comparable to leprechauns,
'little people' or fairies in the folklore of rural Europe. They are a
nuisance that has to be dealt with in a matter-of-fact way, on a
quid pro quo basis. Bargains must be struck with them and they
must be encouraged to keep away or else to stop their annoyances
and their harmful practices. They are not 'devils' in the western
sense, nor are they as implacably evil as the witches. They are not
'angels' or intercessors, or in any way a direct part of divine
providence and governance, and the commerce that takes place
between them and human beings is far from being prayer.

In periods of intensive and extensive social change, new and threatening experiences may be personalized as alien spirits and associated with communities of affliction, liminal rituals (which we have already described), and spirit mediumship. Alien spirits are another example of socio-psychiatric spirits and they may represent alien groups of people or individuals, new social problems or diseases, new technological inventions like the aeroplane which are remote or mysterious for villagers in rural areas. Even famines, droughts, epidemics, or economic ills such as inflation and shortages of commodities can be personalized as alien spirits.

A term which is frequently used by writers to allude to this tendency to personalize experience and to people the world with spirits is *animism*. It was Sir Edward Tylor who coined the word and used it in the first place to describe his own theory of the evolution of religious beliefs from dreams, then to the concept of the soul and finally to disembodied spirits who were objects of worship.[4] Needless to say, this was a wholly gratuitous evolutionist theory which is impossible to verify, but the term animism has survived to describe the mentality which views the world as being 'alive' and most, if not all, experiences as being in some sense 'personal'. Frequently the exponents of non-Christian traditional ethnic religions are called animists, but this does them less than justice. An animistic outlook easily co-exists with beliefs in a creator or supreme being and other eminent spiritual beings. So-called animist religion is usually not reducible to the socio-psychiatric personalizations we have been speaking about, most of which are not, in any case, religious phenomena at all.

Another interpretative concept has been *animatism* which posits the existence of a cosmic impersonal force, analogous to, say, electricity, an unseen living power possessed by beings and experiences in a greater or larger quantity. For some years anthropologists were fascinated by this idea and believed they had identified it in the Polynesian concept of *mana* or ritual power. Such a concept has been verified in other societies and in other parts of the world; for example, J. H. M. Beattie identified the similar-sounding *mahano* among the Nyoro of Uganda in Africa as 'ritual power'.[5] A very popular example of this way of thinking has been Placide Tempels' concept of 'vital force' among the Bantu of central and southern Africa.[6] Tempels went so far as to use this term to refer to the dynamic nature of being itself among Bantu peoples. However, it is very questionable that African peoples conceive of being as 'force'. Vincent Mulago has argued for the idea of beings endowed with the quality of forceful life, rather than vital force and this approach is probably generally true of other cultures in which foreign observers have discerned impersonal forces.[7] Although it may be possible to make abstraction of the quality in question, it is never apprehended in a non-personal way, but is always the endowment of an individual or being conceived as personal. Animatism therefore rests on shaky foundations and possibly more on the speculation of scholars interpreting ideas that are strange to them than upon the beliefs and practices of the people themselves.

In the traditional societies of Third World cultures, then, the forces which are held responsible for physical misfortune which is not attributable to human wickedness are conceived as personal or as qualities with which personal beings are endowed. They are not independently operating impersonal forces. They tend to be seen as morally neutral beings against which one must be 'inoculated', often by entering into communication with them. It is, if you like, a 'spirit theory' of disease, instead of a germ theory.

At many points in this book we have discussed the relationship of sins and moral offences to divine punishment in the shape of sickness and misfortune. A variation on this theme occurs in those societies which practise the veneration of ancestors. We briefly referred to this practice in its various forms in Chapter 4. We saw there that ancestors could be regarded as guardians of the living, ready to mete out punishment if their descendants neglected to remember them or make offerings to them. We also considered the category of wholly malevolent ancestral spirits, people who died with 'a chip on their shoulder', as it were, and who now take it out on the living, of whom they are acutely jealous. Considered rationally, such anthropomorphism could be seen as morbid, although it is merely another aspect of the moral ambivalence attributed to spiritual beings in African and other cultures. For ancestral spirits are ultimately surrogates for God in one sense or another. The amoral representatives of an amoral God? Perhaps. In practice, however, they were not as a group thought to be evilly disposed towards the living. On the contrary. It was only the Christian missionaries who outraged family piety and turned them into devils. It is perhaps significant that the ubiquitous Brazilian god Exu stands for the souls of the departed in Purgatory according to the view of popular Christianity in Cuba.

The Judeo-Christian tradition has developed a belief in cosmic forces of evil which are symbolically, but not necessarily causally, linked to human suffering. They are representations of the elemental forces intrinsically present in experience and they are by definition immoral, that is to say sinful and conducive to sin. Islam, which can also be regarded as an appendage of the Judeo-Christian tradition, appears to have developed a more ambivalent kind of devil. Its *djinn*, led by Iblis, appear to be morally ambiguous and even capable of conversion. In many parts of eastern Africa, for example, the *majini* (*Djinn*) approximate to the socio-psychiatric personalizations about which we have just been speaking. Not so in the Christian tradition. We have already spoken of the experience of evil as being external to the individual and even of the concept of social sin. It is clear that evil is an external objective reality. It is also clear that there is an organized 'mystery' of evil which God in Jesus Christ came to combat and to overcome. The Bible describes this mystery of evil in personal terms and it also sees the deeply rooted human experience of suffering as analogous to the slavery caused by sin, as an occasion for repentance, for purification and ultimately redemption.

The names Satan and Devil derive from Hebrew, Greek and Latin originals meaning 'adversary'. Anybody in the Biblical language and culture could be called a 'satan', as Peter was so called by Christ.[8] It was originally a legal term which, in the Book of Job, is applied to one of the 'sons of God', that is, the heavenly court, whose task it was to accuse, prosecute, test, tempt, and even execute punishment.[9] We see him standing at 'God's right hand', endowed with authority by God to lay bare human wickedness. The picture is one in which the Devil is not yet clearly dissociated from God himself, but it is a stage removed from David's understanding of Yahweh causing him to sin and then sending a pestilence to punish him, or Saul being possessed by an evil spirit sent from Yahweh which makes him throw a spear at the youthful David.

It is chiefly the apocalyptic literature of the Bible which develops the mystery of evil and the empire of sin in the world in terms of the primeval tempter, the serpent, the dragon, the beast, 'the seducer of the whole world', the opponent of God in the cosmic struggle between good and evil and ultimately the Anti-Christ. Yahweh's opponent was also given the names of pagan gods and kings in the Biblical books: Beelzebub, Belial, Lucifer. Finally, in the New Testament, Christ also refers to him as the

'Prince of this world' and he is commonly called Satan and Devil by all the New Testament writers.

Popular Christian tradition has developed the iconography as well as the psycho-social consciousness of Satan from many sources, some of them pre-Christian and pagan. A good example of the popular understanding about Satan in nineteenth-century European circles is provided by the following declaration from a demonopathic medium in 1895:[10]

I cover the world with ruins, I drown it in blood and tears. I deform what is beautiful. I soil what is pure. I overthrow the great. I do all the evil that I can. I would like to increase it to infinite proportions. I am all hatred, nothing but hatred. If you only knew the height and the breadth of this hatred, then you would have a vaster knowledge than any that has existed since the beginning, even if it were all added together. And the more I hate, the more I suffer. My hatred and my suffering are immortal like myself. For I cannot not hate, any more than I can not live forever. But would you like to know what increases this suffering? What multiplies this hatred? It is that I know I am beaten and that my hatred is useless, that I do all this evil in vain.

In vain? No! No! Because I have the joy, if you can call it a joy (if it were a joy, it would be the only joy I have)—I have the joy of killing the souls for which He shed his blood, for whom He died and rose again and ascended into Heaven. Oh yes, I make his incarnation useless, and his death—the death of God—I make them useless for the souls I kill.

Do you understand that? To kill a soul! He created it in his image. He made it in his likeness. He loved it with an infinite love. He was crucified for it and I take it. I steal it from him. I kill it. I kill this soul. I damn it along with myself. It has preferred me to him. I did not come down from Heaven for it. I did not die for it.

How does it come about that I tell you all this, you who may be converted? You are going to escape me. I have to say it. He forces me to do it. He uses me against myself. I always have him before the eyes of my mind, yes God as he was when I adored him with such transports that would break all the saints' hearts if they had experienced them as I did. If only you could have seen that light, that beauty, that goodness, that greatness, that perfection!

How then did I lose all that? I was so happy, so happy and now I am eternally unhappy, and I hate Him. If you knew how I hate him, his divinity, his humanity, his angels, his saints, His Mother above all! It is she who conquered me. Would you like to know how I suffer and how I hate? Well, I am now capable of as much hate and sorrow as I was then capable of love and happiness.

I, Lucifer, became Satan, he who is always contrary. At this moment, I have the whole world in my thoughts, all peoples, all governments, all laws. I hold the reins of all the evil which is being prepared. And I can do nothing against this priest, this old man, the Pope. If I could simply damn the Pope! A Pope who would damn himself! If you could only understand! The Holy Spirit is there assisting him. The Holy Spirit prevents him from teaching heresy, from teaching even a doubtful doctrine when he speaks as Pope. Ah, you see a Pope is something very special!

Well, I also have my Church. In my Church there is a Society of Satan, just as there is a Society of Jesus in yours. Do you know what it is? It is Freemasonry. But they can do nothing against your Church except persecute it like Nero, Diocletian, Julian and the Jacobins. And what do I get out of it afterwards? I am conquered in advance. And yet I have always won this victory, killing his souls. I kill his souls, immortal souls, souls he bought on Calvary. How mad human beings are! They can be bought with a little bit of pride, a little bit of mud, a little bit of gold.

But do you think He would suffer? Tell me, would He suffer, if He could suffer? But he cannot suffer. Never mind, I kill his souls. I kill his souls. I kill his souls.

This remarkable outpouring has several fascinating implications. For one thing it shows how Satan in this case upholds the teaching and discipline of the contemporary Church, from the dogma of the incarnation and paschal mystery, right down to the declaration of papal infallibility and the condemnation of the Freemasons. It also pinpoints the paradox which is the concept of Satan himself, that he both is conquered and yet conquers, suffers and rejoices, hates and yearns for what he has lost. The mystery of evil is still a mystery even when it is removed from the heavenly court.

That Satan and other agents of evil are regarded, and spoken of, as persons, is part of Catholic tradition. In 1975 a Statement from the Sacred Congregation for the Doctrine of the Faith[11] recommended the faithful to believe in the Devil, not only as an objective reality, but also as a personal reality. This recommendation did not invoke the doctrine as being *definitive tenenda* (to be held definitively) but it certainly implied that the personal reality of Satan was part of the faith of Christians. Most theologians today are not prepared to speculate as to what this 'personal' character of Satan actually means. In what sense is Satan personal? Is his personality comparable to ours? Is it comparable to God's personality? Is he a real person or a real personalization? Speculation where Satan is concerned is, in any case, unhealthy. We do not believe in Satan, as we believe in Jesus Christ. Satan is not the object of faith and we do not enter into a dynamic and transforming relationship with him by saying that he exists as a 'personal reality', whatever that may mean. God forbid that we should! We believe in Christ who has conquered Satan and all that Satan represents.

There have been saints, such as the Curé d'Ars, who believed that they were obsessed by Satan, even though authorities during the Church's witch-craze believed that diabolical obsession and possession were a punishment for sin. There have been holy missionaries, like the late Bishop Shanahan of Nigeria, who constantly felt the power of evil in the villages and communities they evangelized and who believed they were sometimes physically prevented by Satan from carrying out their work. How far was such an attitude a product of defective salvation theology rather than a correct interpretation of missionary frustration? There are certainly people who feel that their personalities are submerged by the Devil or devils, and the medium just quoted was among them. In many cases these are psychotic projections. There are certainly people who feel powerless against the whole cosmic 'legion' of devils and who experience the world of suffering and wickedness as a multiplicity of demons: demons of sickness, demons of lies, demons of fornication, demons of drug-addiction, demons of divorce, Hitler-demons, even (in the view of some fundamentalists) theologian-demons and Biblical exegete-demons!

Yet there are limits to which one can go in the demonization of experience, if one wishes to remain faithful to Christian tradition. The Devil is not a direct cause of illness, even though there may be a link between moral and physical ill-health. To credit every misfortune and every inexplicable failure or accident with a diabolical origin is irrational and subversive of the virtues of faith and hope. An overpowering consciousness of Satan and of demonic influence in the world can lead to the kind of dualism and sense of hopelessness in the face of evil which we discussed in the last chapter *à propos* of witchcraft. One sometimes hears scholars of religion praising the sense of the demonic which they discern in traditional ethnic religious systems, but there is a danger of imposing alien concepts on these systems. Although it has been said that 'the African is naked in front of evil',[12] for example, it is not at all clear that the evil Africans fear is perceived as demonic, at least if they are faithful to their tradition. Witches perhaps, socio-psychiatric spirits and personalizations, but not demons in the sense in which the Christian uses the term. We should certainly not be too quick to allocate demons or impute diabolical causes. God is in his heaven and the victory is his.

Which brings us once again to the starting-point of this chapter, the problem of God and the Devil, of moral dualism or moral monism. Karen Blixen in her classic account of Kenya in the 1920s wrote of the Africans with whom she lived:

They had preserved a knowledge that was lost to us by our first parents; Africa amongst the continents will teach it to you: that God and the Devil are one. . . .[13]

God and the Devil are one! That is the simple monistic approach which satisfied King David and the Karimojong and which perhaps sweetened the manners of the Brazilian Exu, turning him into the golden-tongued St Anthony of Padua or Gabriel, the messenger of joy. Evil remains always a mystery but ultimately it is located in God as ultimate cause. It is also located in God in the sense that God swallows it up in his victory. Job's message was: Grasp the mystery but do not try to understand, but the mystery is fascinating as well as fear-inspiring and it tends to generate reaction that runs to extremes. On the one hand, there is the temptation to curse God, as Job's wife in fact did, the refusal to bow before the mystery, let alone to identify levels of secondary causality. To say, as many religious systems do say: God and the Devil are one. On the other hand, there is the refusal to credit God with the victory over evil and the willingness to be mesmerized by its manifestations. As Anthony Storr has written: 'The Devil only remains devilish, if he is dissociated from the Deity from which he took his origin'.[14] The Devil must always be thought of in relation to God, as conquered in advance by him; otherwise his devilishness is overpowering and a religion of God turns into a religion of the Devil. The Christian believes that evil and moral wickedness have no future. The future lies with God and not with Satan.

But there are many aspects of the mystery which are impervious to speculation and probing. Has God triumphed so long as Satan can snatch souls from him? Is Hell part of God's triumph? Theological rationalizations of Hell do not always sound convincing, but so long as we can freely choose to refuse God's goodness it remains a very real possibility, and one that was envisaged by Jesus himself. Purgatory is, of course, the antechamber of Heaven and there is no middle way between Heaven and Hell. This remains true, even though we do not know if there is anyone who has made himself so impervious to God's mercy as to remain in the state we call Hell. All of this means that physical healing and even moral healing are not enough if they merely restore the *status quo ante*. We look to a new life, a wholeness on a higher plane, a plane of existence in which evil has no part and healing is redundant. Satan is part of the picture in so far as his evil is swallowed up in God's goodness. It is to that extent that he is testimony to transcendent wholeness.

In these first nine chapters we have enumerated the various levels at which human beings experience 'darkness' or lack of wholeness—environmental, physical, psychic, social, moral. We have also shown how all these levels, while distinct in themselves, are nevertheless linked to one another. They are linked to one another in terms of ordinary cause and effect, but they are linked at a deeper level. Within the darkness shines the light of God, revealed in Jesus Christ, source of all healing and of ultimate wholeness. Suffering is a paradox because it both limits and transcends our experience at one and the same moment. Yet whatever we suffer in our own lives and through our own human nature cannot be more of a paradox than the mystery of a suffering God. It is this mystery of power exemplified in weakness that dispels the darkness and draws all forms of healing into its own deifying light. The second part of this book concentrates on the various forms of healing and on how they contribute in their different ways to the restoration of wholeness by Jesus Christ, whose life is the light of humankind.

Part Two

Light shines in the dark

And that life was the light of men,
a light that shines in the dark,
a light that darkness could not overpower.

John 1:4–5

Introduction

In Part One of this book we have dealt with the different levels at which human beings experience darkness or lack of wholeness—in the physical world, illness, death, the breakdown of social relationships, psychiatric disorders and moral disorders or sin. We have also considered human speculation about preternatural and cosmic forces of evil. We have shown how all of this experience is essentially ambivalent. Not only does it portray the limitations of the human condition, but it also reveals the reality of power through weakness. God himself, the source of all healing and wholeness, is present in that dark cloud through the redemptive mystery of Jesus Christ.

In this second part we consider various levels and activities of healing and discover how all of these are taken up by Jesus Christ and fulfilled by him. There are deviations which detract from the ideal of integral healing in Christ, and these have to be corrected. In the end it is the vocation of the Church to display the ideal in practice, and the last three chapters discuss how this can best be done.

Chapter 10 speaks about medicine as an agent of divine power. In themselves, pharmacological knowledge and scientific medicine are limited. They are even more limited when taken in relation to levels of healing other than the physical. This is one reason for the rise of so-called alternative medicine, which resembles the pre-scientific practice of the Third World medicine-man. Such types of medical practice involve category mistakes, and it has to be recognized that, while integral healing explores the connections between the various levels at which lack of wholeness is experienced, it should not confuse these levels. Prayer and medicine are not the same things, but prayer is related to medicine and does have a powerful influence in healing. Healing prayer has to take account of medical practice and of the saving value of suffering.

Magic, as Chapter 11 sets out to show, is a form of irrational and self-oriented manipulation. As such, it is opposed to the mentality of prayer or supplication. In so far as it stems from ignorance, it should be subjected to a pedagogy that elevates it towards real faith and away from uncomprehending superstition. Magic has nothing to do with a truly sacramental mentality, nor can it be excused on the grounds of expectations about future parapsychological discoveries. The New Testament reveals magic as 'the enemy of true religion' and completely opposed to the concept of miracle, which is the direct confrontation with God's healing love. Theories of miracle in terms of 'the limits of scientific explanation' are also totally inadequate. God's greatest sign is still Calvary and his real power, the weakness of the Cross.

Third World cultures respect the subconscious, particularly as manifested in dreams. Dreams serve the goal of wholeness in one way or another. Chapter 12 discusses them from various angles, as a corrective of conscious attitudes, as diagnostic of illness, as reflections of culture patterns, as a psychological preparation for future events. Dreams are the workshop in which new cultural forms taken by the Christian faith are hammered out, but they are also reflections of the deeper reality of the world of the Spirit. As such, they relate to transcendental wholeness. The power of dreams to heal, to affirm and to inspire is harnessed in integral healing.

Chapter 13 discusses new religious movements as quests for healing and redemption. Unfortunately, many of them are based on unacceptable dualistic assumptions and on the adventist tendency to situate the millennium in the present. Witchcraft eradication movements and movements for 'world-cleansing' operate in waves and tend to strengthen the paranoid fear they profess to eliminate. They lead to quietism, irrelevance or a 'power-monopoly' religion. Christ's message is not that the definitive victory is immediately available or fully realizable in this world, but that the Kingdom has been inaugurated and will be fulfilled.

Chapter 14 deals with spirit-healing and the pragmatic manipulative rituals of personalized psycho-social realities—the alien and patronal spirits of African tradition. These are the rituals of so-called 'communities of affliction' or clubs of the sick that practise mental dissociation and glossolalia. Glossolalia (speaking with tongues) seems to have a therapeutic value, but it should 'edify' and not divide the community. The dilemma of Christians confronted by these 'communities of affliction' is whether to accept the objective personal reality of morally neutral spirits or to identify them as devils. In the event, they should neither dissimulate nor distort. They have to choose the difficult *via media* of evangelizing the sufferer and building therapeutic communities centred on the healing power of Christ.

The next chapter notes the growing tendency in Africa and elsewhere to take the 'demonic option' and to indulge in mass exorcism of devils. Such practice denotes a strictly pessimistic view of religion and harks back to early missionary assumptions about the 'empire of Satan'. Like the millenarian movements, it strengthens, rather than eliminates, popular fears and, like the communities of affliction, it manipulates the powers of mental dissociation. The ministry of deliverance should be more closely circumscribed and should serve a supplicative, rather than a manipulative approach to healing.

Chapter 16 is the first of three final chapters that attempt to map out a policy for the Christian pastoral ministry. The celebration of the sacraments has to take place in the context of integral healing and not just at the level of morality and spirituality. The sacramental view of reality is essentially linked to the mystery of Christ who inaugurates transcendental wholeness. The Eucharist is the central sacrament of Christian life which binds together every level of healing, physical, psychic, social, moral and environmental.

Healing gifts in the Church are the subject of Chapter 17. Their integration within pastoral practice must not entail abuse of the sacraments or a confusion of categories. The liminal phenomenon of pilgrimages to centres of healing has a privileged place in the Catholic tradition, but the concept of miracle as proof of orthodoxy or sanctity has been misleading. Practical guidelines of how to deal with the alien or patronal spirits are offered and the context of the ministry of deliverance is also discussed. Finally, some guidance for community healing services is offered.

The last chapter considers the need for a seriously organized pastoral care of the sick and not simply Church involvement in medical treatment and health care. Proselytism in this area is totally out of place. What the pastoral care of the sick amounts to is giving them a foretaste of the transcendent wholeness proclaimed and inaugurated by Christ, sharing with them something of the joy, the security, the certainty of Heaven. Healing is fulfilled in the resurrection in which we are all called to share. In this final resurrection the scars of the wounds which Christ has healed will still be there, but they will now be glorious. Thus healing in all its forms on earth contributes to final wholeness.

10

Scientific and pre-scientific medicine

A medicine-man's herbs and potions have no power in themselves of acting physiologically on the patient. They are but the agents through which invisible beings act. They are tools, and when they are thanked for their work they are thanked only as a hoe is thanked for its work.[1]

M. J. Field in her study of the religion and medicine of the Ga people of Ghana thus puts her finger on one of the differences of attitude between a western scientific approach to the use of herbs or pharmaceutical remedies and the approach of a medicine-man in a traditional Third World culture. She goes on to assert that there is no dividing line between using medicine in a simple physiological manner like food and using it to help the super-natural action of an invisible being. Food, after all, does not merely act physiologically, it acts by pleasing the eater. It pleases the *kla* of the eater, the life-soul or spirit-entity. So does medicine in the case of the sufferer, say the Ga people.[2] Moreover, spiritual beings act directly on the patient through the medicines and remedies which are applied. In Africa, healing is probably the most common theme of ordinary prayer and there is no opposi-tion between the use of herbs and the invocation of the Deity. 'We beseech thee, help us through these roots!' goes a prayer of the Luguru people of Tanzania addressed to the Supreme Being in the company of the ancestral spirits.[3] God is in those medicinal roots, producing his healing action. In some cultures a person becomes a herbalist because of the action of a dead relative who was a herbalist before him. Dr Michael Gelfand describes how the Shona of Zimbabwe believed that this happens when a man has continuous dreams about medical matters and about herbs and the places where these are to be found.[4] Every herbalist must hold a ceremony once a year to thank and praise his healing spirit, if his powers are not to fail.

We have already noted how the witchdoctor or traditional medicine-man operates on many different levels at once, the psychic, the social, the magical, the religious, as well as the physical. His is an integrated approach to healing and one in which spiritual powers play an all-pervasive role. The witchdoctor possesses considerable botanical and pharmacological knowledge. He learns this from other herbalists, from relatives who pass their expertise on to him, from a practitioner to whom he may have been apprenticed, and from his own accumulating experience. Yet this knowledge is severely limited and it may play a quite subsidiary role in the diagnostic interview and in the remedy that is prescribed. Often a great deal is left to the patient in the way of finding, mixing, cooking and applying the remedy. The following is a medical prescription quoted by Dr Una Maclean from a Yoruba medical book compiled in Nigeria:[5]

Remedy to kill all guinea worms

String made from the bark of *olorin* tree or *eru* tree. Make nine knots in the rope or tie it in nine places. Cut another rope into pieces. Put on it some white beans. Add some ground whip hide. Then put a snail in and cook them together without water.

> Eat the snail.
> Grind some of the beans, add shea butter and apply to the sore.
> The remaining beans should be eaten gradually.
> Then take the knotted string and use it to rub your body all over.
> Then insert it into the shell of the snail.

Next tie some white thread round your two wrists and ankles. Go near to the hole where you will bury the snail shell. There untie the threads and insert them into the snail shell.

> Then utter this incantation:
> 'I bury the dead of the guinea worm in my body, let it never attack me again, because the dead never rise into the world again.'

Then bury the shell and you will never suffer from the guinea worm again.

Clearly the pharmaceutical properties of this remedy are limited and Dr Maclean notes that it seems to rely more on the magical rationale of like curing like. It must also be very reassuring to the patient, since it provides both an internal and external medication and operates on a complete time-scale of past, present and future.

Western scientific medicine is wholly concerned with the

sphere of physical health and to a much smaller extent with healing in its entirety. Medical scientists tend to be pessimistic or optimistic about the pharmaceutical properties of traditional herbal medicine. Either they see the witchdoctor's emphasis on the psychic, social, symbolical and religious aspects of the cure as a substitute for effective pharmacological knowledge or they credit him with an understanding of physical remedies as yet unknown to medical science. The World Health Organization, Commonwealth bodies and a number of medical foundations and university schools of medicine have launched studies of herbal remedies in various parts of the world. It is a subject that receives considerable press and radio coverage in Third World countries, as if western medical science is about to confer the accolade of respectability and recognition upon the despised witchdoctor. Yet very few positive results seem to emerge. It may well be true that the lack of physical scientific knowledge, as well as a lack of scepticism about the occult, enabled the witchdoctor to develop parapsychological powers untapped and unexplained by western medical science. It is certainly true that, while western medicine is highly valued in Third World countries for its increasingly effective treatment of acute conditions, severe infections and surgical emergencies, the witchdoctor's practice continues to flourish for other than mainly pharmacological reasons, notably his efficacity in treating everyday complaints, and his integrated approach to healing that we have already noted.

We live in a world where medical discoveries and progress in medical science make daily headlines. There seems no limit to what doctors, surgeons and researchers can do: new wonder drugs, organic transplants, complex heart surgery, reattachment of severed limbs, obstetrics, *in vitro* fertilization and biological engineering. Far-reaching success is reported in wiping out smallpox, tuberculosis, leprosy and many other complaints. What we tend to forget is that scientific medicine has a remarkably short history. Two or three hundred years ago medical practice was crude in the extreme, to judge by the blood-chilling surgical instruments one sees in medical museums and by the equally horrifying accounts of treatments given to dying rulers who presumably commanded the best available medical resources of the time. Samuel Pepys's description of the trepanning of Prince Rupert in 1667, for example, and the doctors' fear that the 'whole inside of his head is corrupted' shows what a hit-or-miss affair surgery was in those days.[6] Blood-letting seems to have been the most common form of treatment, while medical theory rested on the concept of the four humours and on astrology, as much as on empirical experience and diagnosis. The advancement of medical science had to await growth in the practice of anatomical dissection, in the study of botany, chemistry and biology and other sciences. It depended on the ability to fashion precision instruments and make exact measurements. It depended as much on the development of communications and on the sharing of knowledge within the world medical community. Before these advances could be made, all medicine was 'alternative medicine'. It was all pre-scientific. Doctors were all of them witchdoctors, struggling in isolation to treat the sick according to their own lights and their own limited experience.

Under the impact of western medical science, the witchdoctor today often becomes more of a herbalist. Harjula's study of the herbalist Mirau in Tanzania demonstrates this.[7] So does Dr Maclean's account of magical medicine in Nigeria where the traditional doctor supplements his inherited ethno-medicinal repertoire with ideas gleaned from modern health education and western practice and where books of traditional remedies are produced with an eye to the reading public.[8] However, as we have said, the witchdoctor's pharmacological knowledge is limited. He has no means of analysing or measuring the chemical components of his remedies in any precise way. Often the therapeutic properties on which his cure relies are present in unequal quantities in the roots, leaves and pieces of bark that he employs. Without any precise instruments, he measures out his medicines with cigarette-tin lids, or small mentholatum bottles. In addition, he may have no very precise intentions about the effects of his remedies. They are vaguely supposed to cure pains in certain regions of the body.

All over Africa and in other countries and continents of the Third World are to be found peddlers of traditional medicines. Laid out on a cloth at a market, you will see bundles of leaves and roots which the peddler will explain to you, often with an exaggerated wealth of detail which does not inspire confidence. At Kumi market in eastern Uganda I once encountered a witchdoctor with a vast array of stones, shells, twigs and leather talismans spread out for sale.[9] There was also a large lump of dried wood and I asked what it could do. 'If you are bitten by a snake', he said, 'it will make you vomit the poison out of your body. It is a very powerful medicine', he added, 'it comes from Tanzania!' The mystique of distance, I reflected. In Dar-es-Salaam, capital of Tanzania, I examined a display of bottles of all shapes and sizes, set out for sale in a stall by the side of the road, a common sight in African towns and cities. The bottles bore labels such as 'stomach medicine', 'childbirth medicine', 'back medicine', 'head medicine', and they were filled with brownish-coloured powders or dark liquids. As it happened, there was no medicine from Uganda, but there could well have been.[10]

The westerner may smile at the crudeness and the *naïveté* of these remedies, but in spite of all its triumphs modern western medical science not only has its own limitations, it creates its own problems and develops its own illusions. Western medical science is, as we said, a recent phenomenon. It is also developing extremely fast indeed. Because of its very newness and speed of development, we are unable to know all the possible side-effects and long-term consequences of the drugs and treatments that are introduced. Moreover, resistance can be built up to the drugs, so that they lose their effect. Drugs may no longer help the patient and new strains of illness and infection appear that are drug-resistant. This is the situation today with malaria, the disease that is responsible for more fatalities in the Third World than any other. A few years ago, doctors were confident that malaria was under control. Today, they are far from sure about that, and opinion varies considerably about which drugs are appropriate in which regions of the world.

In addition to new virulent and drug-resistant strains of illnesses already known, there are also the so-called 'diseases of civilization'. These are illnesses associated with the modern life-style, with too rich a diet, with the rapid pace of modern life and the anxieties it provokes, with petrol fumes, industrial pollution, alcohol, cigarette smoking and drugs, and radio-active waste: cancer, heart disease, sexually-transmitted diseases, alcoholism and the neuroses, not to mention the possibilities of fatal accidents and physical disabilities caused by modern means of transport, the motor car, the motor-cycle, the aeroplane, and by urban violence and terrorism. Scientific exploration in the field of medicine is an on-going and never-ending struggle. It is a hydra whose multiple heads, when severed, produce twice as many in their place.

Limitless faith is placed in the possibilities of modern medical science by ordinary people, and they are surprised when they encounter chronic or terminal illness. Such experiences are more shocking in western countries than in the Third World where life is often cheap and life-expectation brief. There are also many small everyday complaints, simple infections and mild disturbances which sophisticated medicine can do little to prevent or alleviate, and there are the many conditions which in a modern technological society have a psychiatric basis. The modern role of the doctor has become dissociated from earlier comprehensive socio-moral roles. Doctors display a pluralism of ethical standards. They do not have a unified moral understanding of such questions as abortion, biological engineering, sterilization, contraception, euthanasia for severely handicapped infants or the terminally ill, the right moment to switch off a life-support machine in the case of a patient who cannot recover, problems concerning the transplanting of organs and so on. Watching a television programme in Australia in 1983 which discussed advances in developing human embryos outside the womb, I was surprised that only the medical and legal aspects of the question were mentioned, and that there was no reference whatever to religious or moral criteria.

The limitations of modern scientific medicine result in several consequences, one of which is a return to treatments of questionable validity in scientific terms—so-called 'alternative medicine'. In western countries today, alternative medicine in innumerable forms is growing apace: osteopathy, acupuncture, homeopathy, radiesthesia, acupressure or hand and foot reflexology, not to mention natural healing through herbs and health foods. Many of these practices are undoubtedly beneficial and cater for aspects and possibilities overlooked by medical science. Another consequence is to look for other levels of healing, the psychic, the social, the religious. The development of, and popular interest in, psychiatry corresponds to a widely felt contemporary need, as does also the creation of therapeutic communities and a growing interest in the social aspect of medicine. Religion, too, comes into its own, sometimes even as a self-professed 'science' which claims to be an alternative to scientific medicine—Christian Science, Scientology, Transcendental Meditation and the many movements of oriental origin which claim to offer techniques of heightened consciousness, of self-control and personal fulfilment. There is what Peter Nichols has called the morbid belief that religion can settle any and every problem directly without the mediation of human rational activity.[11] Charismatic and Pentecostal prayer groups can develop along these lines, even producing clients for psychiatric hospitals with paranoid psychoses.

This raises the question of category mistakes in healing. It is important to know what category one is dealing with and what are the limits of that category. 'More needs she the divine than the physician', exclaimed the good doctor on hearing the revelations of unnatural deeds by Lady Macbeth in her famous sleepwalking scene.[12] Shakespeare's doctor recognized the relevance of another category of healing for his patient, although, as the poet hints at the very end of the play, his advice was unavailing and the 'fiend-like Queen' by her own hand 'took off her life'.[13] There is always the danger that an integrated approach to healing may result in a confusion of categories. The following announcement appeared in a Tanzanian daily newspaper a few years ago:[14]

Announcement

The general public is informed that Falaki Sheikh Mohamed el Deen—A Sudaneses Professor has come back from *safari*.
The Professor adds that new kinds of medicine have arrived which can cure the following diseases:—

1—The Jin Maradhi of Jin (Spirit Illnesses)
2—Lames [*sic*] or Cripples
3—Stomach troubles
4—Birth Problems can be solved
5—Medicine which can prevent a bullet or a knife not [*sic*] to enter into your body
6—Medicine which makes weak one strong [sexual potency]
7—Medicine which cures evil spirits
8—Medicine which stops a thief not [*sic*] to steal any of your properties

He hereby asks his old patients kindly to come and collect their medicines. The treatment starts at 8 a.m. to 6 p.m. every day.
Contact him at Plot 8, Berkery [*sic*] Road, behind Aga Khan Mosque.
He wishes old and new patients good try.
Falaki Professor Sheikh Mohamed el Deen

There is a wealth of material here on which to comment. The witchdoctor in question clothes his advertisement in a modern western style. He is a Professor and he has regular surgery hours. However, he is also a religious leader, a sheikh, and he claims to cure complaints caused by Islamic spirits. He comes from the Sudan—the mystique of distance again—and his medicines operate at several levels. Apart from the religious level, there is the level of ordinary physical conditions, disabilities, stomach trouble and birth problems, the level of sexual potency and life-force, the level of socio-psychiatric spirits, and the level of protective and retaliatory magic. Disarmingly, he does not claim infallibility but wishes his patients a good try.

African cultures tend to have a loose and inclusive understanding of medicine. The word that is used, *dawa*, *uwuganga*, or whatever, refers to all the different levels of healing at once. Using a mathematical analogy, even physical medicine alone can be plotted on a graph as a co-ordinate of two factors: proximate/remote in effect and literal/symbolical in form.[15] At zero one would find western medicine, designed to cure a person with a cut finger directly here and now. Elsewhere on the graph one would find medicine designed to prevent you cutting your finger again or medicine that symbolizes the wholeness of a healthy finger. Witchdoctor and patient are usually not interested in disentangling the different levels of healing and this is clearly a weakness in their concept of medicine. It *is* important to recognize that levels of healing overlap, physical, emotional, psychic, social, moral, and that they also interact one with another. It is important not to treat any level in total isolation from the others, but it is also important not to confuse the categories. An integral approach to healing must not imply a confusion of categories. It is not even merely the sum total of the categories. Rather it is tracing their interaction and enabling them to lend support one to another. More importantly, when the religious level is recognized, there is an understanding that wholeness is ultimately the consequence of a new dimension of healing.

In an earlier chapter we noted how progress in medical science and developments in medical practice are bringing increased specialization in the western world. The general practitioner who is a real 'family doctor' and who occupies a privileged place in the community is giving way to a medicine practised from hospitals and medical centres with specialized departments. The medical centre is a kind of medical 'supermarket' where the new and increased ranges of treatments and drugs are now available. In many Third World countries, there is not, and never has been, a general practitioner of western scientific medicine. Western medicine in these countries has always been organized from hospitals. Hospitals are obliged to cover the health care of a whole region and to train and support medical assistants and rural medical aides in the village dispensaries. These village 'dres-

sers' are often foreigners, not entirely trusted by the local inhabitants. Because of problems of supply and distribution, they may
actually have few, if any, medicines to dispense. Their medical
world and their resources are thoroughly Eurocentric, since it is
from Europe and the West that their know-how and their drugs
come from. They usually cut a poor figure beside the witchdoctor whose resources are all near at hand and whose medical
outlook is shared by the whole community. If there is a general
practitioner or a family doctor in the villages of the Third World,
it is the witchdoctor. Mirau of the Meru people in Tanzania
operates with 130 local herbs and sees up to fifteen patients on
weekdays, treating their physical complaints and reconciling
their social differences and disputes.[16] Lloyd Swantz estimated in
the late 1960s that there were roughly 700 witchdoctors in the
city of Dar-es-Salaam consulted by up to 10,000 patients a day.[17]

Doctors can achieve nothing if they do not secure social
approval. Earlier this year (1984) I came across a mission hospital
in northern Tanzania which had been virtually abandoned by the
local people because the expatriate doctor from Europe was
unlucky in the first weeks after his arrival. There were several
deaths at that time and the doctor, as yet ignorant of the local
language, was an unknown, inarticulate person who was mistrusted. Doctors have to communicate if they are to be accepted.
They must also be thoroughly aware of the prevailing social
conditions of their patients. Many of the treatments they prescribe impinge on the social sphere, the holiday, or enforced rest,
hospitalization itself, diets, changes in life-style and so forth. The
witchdoctor for his part gives and receives social approval. His
verdict after divination offers the social approval necessary for a
given course of action, the licence to accuse a suspected witch, a
commission to perform relevant rituals, the sanctioning of protective or retaliatory measures. In most cases, also, he shares in
the religious suppositions of his clientele. The story is told of a
doctor from the People's Republic of China who was practising
in a Tanzanian hospital, as part of a medical aid programme. A
patient to whom he had just given a bottle of medicine exclaimed
'God bless you, doctor'. To which the Chinese Communist
replied: 'I don't believe in God'. 'Then', said the African patient,
'I don't want your medicine!' And this is the point at which we
began our discussion of scientific and pre-scientific medicine.
Doctors treat, but God cures. It is not that religion takes over
where medicine reaches its limits, but that medicine, however

scientifically advanced or efficacious, *is* limited. Its healing power is part of God's healing action.

A man who exemplified this truth in his own life was Dr Adrian Atiman.[18] Atiman was born around the year 1866 in a village called Tundurma in Mali, West Africa. He belonged to the Songhai tribe. Captured by Tuaregs at the age of nine, he was carried off to Algiers where a missionary ransomed him from the slave market in 1876 for the sum of 300 francs. After schooling in Algiers, Cardinal Lavigerie, the founder of the Missionaries of Africa (White Fathers), sent him to Malta to train as a doctor in 1882 along with five companions. Six years later, after graduation as a doctor, he set out with a caravan of missionaries to Karema on Lake Tanganyika, covering the 700 or so miles from the East African coast on foot. Atiman lived the rest of his long life at Karema, dying there at the age of around ninety in 1956. He practised as a doctor, performing amputations and abdominal operations with the minimum of hospital equipment. He also practised as a catechist or religion-teacher, combining both a religious and a medical role. He married into the family of a local chief and was immensely respected by everyone who came in contact with him. His zeal in the service of the poor and sick of Karema and his personal holiness are still a byword in Tanzania, the country of his adoption. When he died 2,000 people walked in his funeral procession.

Atiman healed with both prayer and medicine, achieving an admirable balance between them both. There is no doubt whatever that prayer brings about physical healing, whether as one of the many factors which lead to a cure or whether it heals in ways which medical science is not able to explain. God is Love and that Love heals. He is not a God who hands out nothing but sufferings and trials. He wants people to be healed in every way and at every level.

A leper came to him and pleaded on his knees: 'If you want to' he said 'you can cure me'. Feeling sorry for him, Jesus stretched out his hand and touched him. 'Of course I want to!' he said. 'Be cured!' And the leprosy left him at once and he was cured.[19]

God loves us unconditionally. At different times and in different cases, one or another level of healing may have greater importance in God's eyes. It might not be physical healing, for example, but moral and inner healing, as a preparation for being judged by his love and entering into the fullness of that love, dying into

Love. But prayer makes a difference whatever its effect may be.

We must not be too quick to claim a cure from God because we have prayed. The important thing is to enter into the mind of Jesus himself, to read the Gospels and live out his reactions, to respond to God revealing himself in the healing power of Jesus. Matthew and Dennis Linn speak of a 'soaking prayer', prayer as a kind of long-term 'X-ray' which gradually produces the trans-forming encounter with Christ.[20] Intercessory prayer with the laying-on of hands is especially effective, since love is expressed through the sense of touch. 'He stretched out his hand and touched him.' The touch of the one who prays for healing links the sufferer with the Body of Christ, the Church, and effectively symbolizes the channel of God's healing love. It also may act to draw out the sufferer's own potentialities for health, especially faith in that healing love. Probably, as MacNutt and the Linns imply, physical healing is mostly linked with the healing of the emotions through prayer.[21]

If healing is to take place, the sufferer must want to be healed. Jesus asked the sick man at Bethesda: 'Do you want to be well again?'[22] It was a pertinent question, since he had been ill for thirty-eight years and there are many chronic invalids who like to be a centre of attention and shrink from the responsibilities of a healthy life. If healing is to take place, the sufferer and his or her intercessor must have a quiet trust in God's healing love. This healing love is a power in which we have faith and it is this power which heals, not our faith in it. Yet the faith must be there which brings us to Jesus and submits us to the power of his healing love. As we have said, this faith or trust is not a presumption. We do not have a claim on that power because we have faith in it; it is for Jesus to exercise it in the way he wills. Faith-healing is, as Maddocks points out, an 'erroneous conception'.[23]

Unfortunately, this misunderstanding is widespread. It is fre-quently taught that healing fails because of unbelief or because of a lack of sufficient faith. As we have seen, it is faith that gives God's healing power its scope, but God comes to make good the faith of sufferers who cast themselves on his mercy.

'If you can do anything, have pity on us and help us.' 'If you can?' retorted Jesus. 'Everything is possible for anyone who has faith.' Immediately, the father of the boy cried out, 'I do have faith. Help the little faith I have!'[24]

The practice of 'claiming one's healing' is mistaken. Still more unjust is it to condemn the sufferer for a lack of faith when a cure does not take place at the level, or in the manner, desired by those who pray or intercede. There are healers who turn against the sick person when the expected cure fails to happen and blame him or her for the 'failure'. In this way, they provide themselves with a built-in reason for the fallibility of their otherwise infallible theory of healing. Such people have not entered truly into the mind of Christ. Possibly they do not appreciate the redemptive value of suffering and certainly, in many cases, they deprive the sick person of prayer and compassionate support when it is most needed. Faith-healing becomes even more inhuman and irrational when it is presented as an alternative to, or even the definitive replacement for, medicine. An increasing number of independent Churches in Third World countries, many of them under the influence of Pentecostal theologies and healing evangelists, repudiate hospitals and the attentions of doctors or nurses and the medicines they prescribe. In some cases, Jesus is claimed as the only doctor and prayer the only medicine. In other cases, the reality of pain is denied, or the ability to sublimate it through religious ecstasy is affirmed. These Churches and their communities may exercise a truly therapeutic function, particularly through charismatic prayer and speaking in tongues, and we shall return to this aspect of their life in Chapter 17, but, in so far as they repudiate the contribution and religious relevance of the work of doctors and nurses, they are guilty of a harmful category mistake. They also tend to encourage a hope for immediate answers to prayer which may be based on a selfish yearning or manipulation, and not on an entry into the mind of Christ and a genuine surrender to his power.

In practising medicine and applying physical remedies for illness we are entering into the absolute and overall healing action of God. Prayer for healing recognizes this. It also directly channels that healing action in such a way as to confirm, reinforce and even surpass the physical remedies that we apply. This overall healing action has been entrusted to Jesus Christ.

It is the same God that said: 'Let there be light shining out of darkness', who has shone in our minds to radiate the light of the knowledge of God's glory, the glory on the face of Christ.[25]

11

Magic and anti-Church

No subsequent papal visit to Africa was quite like the first one. Paul VI's journey to Uganda in 1969 was a visit to the whole of Africa, and the whole of Africa was there, bishops and pilgrims from nearly all the 54 countries of the continent. The All-Africa Symposium of Bishops which the Pope was to close on the first day of his stay was held at the Institute where I was teaching, and I was personally involved in the preparation of some of the papal spectaculars. Of course there was a humorous, even a ludicrous, side to some of the preparations. There were all too human controversies over commissions and contracts, provocations over protocol and quibblings among choirs. It was hoped to make a substantial profit from Pope badges, Pope shirts, Pope dresses and head-scarves, Pope ash-trays, Pope tea-trays and even Pope umbrellas. As it turned out, there was a surplus of papal cotton print after the Pope's departure and a beauty competition had to be hastily organized for a 'Miss Uganda Papal Visit' with competitors wearing dresses made from the material. The date of the visit had been selected so as not to clash with the landing of the American astronauts on the moon and the inevitable comparisons were made between the Pope setting foot on African soil and Armstrong's 'giant leap for mankind'. There were fears that the Pope might appear too much like a man from outer space and that the whole visit would be one vast irrelevancy. But the papal moonshot was a success. The crowds were colossal, and the expected confusion did not happen. All eyes were focused on the tiny white figure of Paul VI, the small figure with the powerful message: 'You may and you must have an African Christianity'. The visit brought Rome and Africa together, but more importantly it brought Africa itself together first and helped the African Church become self-conscious. The climax of the papal visit was the blessing of the Uganda Martyrs' shrine at Namugongo, twelve miles from Kampala City. The whole site was hung with flags and bunting and enormous crowds massed along the route. Over a shop facing the gateway to the shrine was a sign proclaiming: 'Pepsi welcomes the Pope'. It was there among the milling people that the witchdoctor accosted me when the ceremonies were over. He was a thin, angular man and wore a not very clean cotton *kanzu* or tunic under his threadbare jacket. He pressed a small paper-covered cylinder into my hand, saying it was a relic of the Uganda Martyrs. I was intrigued, knowing that such relics were hard to come by, certainly of the size indicated by the object he had given me. I put it in my pocket, paid him the small sum he asked, and struggled on to find my car.

Back at home, I had leisure to examine my prize. Unrolling the paper I found a cylinder of hardened, grey clay, a type of medicine which the Baganda call *emuumbwa*. It is mixed with water and drunk. On the paper were the following printed instructions:

This Medicine was invented by Mr Augustino Katende of Nnalubudde Bussujju, P.O. Box 153, Mityana, Uganda.

1. This Clay is mixed with soil got from where the Uganda Saints were burnt!!
2. If you believe the Uganda Saints and you have a certain disease, just rub it on [a] saucer where is water, then take that water. You will be cured soon without going to a Hospital.
3. Before taking that water, first say these words 'The 22 Saints of Uganda who were burnt at Namugongo let your blood help me cure my disease.'
4. After getting what you demanded from the Uganda Saints write to the above address.
5. God is our leader in everything and the Virgin Mary is the King [sic] of Saints.

My first reaction was one of disgust. Here was a man making his own private profit from the papal visit. The idea that this clay could cure a person of any illness without hospital treatment appeared magical. 'You must not practise divination or magic', thunders the Book of Leviticus. 'Do not have recourse to ... magicians; they will defile you. I am Yahweh your God.'[1] But then, did not these instructions display an underlying faith in the intercession of the Uganda Martyrs and was not paragraph 3 a prayer for their favour? Did not the final sentence suggest solidarity with the Church, even though the clay was described as a medicine invented by an individual? I thought again of the woman with the haemorrhage.

Now there was a woman who had suffered from a haemorrhage for twelve years; after long and painful treatment under various doctors, she had spent all she had without being any the better for it, in fact, she was getting worse. She had heard about Jesus, and she came up behind him through the crowd and touched his cloak. 'If I can touch even his clothes,' she had told herself 'I shall be well again.' And the source of the bleeding dried up instantly, and she felt in herself that she was cured of her complaint. Immediately aware that power had gone out from him, Jesus turned round in the crowd and said, 'Who touched my clothes?' His disciples said to him, 'You see how the crowd is pressing around you and yet you say, "Who touched me?" ' But he continued to look all round to see who had done it. Then the woman came forward, frightened and trembling because she knew what had happened to her, and she fell at his feet and told him the whole truth. 'My daughter,' he said 'your faith has restored you to health; go in peace and be free from your complaint.'[2]

Here was a woman who had lost confidence in doctors and who had put her faith in the healing power of Jesus, believing it to be a kind of physical emanation from his clothes. Her intention was to touch Jesus surreptitiously and sneak a cure from him because of the embarrassing nature of her complaint and because it made her ritually impure in the eyes of the Mosaic Law. It was an act that bore many of the characteristics of magic. It was individualistic and seemingly irrational. It implied a despair of medical treatment. And, surprisingly, it worked! Jesus cured the woman through his own clairvoyance. Prophets were supposed to know the secrets of those who touched them, as Simon the Pharisee assumed in the case of the woman who was a sinner: 'If this man were a prophet, he would know who this woman is that is touching him and what a bad name she has'.[3] But Jesus made the woman who had been cured of the haemorrhage come out into the open and say what she had done. From a private, individualistic act, it became a public testimony of faith. The 'magical' emanation of power became a verbal command: 'Be free of your complaint'. In this way, Jesus tolerated the woman's superstition in order to convert it into a prayer and a power for healing that was acceptable to the community.

Sometimes the dividing line between superstition and faith, between magic and folk religion, is finely drawn, and it is a short step from one to the other. Faith in Christ is not simply a cerebral exercise. It communicates in ways that are non-verbal. But the manipulation of material symbols holds dangers for the religious believer. Magic is always a kind of occupational hazard where symbolic communication is concerned. In Chapter 8 we discussed evil magic or sorcery in connection with human agents of physical misfortune, but magic is not necessarily harmful. Usually, it aims to cure, protect or profit, rather than to harm, hinder or destroy.

Magicians make little pictures of what they would like to happen. It is the anticipation of an event, implying a belief that the anticipation actually influences the event. One of the difficulties about a magical view of reality is that it does not constitute in practice a clear alternative either to medical science on the one hand, or to *bona fide* religion on the other. Theoretically, it is easy enough to keep the concepts distinct and most cultures and languages do this. In actual fact, magic acts as a corrupting influence on both. Magical practices are rituals or symbolic actions and often take the form of the manufacture of a medicine, made up of highly symbolic ingredients. Magical rituals are not merely expressive, they are instrumental. That is to say, they do not merely make a statement about a given expectation, a cure for example, but they purport to influence events and to bring the expectation to reality.

Magic is essentially self-reflexive. It acknowledges no agent of causality outside itself. It attributes an automatic or infallible effect to a concrete symbol, without invoking or exploring any external agency or causality. It is secular because it does not invoke the direct action of a spiritual being, although it recognizes that magic is part of the general providence or divine order of things. However, magic is equally irrational because it is objectively groundless and evinces no interest whatever in natural forces or psycho-physical causation. Magicians simply refuse to think further than their own ritual and the effect they desire so ardently. It was Bronislaw Malinowski who remarked that there was no Church of Magicians. This is profoundly true. Magic is essentially an individualistic power-ritual. Magicians are far from altruistic and act solely in their own interests. Magic is therefore characteristically anti-Church. It thrives on secrecy and surreptitious self-help. It is an irrational and irreligious form of auto-salvation. It is altogether different from the self-abandonment and self-deprecation of prayer.

Applied to religious worship, magic becomes 'superstition', the tendency to believe too much, to go further than official faith and practice allow. It means indulging in futile actions or vain observances which betoken intellectual laziness and a lack of trust and openness towards God. It relies on a purely human expertise as against God's power and the natural means which God has given to humanity for solving its problems. It is a form of personal irresponsibility and an abdication of genuine human talents—in short, a failure to face up to the true demands of life.

And yet a great deal of magical practice is based on ignorance. The magical 'sympathy' of like curing like is not questioned or rationally worked out. Although a magical rite cannot be efficacious as a result of its symbolism alone, it may 'work' for reasons unknown to the magical practitioner. In the realm of symbols people rely on feeling and on experience, rather than on intellectual analysis. Not all who, objectively speaking, practise magic are guilty of magical error. Hence there is room for tolerance and for a positive pedagogical approach in the area of popular religion even when this has magical overtones. This is especially the case when superstition appears to be a crude extension of the sacramental principle. The sacramental view of the world not only affirms the participatory nature of reality, it also proclaims that all our experiences speak of divine reality, that everything is (in Hopkins' phrase) 'charged with God'. The Church further discerns special instances of the encounter with God through signs. These are the sacraments which place us in contact with God's self-revelation in Jesus Christ, which refer to his historical life and mission and which continue his saving activity. The Christian believes that Christ continues this saving action in and through the sacraments and that, in the case of the Eucharist, he is really and personally present under the species of consecrated bread and wine. The so-called sacramentals are an extension of the sacraments, invoking God's blessing on other aspects and moments of life, through material signs and actions and reminding us that God's grace is unlimited in its freedom and its application. The superstitious may attribute to the sacraments and sacramentals automatic effects that are normally outside their scope, but they attribute these effects to God's power or to the intercession of the saints, if they reflect deeply enough about them. They are like the woman with the haemorrhage perhaps in their misunderstanding of how God saves and heals.

There are many reasons why magic works. Coincidence may be one of them, since often no time limit is set for the ritual to take effect. When the desired event finally takes place by chance, it is claimed as a direct result of the magic. Social convention may also provide for the simultaneous fulfilment of the result which a magical rite anticipates. Society makes the foreseen event happen because the magic demands it. For example, a traditional non-

Christian marriage ritual may have magical aspects which are designed to ensure that the union takes place. At the same time, the community gives legal recognition to the union and brings it into existence. More often, perhaps, magical action is open to psycho-physical causality. There are parapsychological phenomena which are experimentally proven but which are not yet explicable in terms of contemporary scientific theory. These include telepathy, water and mineral divining, table-tapping and certain gifts of healing (not necessarily in a religious context). Perhaps the story of Ntekilomo's rotating stool, which we cited at the beginning of this book, concerns a parapsychological phenomenon of this kind. However, we cannot justify magical practices in terms of a science yet to be discovered. Magic by definition is uninterested in psycho-physical mechanisms, even though it may unconsciously exploit them. Moreover, the appeal to an unknown future scientific discovery may be an act of faith in the evolution of science and technology, but it is unconvincing as it stands. Evolutionary optimism is a spur to discovery, but the mysteries of creation will never be completely explored and comprehended in this life.

Magic remains an irrational attitude since it does not look for causes outside itself, whether these are scientific or theological. It is an abdication of the human reason. The magical is the antithesis of the miraculous, which is not only not afraid of scientific explanation, but even invokes it as part and parcel of its definition. In natural terms, the miraculous is what contemporary science is unable to explain, and although scientific discovery may circumscribe the miraculous to a greater or lesser extent, it also reveals the miraculous for what it is. A conviction should not be a blind conviction, but the magical practitioner is as happy as an ostrich with its head in the sand. To be human and rational one must know what one is doing, even if one cannot satisfactorily explain its workings, its causes and its consequences. Magic is a form of agnosticism which does not wish to know.

Religions are symbol systems, that is to say they constitute a tradition and a framework of images and meanings which is seen by the believer as shaping itself to psychological reality and shaping that reality to itself. As Geertz explained in a classic essay, religion is both 'model of' and 'model for', a replica and a mock-up, of reality.[4] Through these symbols the believer has a direct and total psychic experience of divine reality, and is enabled to participate in the inner life of that reality, thereby constructing his or her own human life in this world. Religious symbols, be they words or images, sacraments or sacramentals, are not ends or values in themselves. On the contrary, they are channels or vehicles for the reality in which the believer participates. Magic makes the mistake of turning a symbol into an objective power—something which exists and acts on its own. There is always the insidious danger that a magical interpretation will subvert Christian sacraments and sacramentals. From time to time one comes across examples in the popular stratum of Christianity, a leaflet, for example, about the Miraculous Medal. After a first paragraph about Our Blessed Lady, her appearances to St Catherine Labouré in Paris in 1830 and her revelation on that occasion of the Miraculous Medal, there then follows (at least in a sample I have seen) a description of all the things 'it' will do for the person who wears or uses 'it'. The substitution of an 'it' for 'her' who is the Mother of God can easily come to reflect a magical attitude. This is basically a manipulative attitude, rather than a supplicative one. It is an attitude which tries 'to put God into one's pocket' or to draw him to do what one wants through the manipulation of material things. It is, in the truest Biblical sense, an act of idolatry or a reduction of God's infinite and spiritual power to the level of a natural force that can be appropriated and applied by the practitioner. Prayer and ritual action, under the influence of magic, become a technique for constraining and distorting God's nature, if such a thing were possible.

Throughout the history of Judaism and of Christianity, holy things have been used magically at various times. The Israelites used the Ark of the Covenant in a magical way, when they carried it into battle in order to gain an automatic victory over the Philistines, and Yahweh taught them a lesson by allowing the Philistines to capture it.[5] The English were more successful at the Battle of the Standard in 1138 when they carried a mast fixed to a cart into battle. The mast or 'Standard' from which the battle took its name was bedecked with banners and bore the Sacred Host itself. The English, however, failed to follow up their victory over the Scots, with or without the presence of the Blessed Sacrament. There were, of course, numerous medieval battles in which the Eucharist was celebrated by both sides and the Blessed Sacrament carried. Introducing a magical element into worship is the essence of false worship. Idolatry is its extreme form and the worst form of idolatry is Satan worship because it suggests that God's victory over evil is not absolute and complete. Satan worship, where it is genuine, typically involves the grossest magical formulations. Magic is therefore 'anti-Church' in more senses than one.

Mention has been made several times in this book of parapsychological phenomena. These include forms of extrasensory perception such as clairvoyance or the perception of events and objects by paranormal means, telepathy or the perception of the thoughts and mental states of other people and precognition of future or remote events. Another type of parapsychological phenomena is collectively known as psychokinesis. This refers to the idea that physical objects can be influenced by the will. It is the proverbial power of mind over matter and it may include the possibility of healing through the use of psychic power. Most scientists tend to regard parapsychological phenomena as an unproved possibility, rather than as an out-and-out impossibility. The theories which are put forward, including that of the collective unconscious—a common, unconscious source of knowledge in which individual minds participate—seem to raise more questions than they answer. Experiments that have been carried out favour the existence of extrasensory perception, more than psychokinesis, although it cannot be said that the latter's existence is improbable. More experimental evidence has to be collected, if the theorizing is not to remain premature.

Healing gifts and healing powers may operate with natural factors up to a point. Many—probably most—illnesses and disabilities are psycho-somatic and are open to the power of suggestion. Many forms of treatment and/or ritual are physiologically therapeutic, whether they include medically active herbs or techniques of manipulation. However, there are so many anomalies in the human make-up that it is impossible to exclude apodictically the parapsychological elements in healing. Hypnosis is, of course, accepted and used by psychiatrists and there is no doubt of its existence. Nevertheless, there is no theoretical agreement as to what makes a hypnotized patient susceptible to the psychic influence of the hypnotist. Some argue that the altered state of consciousness is due to neurophysiological causes; others, to the social relationship of hypnotist and subject. Modern psychiatrists, in any case, regard the therapeutic use of suggestion and hypnosis as inferior to analysis.[6] If treatment relies on the domination of the patient by the strong personality of the doctor or healer, then emotions and neuroses are unlikely to be permanently healed. The effectiveness of much healing ministry and prayer is due, in natural terms, to the conversion of the subject, the acquisition of new convictions about his or her state, and the adoption of new attitudes towards it. 'Soaking prayer' which brings about a gradual change of mentality is more likely to have a lasting effect than a sudden conversion which may denote an unstable personality or condition. It remains clear, however, that in the as yet unproved and unintelligible area of parapsychological phenomena, there is considerable scope for charlatanism and for the blind credulity that is magic.

Jesus Christ may have shared some of the techniques of the pre-scientific medicine-man or witchdoctor, but he was no magician. There are two episodes concerning magicians in the New Testament. One was Simon the magician:

Now a man called Simon had already practised magic arts in the town and astounded the Samaritan people. He had given it out that he was someone momentous, and everyone believed what he said; eminent citizens and ordinary people alike had declared, 'He is the divine power that is called Great'. They had only been won over to him because of the long time he had spent working on them with his magic. But when they believed Philip's preaching of the Good News about the kingdom of God and the name of Jesus Christ, they were baptized, both men and women, and even Simon himself became a believer. After his baptism Simon, who went round constantly with Philip, was astonished when he saw the wonders and great miracles that took place. . . .

When Simon saw that the Spirit was given through the imposition of hands by the apostles, he offered them some money. 'Give me the same power' he said 'so that anyone I lay my hands on will receive the Holy Spirit.' Peter answered, 'May your silver be lost forever, and you with it, for thinking that money could buy what God has given for nothing! You have no share, no rights, in this: God can see how your heart is warped. Repent of this wickedness of yours and pray to the Lord; you may still be forgiven for thinking as you did; it is plain to me that you are trapped in the bitterness of gall and the chains of sin.' 'Pray to the Lord for me yourselves' Simon replied 'so that none of the things you have spoken about may happen to me.'[7]

The other man, Bar-jesus or Elymas Magos, was dramatically punished by Paul and Barnabas. The incident took place in Cyprus.

They travelled the whole length of the island, and at Paphos they came in contact with a Jewish magician called Bar-jesus. This false prophet was one of the attendants of the proconsul Sergius Paulus who was an extremely intelligent man. The proconsul summoned Barnabas and Saul and asked to hear the word of God, but Elymas Magos—as he was called in Greek—tried to stop them so as to prevent the proconsul's conversion to the faith. Then Saul, whose other name is Paul, looked him full in the face and said, 'You utter fraud, you impostor, you son of the devil, you enemy of all true religion, why don't you stop twisting the straightforward way of the Lord? Now watch how the hand of the Lord will strike you; you will be blind, and for a time you will not see the sun.' That instant, everything went misty and dark for him, and he groped about to find someone to lead him by the hand. The proconsul who had watched everything, became a believer, being astonished by what he had learnt about the Lord.[8]

Magic is a technique, a transferable or saleable commodity. This explains why Simon thought he could buy the power of the Spirit with money. His understanding of the sacraments had not risen above the level of magic. He was 'trapped in the bitterness of gall and the chains of sin'. Bar-jesus or Elymas, as he was called, was fearful of losing his influence over the proconsul. His was a professional rivalry, and his interests were equally financial. Paul exposed the fraudulent character of his practice and called him the 'enemy of all true religion'. Magic is always fraudulent, since it invests ritual actions with a power they do not possess. It is also the enemy of all true religion since it is based on self-interest and not on abandonment to the will of God.

Jesus of Nazareth was a worker of wonders or miracles. Whatever the factual basis for some of the miracle stories may have been, his contemporaries experienced him as a wonder worker and wonders were attributed to him. As we have already seen, there are a number of such stories which cannot be explained or 'explained away'. Textual criticism is not able to reduce them to a normal experience nor to tell us how far they were impervious to the scientific explanations which we accept in the twentieth century or that were accepted in any century. The ultimate criterion of what is, or what is not, a miracle does not depend on scientific observation. This is obviously relative. There are phenomena which at one time in human history can be explained by the contemporary scientific knowledge, and which at another time cannot. There is a naïve evolutionist attitude towards miracles which sees them as gradually receding as scientific discoveries provide more and more natural explanations for the wonders that mystified earlier, ignorant generations. Of course, scientific discoveries also provide us with an ever-increasing number of wonders that still mystify us and for which no ready natural explanation is yet to hand. Our evolutionary optimism may persuade us that explanations will eventually be found, but, to cite only the case of the parapsychological phenomena, for example, we are not very much nearer to a satisfactory explanation than we were fifty years ago. Science, in any case, does not establish immutable natural laws. On the contrary, it sets up hypotheses or paradigms which it tests and applies through experiment until the discovery of too many anomalies forces the abandonment of the reigning paradigm and the need to search imaginatively for another. Thus Aristotelian physics gave way to Newtonian and Newtonian to that of Einstein. Miracles are marvellous, in the sense that they are designed to attract attention, but they are not breaches in a natural law which compel assent because of their scientific inexplicability. Moreover, they are not marvellous just for the sake of being marvellous.

It is clear in the New Testament that the miracles of Jesus were not intended to pander to the escapist human thirst for the marvellous. They were not compulsive, but were essentially ambiguous. Instead of compelling the observers, they summoned them to respond in faith and love. They challenged them to throw in their lot with Jesus and to proclaim the kingdom of God. Miracles were essentially signs of authenticity. In fact, John consistently calls them 'signs'. They expressed who Jesus was and translated his message into action. They were acts of service towards those in need, the sick, the disabled, the poor, the hungry, the sinful. They were unselfish acts of service and typically they were cures. But they were also signs of saving power, Jesus' power to save humanity from definitive evil and definitive suffering. Jesus deliberately played down the marvellous aspect of his signs. He tried to get rid of all showiness, all eye-catching 'fireworks', because his saving power was one of service and love. His miracles were not intended to exalt himself, and that is why his greatest sign was his death on the cross, his complete self-emptying. Nevertheless, the miracles did remind the onlookers that human beings are finite and that the whole of reality is under God's dispensation and control.

Pierre Simson takes the example of Jesus' walking on the water to demonstrate the sign-value of a 'miracle'.[9] The story is told by Mark and John, and especially Matthew who accentuates the wonderful character of the episode and adds the detail of Peter sinking in his attempt to emulate his master. John McHugh has suggested that the words 'walking on the sea' could equally be taken to mean 'walking by the sea'.[10] This explanation is grammatically possible and would mean a considerable lessening of the marvellous element in the story. But the meaning of the sign is contained in the words: 'Fear not. It is I' or 'Fear not. I am he', the revelation of the person of the Saviour in whom we place our faith and trust when we are in difficult circumstances.

Jesus was tempted in the desert to use his powers to make his Messianic task easy, to offer a show to the people of Jerusalem by jumping unharmed from the pinnacle of the Temple. This would have been a short-cut to the achievement of his mission by compelling his onlookers to accept him. But it would have defeated its own purpose by turning his followers into robots, by stopping short at the mere marvellous, and by accepting the short-sighted popular understanding of the expected messiah. Jesus was also tempted to use his powers to satisfy his own hunger by turning stones into bread. Jesus multiplied loaves for others, but he would never perform a miracle like that to escape from the pangs of his own hunger. His miracles were for others, not to make life easier for himself.

We live in an age when science and technology reign supreme. They shape our understanding of reality and even of what is, or is not, a miracle. That is why the Lourdes Medical Bureau only accepts as miracles cures which have no known scientific explanation, and why the miracles accepted for the beatification and canonization of saints must be scientifically inexplicable. But that is our own twentieth-century problem. A miracle is not just an inexplicable phenomenon to which a subsequent religious interpretation is attached. It is apprehended first of all as an instance of God at work, as an answer to prayer.

As we have noted, the greatest sign that Jesus worked was on Calvary. Once again he refused to take the short cut and to come down from the cross when challenged to do so by the priests and elders of the people. How much less credible a crucified and revived Christ would have been than a crucified, dead, buried and risen Christ! A three-day postponement of the 'magic trick'? No, the revelation of a totally new dimension of Christ's humanity, his unlimited availability and universal personal presence. He continues to challenge us, to serve us, to call us—and all without the need of magic! Magic is the enemy of true religion. It is a form of irrationality and selfishness which deforms worship. It has nothing to do with miracle, which is a confrontation with God's healing love and with his power exercised in weakness.

12

Dreaming and healing

One of my responsibilities at the Institute where I was teaching in Uganda in the 1960s and 1970s was the library. I engaged as library assistant a quiet and dependable man whom we may call here Bonaventure Opio.[1] One night I had a vivid dream about Bonaventure. I dreamt he was taking the shoe off his right foot and as I looked at his toes I noticed that they had become writhing snakes. I do not remember how the dream ended, but being an inveterate breakfast-time dream-teller, I described the dream to Bonaventure in a lighthearted way. I was not prepared for his reaction. He was horrified and I dropped the subject immediately. A few days later, Bonaventure came to my office and asked for permission to rest an hour or so from work, and when the hour was up I went to see how he was. 'I am not well' was the reply, 'but there is nothing wrong with my body.' I told him not to come to work next day if he did not feel like it, but he showed up as usual. Later in the day he was in my office again. 'There are wild animals following me. It's because of your dream.' I got him to see a doctor at the mission hospital and he felt well for a week or two. Then he went suddenly and violently berserk at home and was taken by the police to the psychiatric hospital, where schizophrenia was diagnosed. I resolved never to tell a dream to an employee again.

Some time during 1974, about a year after these events, I had another vivid dream concerning a young secretarial assistant I was employing. Let us call him Sylvanus Kateregga. The dream was so vivid that I can still remember the details clearly ten years later. I was driving a car with Sylvanus sitting beside me. It was not my own Volkswagen Beetle, but a large car with four doors and a boot at the back—a Peugeot or a Fiat. We drove together along a road that skirted a steep escarpment, the kind of road one sees in many parts of East Africa. On our right was a sheer cliff of rocks and trees towering above us, while on our left was a sheer drop into the valley below. Presently we came to a convex section of the road bordering a re-entrant in the side of the slope. I stopped the car and we both got out. At this juncture I noticed that we were both in military uniform. I was in service dress, with a forage cap. We opened the boot of the car and pulled out a heavy sack which seemed to have a human body in it. There was a parapet of cement at the roadside and we threw the sack over it and down into the valley below us.

Then we got back into the car and drove on to a small trading station and pulled up outside a shop that had had its windows smashed. I remember that, as I stopped the car, the wheels passed over some flattened cartons and other bits and pieces that seemed to have been tossed out of the shop. In front of the car, by the side of the road, was a tall, ornamental sign made of wrought iron. There seemed to be a drinking fountain connected to it and we both drank from it. At this point I awoke.[2]

In so far as the dream was a personal message about my own life, a quite rational interpretation presented itself. The alien car possibly stood for the current research project which had been entrusted to me and in which Sylvanus was assisting me. The uniforms may also have expressed our roles in this programme. I was in complete control of the car, feeling confident therefore about the way the research was going. The disposal of the body in the sack seemed to be a rather grim image of my reorganization of the co-ordinating committee, in which a member who had been an embarrassment was obliged to resign. The flattened cartons were presumably other obstacles easily overcome and the water we drank may have been the satisfying fruits of the work.

The dream was unlike my anxious dream of Bonaventure in which my deep-seated fear of finding snakes in a shoe had reappeared and had possibly expressed an unconscious concern for my employee. In the dream of the car there was no concern felt for Sylvanus. Yet when I considered the framework of images in which the message of the dream had been given, I was disturbed. We were living under the bloodstained rule of Field Marshal Idi Amin Dada, and bodies were frequently being put into the boots of cars and shops looted and ransacked. The military uniforms took on a sinister significance, and I recalled several incidents reported in the press where bodies had been thrown over the side of an escarpment in just such a place as I had seen in the dream. I had myself seen dead bodies lying in hollows beside a main road.

Remembering the impact of my other dream on Bonaventure, I resolved never to breathe a word to Sylvanus, and I have kept my word until this day. I quickly forgot the whole thing.

Three days later, Sylvanus appeared in my office with a worried look. He told me that two of his father's brothers had been arrested by the army and taken to the killing ground at Nagulu. The elder brother was a shopkeeper at Kireka, a few miles outside Kampala, where a large wrought iron metal sign stands, indicating the turning for Namugongo and the Uganda Martyrs' Shrine. His shop had been pillaged. I was thunderstruck and immediately identified the pillaged shop and village of my dream. I also instantly recognized the wrought iron sign. I tried to comfort Sylvanus, but said nothing of the dream. A week or so later we heard that the younger of the two uncles had been released, having bribed his way out of detention, but that the elder one had disappeared. Eventually, his body was found in a ditch or hollow beside the main road. I stuck grimly to my resolution to say nothing about the dream.

Was this dream a coincidence or was it prophetical? Were there two messages—a reassuring one for my own life and a message for Sylvanus who would receive moral support from an employer already psychologically prepared for his bad news? The idea of identifying paramnesia, the *déja vu*, or 'I've been here before' feeling seemed to be ruled out, because I remembered clearly my decision not to speak to Sylvanus about the dream when I awoke. Sigmund Freud, the father of scientific dream analysis, was convinced that dreams were concerned with the past but he also quite candidly confessed that psychological explanations of the premonitory character of some dreams were inadequate.[3] J. W. Dunne conducted extensive experiments with dreams and dream fulfilment and came to the conclusion that 'there is considerable evidence to indicate that the dream occasionally goes forward instead of back to find its material'. He thought that past and future images were blended in dreams in about equal proportions.[4] Anticipatory dreams may, of course, be the simple outcome of imagining the various possibilities of the future, one of which is actually verified. A really prophetical dream, in the sense of foretelling future events, belongs to the class of precognitive phenomena, in the opinion of a modern psychiatrist like Charles Rycroft.[5] Quite a number of different types of dream express an attitude of the dreamer towards the future: anxiety dreams, dreams about physical illness and the so-called convenience dreams which come nearest to Freud's idea of dreams as wish-fulfilment.

Not all dreams are about future fears and yearnings, and not all dreams by any means are vivid or important to the dreamer. There is a hierarchy in dream material. C. G. Jung liked to talk about the 'big dream'.[6] All dreams, however, have something to say and they perform their functions even if we do not understand them or cannot translate them into rational discourse. Dreaming is an imaginative activity of the intellect which employs the symbolic mode. It is a private mythology which must be placed in the context of the dreamer's own life-situation. It requires what the Jungians call a personal amplification in which the dream can be developed and used in rational, waking life. Dreams are not symptoms of neurosis, as Freud believed. They are the personal documents of healthy people. They are 'a letter to oneself', a meaningful message from one aspect of the self to another, from the unconscious to the conscious aspects.[7] Dreams come in series like myths and they undergo transformations in the same way. In so far as they echo culture patterns they may have social uses and may be susceptible of socio-cultural analysis, but ultimately it is the dreamer who must ask: 'What does this dream mean to me?'

The fact that very often dreamers are scandalized by their own dreams, embarrassed by them or dismiss them as nonsense, shows that they may have something important and unpalatable to say to them. Dreams are not just an overflow from a living rubbish-heap of repressions (the unconscious), they may, as Storr remarks, be attempts of the mind to correct its own errors, efforts to correct a one-sided conscious attitude.[8] Dreams often express what the dreamer is afraid to face up to in waking life. They open up new possibilities, new means of action. They affirm courses of action and prepare for new developments. They resolve conflicts and consolidate life-choices. In a general sense then, all dreams are healing dreams. All dreams strive to integrate the personality and to bring about a healing of social relationships to a greater or larger degree. All dreams serve the goal of wholeness.

In the traditional cultures of Third World countries, dreams tend to have an abiding importance which they do not enjoy in the cultures of the industrial west. I found this out to my cost when I treated my snake dream as a joke and retailed it to my employee in the library. Dreams are treated as prophetical, but not always in the sense of being oracular or premonitory. Whether or not they are held to deal with future events, dreams are thought to reflect a deeper reality, a continuum which takes no account of time past or time future. The concept of 'dream-time' of the Australian Aborigines is an extreme form of this idea, according to which dreams are windows into the real world. They are glimpses of the archetypal world, the original creative dreaming by the totemic ancestors and creator spirits. Dreams participate in the original creative imagination and their involuntary character reflects the givenness of creation, its divine origin and purpose.

We have seen that dreams reveal new potentialities within us, even perhaps a precognitive power of which we are not aware when conscious. In Africa, I have found that dreaming and the telling of dreams are often related to vocation stories and religious crises. Bengt Sundkler believes that a whole new dimension of the spiritual life has emerged from dreams in Africa.

Catholics and Protestants may differ in many things in Africa, but in one essential respect they share the same experience all over the continent. Many vocations to serve in the church were inspired through dreams. This was God's way to get to grips with a possibly stubborn young man.[9]

Sundkler sees the dream as a 'workshop' in which the artefacts of traditional and modern worlds are combined. Analysing 850 dreams, he comes to the conclusion that many of the conflicts between old cultural frameworks and new religious meanings in the crises of conversions and vocations are resolved at the unconscious level through dreams.[10] Initial dreams are often an important element in the originating experience of an independent church or new religious movement. To give only one example, Simeo Ondeto, a principal founder of the *Maria Legio* Church of Kenya, was much given to dreams, and his church owes its beginnings to his dream visit to Heaven.

I have listened to the vocation stories of a number of African priests, seminarians, sisters and catechists, many of which contained a reference at some stage to a dream, and clearly the recognition of an inner call from God often occurs in the conscious response to a dream, as Sundkler reports.[11] Dreams played a role in the charismatic movement known as *Jamaa* in Zaïre, founded by the Flemish Franciscan Fr Placide Tempels. In this movement, the initiant is required to have a dream-encounter with Christ before he can proceed to the second stage.[12] In the heterodox Catholic sect of the Bachwezi in Uganda, initiants expect the Blessed Virgin, saints or angels to reveal the ingredients of medicines during the course of a dream.[13] This idea brings us to a discussion of the relationship of dreaming and physical illness.

In an episode of the B.B.C. television series *The Long Search*, the principal of a Lutheran theological college in South Africa was interviewed and told how, during an illness in which everyone despaired of his life, he had dreamed of his deceased grandmother. In the dream she commanded him to get up and continue his work for the Church, striking him on the back as she did so. He awoke completely cured, but with a bruise on the spot where the old lady's hand had fallen in the dream. The programme ended with an earnest plea for the Christian Church to come to terms with dreams.[14] The association of dreaming and illness has a long history. Aristotle and Hippocrates believed in the existence of prodromal dreams in which the dreamer had precognition of an impending illness.[15] Perhaps the Lutheran pastor's dream of his authoritarian grandmother was a premonition of his recovery. Perhaps it was even a message to co-operate psychologically with treatment being given to him and to reawaken his interest in living.

Freud noted that the painful stimuli provided by illness were a somatic cause of dreaming, and he was prepared to accept the diagnostic power of some dreams.[16] In many traditional cultures like those with which I am familiar in Africa, the diagnostic dream is generally recognized. A traditional healer like Mirau of Tanzania regularly listens to the dreams of his patients and even takes note of his own dreams.[17] If a patient has no dreams to tell which can help a healer in his diagnosis, some African witchdoctors give a medicine to induce dreams. This practice is known as dream incubation, and there may be (as there used to be in the ancient classical world of Greece and Rome) special dream-places or dream-temples where dream incubation can be practised. Certainly, the Australian Aborigines practise dream incubation and preserve totemic sites where dreams are expected to occur. The diagnostic dream may reveal problems of physical illness, but also problems and potentialities in the unconscious concerning the patient's psycho-social life. In dreams a person suffering from illness may have a far wider and deeper sensory awareness of the complaint than when awake. The dream may also help in the healing of the subconscious of the sick person, as it seems to have done in the case of the Lutheran pastor. Diagnostic dreams, therefore, and dreams directly related to healing, appear to be an established fact.[18]

If dreams are a natural phenomenon in which people give and receive messages within their total self, there is no reason at all why God may not be thought to use them in order to reveal his purposes and issue his challenges to individuals and groups. Christian missionaries have usually been intolerant of dreams and dream-telling, sharing in an attitude which used to be popular in the western world that dreams are absurd. To take a dream seriously was regarded as going against the First Commandment, and was condemned as vain and foolish, along with other superstitions such as charms and omens. The usual advice given by confessors and spiritual directors has been to ignore dreams altogether on the grounds that they are involuntary and irrational. This Christian rationalism is in sharp contrast with the impression that a Third World person receives from a reading of the Bible. The Old Testament is filled with innumerable instances of dreams and dream-interpretations, the implication being that the dream is a favoured channel of divine communication.

It is obvious that dreams can be used naïvely and irresponsibly. They can be accepted as crudely oracular and as part of the divination process. Dreamers can take great account of their dreams but fail to use them constructively. Dreams are a dialogue between the conscious and unconscious parts of ourselves, and there is a real danger of allowing the unconscious to dominate the conscious. The popular dream-books which one sees for sale on the pavements of Third World towns and cities tend to create the impression that dreams are a whole rule of life. My favourite dream-book is *Secrets of Dreams* by Sheikh Yahya Hussein, which I picked up from a pavement bookseller in Nairobi, the capital of Kenya.[19] Such popular books present dreams as pieces of advice for any and every situation in life.

Perhaps the Old Testament is so dream-dominated that the writings of the New Testament are perforce somewhat of an antidote. As Rycroft notes, there are no dreams dreamt by Christ recorded in the New Testament and this is in sharp contrast to Muhammad and the Buddha.[20] Much of the Koran itself was said to have been revealed to Muhammad in dreams. Can one go further, as Rycroft does, and say that because of Christ's lack of interest in dreams, dream interpretation plays no part in Christian religious theory or practice? I think not. Jesus Christ certainly made use of material from other people's dreams, witness the case of his citing the dream of Jacob's ladder to Nathanael.[21] Of the Synoptic writers Matthew is the most Jewish in his attachment to dreams. Not only are there the dreams of Joseph and the wise men in his infancy narrative, but he also mentions the dream of Pilate's wife, cited in evidence of Jesus' innocence.[22] 'Have nothing to do with that man; I have been upset all day by a dream I had about him.'[23] In Acts Luke records both Peter and Paul as being subject to night visions and miraculous events that occurred in sleep. For example, the angel of the Lord appears to Peter at night when he is sleeping in prison.[24] On being released from prison, Peter still believes it to be a dream. Paul has night visions of the man from Macedonia which lead to a whole new enterprise of evangelization and he also experiences the Lord standing by him at night and saying: 'Courage! You have borne witness for me in Jerusalem, now you must do the same in Rome.'[25] A dream affirmation perhaps. In the history of the Church we find saints like St Francis of Assisi who paid considerable attention to dreams and dream symbolism.[26] Francis took several crucial decisions on the basis of dreams. For example his resignation from the official leadership of the order in 1220 was due to a dream. Everyone who has studied Giotto's frescoes in the upper church at Assisi will remember Pope Innocent III asleep with his tiara still improbably on his head, dreaming of Francis holding up the Church. And there is Francis depicted as taking the place of a column under a threatened cornice. The Christian tradition does not, I think, exclude, let alone oppose, dream interpretation. Rather it encourages a balanced rational approach to dreams, not a rationalism that attempts to ignore them.

Dreams are problem-solving and healing and they are a form of personal mythology. Ultimately it is only the dreamers who can say what they mean in their own life-situation. The psychoanalyst is there to help them make sense of their dreams and to discover the shape of psychiatric disorders if there are any, as revealed through the dreams and the patient's reactions to them. Normal people can be their own psycho-analyst, and this does not entail complicated processes or specialized knowledge. It is not necessary to dig up buried complexes. That is for the psychiatrist in dealing with pathological cases. It is enough for the dreamers to situate the dream symbols in the immediate context of their waking life and to amplify them in the light of conscious experience. 'What do the symbols in this dream mean to me?' 'Does this dream hold a special vividness or importance for me?' A dream must provoke a conscious activity of reflection, discernment, even prayer. In the critical use that we make of dreams, recognizing new potentialities, choices, possibilities, God may be revealing his purposes to us, as he did through Paul's night vision of the Macedonian. 'Come across to Macedonia and help us.'[27]

Symbols are polyvalent. That is to say they mean different things at different times to different people. Dream symbols are no exception and that is why a dream-book like that of Sheikh Yahya Hussein has value only to the extent that symbols are shared. Otherwise, the writer of the dream-book indulges in unhelpful generalizations such as: 'If you dream that you are married to a European wife, it means that you will have troubles in your life'.[28] But symbols *are* shared and even shared dream symbols recur in the dreams of different individuals. This phenomenon is called the culture pattern dream and it is associated with the social uses of dream telling. A dream has to be told in order to be communicated and no distinction can be drawn experimentally between dream, dreamer and the process of dream telling. If a big dream can become a living myth for an individual it may also be thought to have a message for other members of the community. This would be because of the shared symbols and meanings of the dream, but also perhaps because of the social status and role of the dreamer. In African tradition the social importance of a chief's dreams is unquestioned and he is expected to dream relevant dreams for the edification and guidance of his people. When Jung himself visited East Africa in the 1920s, a chief of the Elgonyi tribe told him that no dreams were being dreamt after the British had colonized the country. 'We have no dreams any more since the white man is in the land.'[29] This was synonymous with saying that the leadership had been taken away by the British and that the Africans were no longer allowed to think and plan for themselves. The transforming symbol of the dream was traditionally used by leaders to invest their decisions with a mysterious and unquestionable finality, and also presumably to appeal to the action language in the unconscious of the ruled. Culture pattern dreams are nourished on the sharing of imagery through dream telling itself. Dream-places and techniques of dream incubation may also account for the dream pattern. Without suggesting that the telling of official dreams is fraudulent, it may also be that the structure and framework of images demanded by the spoken form of the dream influence the content that is presented. In other words, the imaginative thought process of dreaming links up with the creative literary imagination.

Once one is in the realm of culture pattern dreams the way is open for the structural analysis of dreams on the model provided by the structural analysis of myth. Myths occur in sets and the principles governing the transformations can be identified. The same can be done with culture pattern dreams. Adam Kuper, in an article that appeared in 1979, made a structural analysis of the dreams reported by a Plains Indian from North America.[30] Instead of focusing on the solutions which a dream presents to the dreamers themselves, Kuper's analysis stressed the argument of the dream, the way in which the dreamers move from an initial dream premiss to a final dream resolution. This has significance not only for the analysis of dreams as personal phenomena, but also for the understanding of unconscious thought processes in general, as well as for the appeal which a culture pattern dream makes at the social level. My ignorance of culture pattern and of the social uses of dream telling allowed me to blurt out my snake dream to Bonaventure. He took it to be diagnostic of his own mental condition and it may also have revealed precognitive powers on my side. In my case, it was a question of intercultural misunderstanding, since the idea of the culture pattern dream is unknown in the West. Unknown, or unrecognized? We are products of our society, and apart from the universal body symbolism occurring in dreams, there is a certain amount of shared imagery deriving from our culture. My dream of driving a motor car, for example, is far from exceptional. Modern westerners frequently dream of driving cars and this may represent the various relationships dreamers have with their own passions.[31] According to Rycroft, the automobile dream replaces the earlier rider-and-horse dream, which had much the same connotations. The cultural fact of the motor car replacing the horse has inevitably influenced the imagery of dreams. If dreams reflect social change and social values, maybe they can tell dreamers something about their social roles and maybe they can also indicate an appropriate social use for dreams.

The dream world is not more or less real than the world of consciousness. It is a different mode, and—because of the involuntary character of dreams—it tends to be more innocent, more honest. The fact that so many writers have used the dream format for their stories and poems—Coleridge, Lewis Carroll, Newman (*The Dream of Gerontius*)—illustrates the link between the imaginative process of dreaming and the creative literary imagination. The dream format also allows speakers or writers to be more honest and to get away with saying things they could not say otherwise. This is a not unimportant consideration in the social use of culture pattern dreams—the shift of responsibility on to an involuntary process which one can do nothing about. A nice example of this was provided by Cardinal Basil Hume at the 1980 Rome Synod of Bishops. The dream format allowed the Cardinal to make a pointed address about the different models of the Church without appearing to offend authority. He began:

I speak in my own name, in my own name alone. I have listened to many speeches intently and attentively—well, that is not quite true. I confess that from time to time I have fallen asleep. During one of these I had a dream. I will speak of my dream.[32]

Having made his point, the Cardinal concluded:

I awoke and I said *Vidi, Gratias*—I have seen, thank you.[33]

A creative writer from Africa who has made extensive use of the dream format is Camara Laye from Guinea, who spent most of his life in exile either in France or in Senegal, and who died in 1980. His first book described the dream-like world of his enchanted childhood, the sense of wonder and discovery which made him see visible material things as glimpses of an inner more real world of the spirit.[34] Another book, *A Dream of Africa*, enabled him to criticize the cruelty of Sekou Touré's rule in Guinea through the dream format.[35] But his most influential book was *The Radiance of the King*.[36] This is an extended dream which explores the experience of human alienation, his own in Paris and that of the white man in Africa. Through the dream format, an imaginative modern mythology or dream journey, Camara Laye rediscovers for Africans their hidden springs of life. It is a kind of map of Camara Laye's 'inner world'. The dream is again a healing dream, healing the rift between rich and poor in Africa, between white and black in the world. It proclaims an openness to all that is positive in other cultures while stressing the need for African cultural authenticity. At a time when many, if not most, African writers are expressing aggressivity and self-sufficiency towards the erstwhile colonial cultures, Camara Laye's dream format makes his constructive message more acceptable perhaps to his fellow Africans.

The witchdoctor, to my mind, is right about dreams, right about their healing character, their power to affirm, to inspire, to assist discernment, even—up to a point—their power to predict and to diagnose. He is right to think that dreams point to an inner reality, to a sharing of values and ultimately to the revelation of human reconciliation in God or, as Camara Laye would say, the 'world of spirit'. Christian healing must not merely be tolerant of dreams, still less confine dream telling to the psychiatrist's couch. Dreams must be recognized and used for what they are, powerful aids for healing and wholeness at many levels.

Let me conclude with another piece of dream telling, this time not my own. In mid–April last year (1983) a young man of the parish where I was living in Nairobi asked to see me. His name was Michael and he had just completed his Sixth Form examinations and was preparing to take up a job in a bank. His visit was by way of a warning to me. He had had a dream, he told me. In the dream I was driving my car (the car symbol again). Suddenly my car had taken to the air, like an aeroplane, but the next moment it had crashed. Michael was diffident about telling me the dream, but he believed he had a duty to do so. He firmly believed that something unpleasant was going to happen to me connected with my car. I told him that it merely indicated his unconscious concern for me and that I was very flattered by it. That was not Michael's interpretation. To 'exorcize' my own doubts as much as anything else, I added: 'It could mean that something nice is about to happen'. I then invited Michael and another youth to the cinema with me and said I would buy the tickets in advance three days later.

On the day in question, I drove into Nairobi City and bought the tickets. I also collected a registered envelope at the Post Office that contained a cheque for the parish, a large sum. I started back and took a detour through a part of town I hardly use in order to avoid a traffic jam ahead. I had not been clever. I soon found myself at a standstill in heavy traffic, but eventually got free. A car passed me and the lady motorist shouted across to me: 'Your bag! They took your bag!' I looked down at the seat beside me where my bag had been. It was no longer there. It had contained the big cheque, my cheque book, the cinema tickets, my driving licence, about £20 in cash and worst of all my reading spectacles.

Two small boys had seized the bag without my knowledge through the open window when I was caught in the traffic.

I drove back to the parish in the kind of shock one feels after being robbed. The first person I saw there was Michael and I told him my story. 'You see' he said 'my dream came true.' I had forgotten about the dream and here was Michael comforting me with the same kind of precognitive assurance I had exercised in the case of Bonaventure. More tickets were bought and we went to the cinema that evening. Michael's dream helped my self-composure and we enjoyed the evening.

13

Yearning for the millennium

The Eastern Highlands of Papua New Guinea lay below me, green folds with deep blue shadows between the ridges. As the plane began its descent to Goroka, the provincial capital, I could see clusters of garden hamlets, with round beehive huts and fenced taro patches. The earth was a deep red in these mountain gardens and the numerous tree stumps showed that the land had been newly cleared. We approached the small highland town and the plane landed on the runway almost effortlessly. I had come for a ten-day consultation on pastoral research and my host received me graciously at the airport terminal.[1] I was surprised to find that the airport buildings opened directly on to the town's shopping centre, rather like a railway station, and I reflected that this was possible since planes and runways were small and air-travel the only means of getting to and from Port Moresby, the national capital. There were no roads or railways.

I found Goroka an attractive town, reminiscent of highland towns in East Africa, but straight out of airport 'Arrivals' I came face to face with the body-art of Papua New Guinea. A near naked man was standing by the roadside, his face, body and hair a riot of brilliant colour. There were red, yellow and white markings on forehead, nose and cheeks, and other splashes of colour on his chest, arms and thighs. He had a fine pair of pig-tusks through his nasal septum and bands of shells and beetle shards around his head. He wore a tasselled black waistcloth and round his neck was a broad collar of intricate beadwork. His head was crowned with a great headdress made of brightly coloured parrot feathers and plumes from the bird of paradise and the forest cassowary. I had no idea whether this gorgeously accoutred man was on his way to a traditional dance, or was a do-it-yourself tourist spectacle, but he represented an ancient culture that was locked in those highlands for centuries, out of the mainstream of European and Asian history. As we passed an elderly European coming out of the post-office, my host remarked that this was the man who made first contact with the tribes of these parts some fifty years ago.

Papua New Guinea is one of those countries which have been subjected to the most accelerated rate of social change imaginable. In the space of a few years the curtain was drawn back on these hidden cultures of the past and the befeathered denizens of forest and mountain were introduced to aeroplanes and all the technological marvels of the western world. It is small wonder the socio-psychological impact has been bewildering and Papua New Guinea has experienced the 'paranoia' of a disintegrating society. Papua New Guinea is one of the regions made famous by the so-called Cargo-cults. These are movements based on the dualism of the haves and have-nots. Frustrated by the colonial experience which introduced them to the luxuries and wonders of European technology without allowing them to enjoy them, the people turned their hopes towards a saviour who would bring them millenary bliss. One day the cargo would arrive; all the gleaming goods would be there and, with their possession, the success and esteem which they conferred upon white people. Myth and its tendency to produce successive transformations helped these people to cope with the paranoid reactions to socio-economic change.

Peter Lawrence has described the successive phases of a cargo-cult in great detail.[2] In the first phases of the movement that he studied the attempt was made to obtain cargo through the beliefs and practices of traditional religion. Eventually, adepts of the cult tried to use Christianity which had been recently introduced by western missionaries. It was felt that white people who had crucified Jesus had forfeited the right to cargo. It was now the heritage of the black race. Soon it would arrive from Heaven, a mysterious country vaguely associated with the Australian city of Sydney.

Christianity, however, was impervious to cargo interpretation, and a new phase of syncretism appeared. The prophet Yali had seen cultural items from Papua New Guinea in a Brisbane museum which became confused in the minds of his followers with the ethnographic museum of the Lateran in Rome. The goods of the black peoples had been taken to a new heaven called

Rome and would shortly be exchanged for cargo. The syncretist phase however proved no more satisfying than the previous phases and it was replaced by another nativistic phase which returned to traditional religious practice. Cargo-cults are soteriological quests—quests for salvation. They predict a total reversal of world order, as one millenary saviour after another appears and different means succeed one another for the attainment of the millennium. The mythical transformations and the waves of enthusiasm generated by the different saviours serve to strengthen faith in the millennium. Cargo represents a definitive revelation of future bliss, but it does not rule out the possibility of beginning to taste that bliss at the present time. Nor is the desired salvation purely a question of material goods and the status that accompanies their possession. It is a deep-seated desire for healing and wholeness at many levels, an integrated healing of the whole psycho-socio-somatic being of man.

Cargo is symbolic of a salvation which is ultimately otherworldly. It represents the desire to escape not only from social despair, but also from social sin and its effects, from the unjust imbalances between races. The paranoid character of the cargo-cult resides in its dualistic assumptions, the war between good and evil, the triumph of the black race over the white, rather than the integration of both in a new order. In this the cargo-cult resembles witchcraft belief, although its aims are focused more upon the acquisition of cargo than on the deprivation of the oppressors. The latter is a concomitant of the former.

Where witchcraft beliefs and practices are tenacious, as in many parts of rural Africa, millenary bliss is often equated with the total eradication of witches. Social disintegration has often brought in its wake the appearance of witchcraft-cleansing or witch-eradication movements. These movements employ new and sometimes syncretist techniques for exterminating all the witches in an entire village or region. Desperate times require desperate measures and witch-eradication is a kind of supernatural pest-control, carried out by travelling professionals. A good example is provided by Kavwela, a travelling witch-eradicator in southern Tanzania. The following is an account of Kavwela's activities in 1962, given me by Angelo Manyanza four years later, and so far unpublished.[3]

Angelo was a Catholic catechist at that time, in a remote Tanzanian forest village called Mkombwe. He had started an outstation there and, although he had a few people under instruction, as yet he had no baptized Christians. Towards the middle of December the village headman, an elderly man called Kayola, announced that a celebrated witch-eradicator from Zambia would be visiting Mkombwe and that his name was Kavwela. Kayola also announced that if anyone absented himself from Kavwela's séance, it would be a sure sign that he or she practised witchcraft or sorcery. Angelo prudently decided that this would be an opportune moment to visit relatives at a village 40 miles away. He intended, however, to return to Mkombwe for Christmas, in the hope that Kavwela would have been and gone.

When Angelo reappeared at Mkombwe three days before Christmas, he was disconcerted to learn that Kavwela was expected there the very next day. There was no turning back now. Kavwela was as good as his word. He duly arrived and again announced that anyone who departed was surely a witch and that the whole village must attend his séance. Angelo decided on passive attendance, but he had reckoned without Kavwela. He was an immediate focus for Kavwela's interest. Kavwela made a dramatic appearance, wearing a headdress of feathers and a costume of animals' tails. He lined the villagers up and began smelling out the suspects. His method was to bind strips of skin on to the foreheads of the suspects. These strips would reveal their guilt, he announced. At this point he demanded a secretary who had paper and pen to write the names of the suspects and his eye fell on the luckless Angelo. Angelo refused to co-operate and Kavwela announced in a loud voice that he was certain Angelo had a horn of witchcraft buried in the floor of his hut. He would come later to smell it out for him. Angelo could not run the risk of refusing to have the horn removed, but he persisted in his refusal to be secretary. Kavwela then commanded him to hand his pen over to another man who was literate, adding that if he refused he would be a sure suspect himself. Angelo obliged.

The eradication ceremony continued. One by one Kavwela announced the names of the suspect witches and one by one their heads were shaved and they were obliged to undergo a humiliating purification rite. It was a catalogue of recent petty misfortunes. Typical was the case of a girl who had had a miscarriage, said to have been caused by the boy-friend who had made her pregnant. The boy was duly shaved and purified. Then, to the consternation of all present, Kavwela announced that the headman Kayola and his wife were witches. Why else, he asked, would Kayola have given him money before the ceremony begging him not to humiliate him in public? Kayola protested that it was a lie, but the witch-eradicator's decision is always final and Kayola was led forward to be shaved, seething with rage and vowing fearful vengeance, all of which confirmed his guilt in the eyes of the beholders. There was no doubt that Kayola was the source of most of the information used by the witch-eradicator. There was equally no doubt that he had paid the money and that Kavwela had double-crossed him.

After this, Kavwela told Angelo he would come to smell out the horn in his house for the sum of fifty shillings. Angelo, who did not have such a sum, but who remembered the story of Nebuchadnezzar and the Babylonian sages,[4] replied: 'If you know there is a horn of witchcraft in my house, you must also know that I do not have fifty shillings'. Kavwela replied that his clairvoyance did not extend to financial matters and reduced his charge to twenty-five shillings. After further bargaining, Angelo made a final bid of two shillings which was accepted. Kavwela duly appeared at Angelo's house in the evening and said that the place reeked of horns. He pottered and poked around the hut and at length sat down near the open doorway announcing that the horn was buried there beside him. He planted a nail to mark the spot, warning Angelo not on any account to try and dig up the horn himself, as it could be very dangerous without the proper medicines. He would return next day, Christmas Day and take the horn away. Angelo was busy with the Christmas services and Kavwela never came to dig up the horn. His two shillings had been paid in advance. When the witch-eradicator left the village two days after Christmas, everyone was glad to see the back of him. The village had been cleansed of witchcraft and Kavwela had collected money from nearly everyone. Four years later Mkombwe village was the scene of one of the worst witchcraft accusation and witch murder cases in the history of the region.[5]

Witch-eradication often results in making people feel secure for a time but its chief consequence is to reinforce people's fundamental belief in witchcraft itself and so, sooner or later, witchcraft accusation reappears and the witch-cleanser's services, like those of the rodent-controller, are required again. Witch-eradication requires that a whole village or region concentrates on the belief and searches for any and every shred of evidence of witchcraft activity. In the general enthusiasm to be purged of witchcraft, the most harmless everyday occurrences are given a sinister interpretation. Magical charms normally thought to be beneficial are suddenly discovered to be harmful, and people are willing to put up with blackmail, extortion and humiliation in the cause of a temporary security or the illusory millennium of a witch-free community. There are lessons to be learnt from witch-eradication, particularly in the context of deliverance and the Christian healing of demonic experiences, as we shall see in a later chapter.

Zambia is a country where there has been a remarkable interaction between Christian and indigenous millenarianism. As early as 1925 a Watch Tower preacher called Tomo Nyirenda turned imperceptibly from denouncing witches to detecting them.[6] He was hailed as Saviour and was called Mwana Lesa or 'Son of God'. His Mwana Lesa movement spread rapidly throughout the Lala people and it is alleged that he killed hundreds of witches before he was captured by the British administration, tried and hanged. His secretary was called Kabwela (Kavwela), already a well-known name in the witch-eradication tradition. In the early 1960s Alice Lenshina became the prophetess of a new religious movement known as the Lumpa Church. It was a movement that spread rapidly in northern Zambia, causing large-scale defections from the Catholic and other Churches. Its most important characteristic was the cleansing of its adherents from witchcraft and sorcery. People came forward to renounce their magical practices and heaps of charms and magical medicines were burnt.

In South Africa, where Sundkler notes that more than 2,030 independent churches were known to the authorities in 1960, the new religious movements are characteristically 'institutes of healing', rather than institutes of sacramental grace or of teaching and preaching.[7] A large number are distinctly millenarian in character and the vast majority heal people from the effects of sorcery or evil magic as well as witchcraft. Many require a dramatic renunciation of magical and other pagan practices and also practise divination, renamed 'prophecy', to detect witches and sorcerers. The same is true of a country such as Nigeria where Barrett in 1968 counted more than 500 independent churches.[8] Barrett optimistically compares the rise of independency in Africa to that of the Reformation churches in Europe and cites the link with witch-eradication as one element in the comparison.[9] In East Africa, Kenya had only 210 independent churches in 1977.[10] It is estimated that there were well over 300 in 1984. One of them is the *Maria* [sic] *Legio* Church or Legion of Mary Church. Although this movement borrows many concepts and externals from the Catholic Church and from its apostolic lay movement the Legion of Mary, it owes its fundamental orientation to the religious traditions of the Luo people and, in particular, to the struggle against evil forces and evil spirits. Indeed the *Maria Legio* Church sees its own role as that of a 'world-cleansing' movement.

African countries, with their relatively small populations, have a much higher proportion of independent churches or new religious movements than the United States of America which boasts 700 denominations in a population of 200 million. Nigeria alone, with half the population of the United States, must now have near to 700 separatist churches. The concept of definitive cleansing, or world cleansing, which animates so many of these movements holds several dangers, apart from those which derive from the reinforcement of witchcraft belief or fear of sorcery. The neutralizing of evil powers by a definitive removal of the agents of evil is calculated to inspire hope and trust in the liberating power of God, but efficacity and finality are confounded. In the struggle between the powers the final victory of good is purported to be immediately available via the divinatory and healing practices of these churches. Power, and not prayer, is the emphasis; and power—even when it is the power of God, or the power of the Holy Spirit—can be 'stored away' in people, especially in the founders and prophets who control the churches.

Many African independent churches strongly resemble the so-called communities of affliction, and like them, manipulate the phenomena of spirit-possession, dissociated personality and glossolalia (tongues). We shall deal with this aspect of their practice in the following chapter. People very often join the independent churches because of illness. They stay on as members if they are cured and they are frightened to give up their membership in case the illness recurs. The independent churches are virtually owned by the founder-prophet and, just as African chiefs and witchdoctors often have hereditary successors, the prophets are succeeded by their own sons or daughters. This appears perfectly natural in the context of these movements which are very often strongly ethnic in origin, in language and conceptualization. The prophet presents himself or herself as the repository of invincible power. He denounces traditional spirits as 'Satan' or 'devils' and he directly challenges the role of traditional spirit-mediums and doctors. His powers are prodigious and, besides healing, may include divining and rain-making. He appears as a new incarnation of the divine king and, indeed, may claim divinity in more or less explicitly Christian terms, as the 'Messiah' or even 'Black Christ'.

Zimbabwe is a country where every ethnic group possesses numerous independent churches in which secessions take place every year. Bishop Hubert Bucher has made a study of the Churches of the Spirit among the Shona people of Zimbabwe in the context of Shona spirits and Shona conceptualizations of power.[11] The power principle in the Churches of the Spirit is the reason why rank and authority are so important and why threats on behalf of the founder-prophet against his rivals, or challenges to his authority, are couched in terms of revelations by the Holy Spirit or based on allegations of witchcraft which result in secessions. Once power becomes the guiding principle, rather than prayerful service, secession and proliferation also become the order of the day.

In the independent churches every activity and every aspect of church life is harnessed to healing from a complex of sin, illness and evil magic or witchcraft. God is a God of power who enables the believer to 'live in strength'. Sickness and weakness have no place because they are directly linked with the powers of evil. The sacraments, when these are celebrated—especially Baptism—are rites of integrated healing. One of the arguments of this book is that the Christian Church *should* adopt an integrated approach to healing, and a consequence of this is that such an approach should be reflected in the celebration of the sacraments. The human sufferer is a physical, psychical, social, spiritual entity, and these various levels of existence cannot be separated. However, the integrated approach of the independent churches of Africa often involves what we have called category mistakes, the confusion of levels rather than a discernment of the way they interact. There is also the fundamentally anti-sacramental tendency to manipulate experience in a magical manner, as well as the unshakeable belief in a direct and literal connection between physical and moral evil, an idea that Jesus repudiated. Finally, there is the tendency to pander to social paranoia represented by the fear of sorcery and witchcraft.

The new religious movements have many positive things to teach the Christians of the mission-related churches, particularly in the field of liturgical inculturation and community building, but they also represent attitudes and beliefs which are unacceptable. The belief in a millennium, a future reign of the saints on earth, a utopian society or perfect community that is imminent or already attainable in this world can lead to a number of religious deviations. Present misery caused by social disintegration or disorientation nourishes a faith in the millennium, as the Book of Revelation in the New Testament itself testifies. But belief in an imminent millennium may lead to quietism and the passive acceptance of the very evils one is seeking to escape. Millenarian faith may equally lead to unreality and irrelevance. Believers may be content to create an alternative society, cutting themselves off from the rest of the world. Their community affords them great social and psychological security and they regard themselves as the 'elect', the faithful remnant chosen by God. Many African independent churches adopt this attitude which also helps to account for their proliferation. A more sinister consequence of millenarian belief occurs when the inevitability of the millennium and the exaltation of the power principle induce aggressivity. Echoing the violent imagery of the Book of Revelation and of many Old Testament writings, such forms of aggressive adventism may inspire the use of force to install the expected utopia and the eradication of those opposed to it. Dualism is the consort of millenarianism. There is no middle path. Those who oppose the elect represent the forces of evil, Satan, Anti-Christ or the ubiquitous witch.

A few new religious movements are recognizably Christian in theology and doctrine, being separatist only in the sense of enjoying an autonomy apart from worldwide communions. These may be influenced in some degree by missionary forms of adventism in the conservative Evangelical churches. A large number of new religious movements are typically 'Old Testament Churches', taking their inspiration mainly from Judaic models. An equally large number of new religious movements are in some degree neo-traditional, being straightforward revivals of traditional ethnic religion, racially and ethnically conscious movements (sometimes of the 'cargo' type), or frankly syncretist, incorporating elements from ethnic and Christian traditions without any profound integration of meaning.[12] As a general rule, new religious movements become more sophisticated as they liberate themselves from their original ethnic identity and become poly-ethnic churches. The formal training of their leaders, especially Biblical training, also assists the process of sophistication and the growth of their appeal to the better educated. In particular, claims to divinity, to messiahship or to the role of 'Black Christ' tend to be abandoned and there is a dilution of the power-monopoly.

Two examples must suffice. The Massowe Apostles, otherwise called the Korsten Basketmakers, were founded by John Massowe in Zimbabwe as long ago as 1932.[13] Persecuted, they wandered into the South African Republic, settling at Korsten, Port Elizabeth, until their expulsion in the 1960s. Originally a Shona ethnic church from Zimbabwe, they have now spread to Mozambique, Tanzania, Zaïre and Kenya where they maintain their headquarters. Although the teaching and person of Jesus Christ receives scant attention in this church, the founder, John Massowe, eventually resisted deification and came to be regarded as a type of John the Baptist, a special prophet or angel for black Africans at a time when Christianity in southern Africa seemed to be the exclusive preserve of whites. This identification was weakened when, because of church growth, the founder was no longer able to baptize each member personally and when his death in 1973 caused a secession of younger members.

The Church of Jesus Christ on Earth through the Prophet Simon Kimbangu now enjoys a following in many parts of Zaïre and was among the first African independent churches to be admitted to the World Council of Churches.[14] Simon Kimbangu exercised a brief ministry in September 1921 in his home village of N'kamba, after undertaking a healing ministry that alienated him from the Baptist Church of which he had been an evangelist. He quickly earned a reputation for miraculous cures, including the raising of a dead child to life, and crowds flocked to N'kamba to be healed by him and to hear him preach. The Belgian authorities suspected a revolt against their colonial régime and sent an officer to arrest Simon. For a few days Simon went into hiding and a state of emergency was declared in the region. Simon then claimed to have received a revelation from God telling him to surrender to the Belgians and imitate Christ in his passion. This he did. He was sentenced to 120 lashes and death for sedition and hostility to whites. King Albert I of the Belgians commuted the second part of the sentence to life imprisonment and Simon died in prison in 1951, at the age of sixty-two, of which thirty years had been spent in prison.

While Simon was in prison, his son Joseph Diangienda, who is now Archbishop and leader of the Kimbanguists, brought the church into existence and organized its membership in the face of violent colonial opposition. The church was finally accorded toleration on the eve of political independence in 1960. Although there is some ambivalence about Simon's messiahship in early hymns and writings, the church, as it has developed, tends to view him as God's special emissary to Africa, following Christ in his passion like Simon of Cyrene and leading black people to him. I was privileged to meet Archbishop Diangienda in 1975. The Church of Simon Kimbangu is more overtly Christian than that of the Massowe Apostles, but they are both movements that have been in existence for more than fifty years and have thus had ample time to develop in size and in sophistication of doctrine. Significantly perhaps, in both cases prophetical power has been tempered by persecution. Tempered also is the millenarian emphasis. These churches have re-experienced a lessening of faith in an instant or imminent millennium, just as the early Christians also did.

The strong expectation in the early Church of an imminent *parousia* or second coming of Christ was a source of considerable embarrassment, as this text of St Peter shows.

We must be careful to remember that during the last days there are bound to be people who will be scornful, the kind who always please themselves what they do, and they will make fun of the promise and ask, 'Well, where is this coming? Everything goes on as it has since the Fathers died, as it has since it began at the creation.' They are choosing to forget that there were heavens at the beginning, and that the earth was formed by the word of God out of water and between the waters, so that the world of that time was destroyed by being flooded by water. But by the same word, the present sky and earth are destined for fire, and are only being reserved until Judgement day so that all sinners may be destroyed.

But there is one thing, my friends, that you must never forget: that with the Lord, 'a day' can mean a thousand years, and a thousand years is like a day. The Lord is not being slow to carry out his promises, as anybody else might be called slow; but he is being patient with you all, wanting nobody to be lost and everybody to be brought to change his ways.[15]

The author answers the complaint that the *parousia* is a long time coming by reminding his readers that we have no knowledge of the date, that the universe is not unchangeable and that God's mercy is also a cause for the delay. Nevertheless, it was thought the *parousia* would take place very soon and people were advised to live as if it were imminent.

Much of the discussion about New Testament eschatology turns on what expectations of the future are attributed to Jesus himself. But whatever these may or may not have been and whatever link there may be between them and the eschatological hopes of early Christians, New Testament writers are clear in their proclamation of the definitive event of salvation as something that has already happened. The kingdom has been inaugurated and in essentials realized already as a result of the passion, death and resurrection of Jesus Christ. Christian churches that reject critical Biblical scholarship are more open to speculation about the future *parousia* and about the millennium (which appears to be an element in Jewish apocalyptic used by the author of the Book of Revelation to refer to the period of God's Kingdom on earth that lasts from the end of Nero's persecution to the Last Judgement). The Seventh Day Adventists are the principal missionary adventist group in the Third World. Originally they believed in a literal millennium that would take place in 1844. This now receives a spiritual interpretation. Together with the Witnesses of Jehovah and the Watch Tower movement (which helped form Tomo Nyirenda's Mwana Lesa movement in Zambia), the Seventh Day Adventists are the major missionary influences where millenarianism is concerned.

The millennium yearned for by adepts of the cargo-cults, the witch-eradication movements and the independent churches is a time of messianic wholeness when the blind will see and the lame will walk again. It is a time when the inequalities between whites and blacks will be removed and the oppression of one race by another will be ended. In these aspirations millenarianism joins the Black Liberation Theologians, even to the extent of proclaiming a Black Christ.[16] The Black Liberation Theologian does not, however, subscribe to a literal millennium, still less to a modern African rival to Jesus Christ. Christ himself is black because he sides with the black oppressed and because the image of a 'white Jesus' is demonstrably false. Christ is black because blackness is God-given, not something to be ashamed of in front of whites. Christ is black because he is human and in the transformation of his humanity by the resurrection he assumes all the burdens of suffering humanity.

To yearn for liberation should be both a prayer and a commitment. This yearning relies on God's power-in-weakness, not on the power of rivalry and conquest. It is not to be equated with a political programme, still less with a rendering of evil for evil. To realize the reign of God on earth the poor must not dispossess the wealthy in order to enrich themselves. The kingdom belongs to those who repent and who remain poor in the sight of God. Yearning for the millennium is a legitimate attitude for a sick society, but it is an attitude of worshipping faith, a dependence on God, not an arrogation of political or ecclesial power.

14

Spirit healing

My first sight of Maji-ya-Soda son of Iswijilo, the most famous spirit-medium in south-western Tanzania, was nothing if not dramatic.[1] It was 28 December 1968 and I had walked eleven miles through the Kimbu forest before dawn, at one point wading through a river up to my thighs. The medium lived by himself in a large forest clearing and all who would visit him were obliged to make this pilgrimage. The early morning light was streaming through the trees on the edge of the clearing as the sun rose over his homestead. Then I caught sight of him. He was seated on the summit of a rocky outcrop at the edge of the clearing. He was swathed in a brilliantly coloured cotton print and wore on his head a crown of beads from which hung over his face a veil of beaded strands. Two assistants wore headdresses of simpler design, while at the foot of the rock sat a party of clients. Maji-ya-Soda was in the midst of a divining rite, involving the use of the poison-bark known as *mwavi*.

In the sixteen years since that first meeting, I have come to know Maji-ya-Soda, his family and his lifework. He is the founder and leader of a community of affliction, a professional healer of great dedication, gentleness and assurance. The community he founded is an adaptation of a movement already known in several parts of western Tanzania, a skilful blend of old and new elements to form a liminal phenomenon that meets the therapeutic needs of a society in the throes of far-reaching social change. The theory and practice of Maji-ya-Soda's community of affliction centres on a hierarchy of neutral spirits or socio-psychiatric beings called *migawo*. We have already encountered this category of spirit in Chapter 9. The *migawo* are 'water-spirits' associated with the lakes that lie in western Tanzania and with epidemics of sleeping-sickness and other plagues that come from the west. It is sometimes said that the chief of the water-spirits keeps a bag full of locusts, tsetse flies and other evil things, releasing them from time to time like Pandora and her box. In Maji-ya-Soda's community the water-spirits are thought to cause a number of social and individual ills, anything that carries with it some kind of social stigma. As a result, the members comprise people with nervous ailments, depressed and deprived people, epileptics, people with psychiatric disorders and people burdened with any and every form of anxiety, medical, moral and social.

Theologically and morally water-spirits are neutral. They are simply a fact of life, like germs, and Maji-ya-Soda deftly tailors his rituals to suit the susceptibilities of Muslims, Catholics and other sorts of Christian, as well as those who profess the traditional ethnic religion. There are three grades of initiation into the community and the ritual centres on the drug-induced mental dissociation of the initiants and on the dialogue that ensues between them and the medium. I came to learn a fair amount about water-spirit rituals and those who participate in them, and I was even given the privilege of a command performance on one occasion. Divination of the kind I witnessed at my first encounter with the spirit-medium determines whether or not the patient's condition is caused by the water-spirits. If so, preparations are made for the initiation. Until 1970, this used to be a lengthy process taking several days. There were ceremonies connected with drawing water, collecting firewood, and brewing beer.

On the evening of the initiation, a kind of 'holy' fire is lit and blessed, before placing on it a decorated pot filled with specially prepared roots and leaves. When the contents of the pot begin to boil, the patient is made to strip, incisions are made on the chest and medicine rubbed into the cuts. The patient is also made to drink a draught from a bottle containing a very secret and highly prized medicine. Maji-ya-Soda has allowed me to handle this bottle from time to time, but it is usually kept wrapped in a special cloth and is given a stool of its own. The liquid in the bottle is a rich golden colour and is probably a drug. The patient is then made to sit on a stool with his or her feet on either side, toes, but not heels, touching the ground. In this posture he has no support when he begins to topple off the stool. The steaming pot of roots and leaves is placed under the stool and a blanket thrown over the patient's head. Under the blanket the patient sweats and chokes in the steam. Meanwhile, the spirit-medium squats on the ground facing the patient and the circle of initiated water-spirit members shake rattles in a circular motion, their whole body vibrating as they sing an ancient Kimbu song: 'The lion roars and sways from side to side'. Everyone including the patient is swaying until finally the latter loses balance and falls off the stool. Sometimes, a patient resists, struggles to escape the choking steam and refuses to stay on the stool. Maji-ya-Soda's method of preventing this is fairly drastic. The patient is wrapped in a mat and tightly bound with ropes.

Dissociation follows. In this Maji-ya-Soda achieves a near 100 per cent success with his drugs and steam bath. Water-spirit regulars who participate with rattles and song develop a facility for dissociation without the need for drugs and there is a confused babble of noise. Patients feel a constriction in the chest but appear to enjoy an enhanced awareness of all that is going on. They answer the questions put to them by the medium in a voice that does not sound to them like their own and they can exercise no control over what they say. The medium addresses them as if talking to the water-spirits themselves and the patients accept the imputed identity. Since water-spirits are alien or peripheral spirits, the medium employs a 'foreign' language such as Swahili or Nyamwezi, rather than the Kimbu language. In fact, most people in the area speak all three languages. Sometimes the patients' glossolalia is slurred and unintelligible and when this happens it is said that they are speaking one of the vernaculars from western Tanzania, or even 'English' of which water-spirit members are ignorant. The medium's questions are leading questions which already suggest the answers, or which invoke the themes of water-spirit theory already known to the patient. Are the water-spirits causing this suffering to the patient? Why are they doing it? What do they want? Do they want a goat? Will they co-operate and give relief to the patient? Will they accept to be the guardians of the patient? At length the medium and the water-spirits bid farewell to one another and the patient is left to sleep off the trance.

Initiation to further degrees depends on what is revealed at the first session. Patients may exhibit a facility for dissociation. During the trance, they may communicate more or less hidden knowledge and it may be concluded that the water-spirits want to use them as diviners and mediums. The water-spirits themselves may confirm this when asked by Maji-ya-Soda. Patients who go through all three stages may eventually be allowed to set up a water-spirit lodge in their own village and act as mediums themselves. Once initiated, the patients are in any case subject to an elaborate set of rules and rituals which must be faithfully observed if they do not wish to anger their new water-spirit guardians. They must consult them frequently through the medium and they must obey the medium implicitly in whatever they are ordered to do.

The period at which I came to know Maji-ya-Soda in his remote forest homestead was the heyday of this spirit-medium. 1968 to 1970 was a period of uncertainty and anxiety for the people of the region and Maji-ya-Soda's community of affliction corresponded to social and psychological needs. The government was threatening to resettle people in new and enlarged villages and everyone was apprehensive. To the government, Maji-ya-Soda represented a power in the land, a power with which they had to reckon. He had numerous water-spirit lodges dotted around the region and a hierarchy of mediums ready to do his bidding. The path through the forest to his homestead was well trodden and, remote though he was from the lines of communication and centres of distribution, he lived in style. His house was roofed with iron sheets. He was well dressed. He owned several shotguns, and he never lacked an army of patients or would-be patients to cultivate his fields for him. Then in 1973 the blow fell, the people were forcibly moved to new settlements, the surrounding villages were razed and the whole water-spirit structure collapsed.

In 1973 I was told that the water-spirits had deserted Maji-ya-Soda. He had frequently told me that he was powerless in the hands of the spirits, and although I am sure he believes this, it is also clear that he manipulates them as a shaman or master-of-spirits is said to do. In 1973, however, the water-spirits disappeared as suddenly as they had arisen in the 1950s and 1960s. When I first came to know Maji-ya-Soda water-spirit beliefs were a generally accepted explanation of a variety of ills, now the theory was in abeyance. No doubt to some extent the villagization programme removed the state of uncertainty that had reigned in the late 1960s. No doubt, too, people had other problems to fill their minds as they cleared new fields, built new houses and organized a new social life. In the Swahili tradition there is a proverb which goes: 'The cure of the sick man depends on the doctor's deceit'. Proverbs are cynical and Maji-ya-Soda was nothing if not sincere. However, there is truth in the idea that illness is only recognized when a theory and a treatment are offered.

The government decided to leave Maji-ya-Soda alone for a few years. They were not anxious to have him around during the formation of the new villages. At length, pressure was put on him to move to Mtanila village, a very large new settlement some fifteen miles from his forest hideout. He was to come as an ordinary settler to farm tobacco with the rest of the village. He moved at the end of 1975, and I confidently celebrated the demise of his water-spirit community with a paper which I read on the subject to the Commonwealth Institute in London in early 1978. A year later, I visited him at Mtanila village and found that the water-spirits had been restarted. The new village was not going well. Promised facilities had not materialized, the price of tobacco had not improved and even the newly built dispensary was short of medicines. Maji-ya-Soda had been quick to exploit the situation. Before long he had persuaded the village leaders to petition higher authority on his behalf. The result was an official authorization allowing him to practise traditional medicine in cases which the dispensary was unable to treat successfully. The only condition set was that the spirit-medium should not interfere in village politics and have no place in the leadership.

Adaptable as ever, Maji-ya-Soda produced a streamlined version of the water-spirit ritual. Initiation now took one night instead of several days. Clients paid new and higher fees in cash, instead of in labour or kind, and practices such as binding initiants with ropes and mats during their ordeal were discontinued. By the early 1980s Maji-ya-Soda's clientèle was more numerous than it had been at any time. Villagization had greatly aggravated people's fear of witchcraft and Maji-ya-Soda announced that members of the water-spirit community were protected against witches. Several of Maji-ya-Soda's junior mediums were also living at Mtanila without being able to practise. Others, however, had moved to new villages elsewhere and were practising water-spirit medicine with Maji-ya-Soda's approval and under his control. A new and improved model of the water-spirit structure had now come into being.

The story of Maji-ya-Soda is instructive in many ways. It is the story of how such liminal rituals arise and are transformed in periods of intense social change. It is a commentary on the power of explanatory medical theories and especially on the harnessing of dissociative powers for therapeutic and social purposes. The water-spirits of Maji-ya-Soda's community of affliction are not objects of religious worship and his clients' attitude towards them is not supplicative. It is a matter-of-fact transaction through which illness and misfortune are made intelligible and controllable. In some cases the spirit which is alleged to do the possessing is an object of religious attitudes and judgements. This was the case for the Ugandan medium I consulted in 1975 (mentioned in Chapter 1). It is not even necessary to practise mental dissociation in order to be possessed by a spirit, as is proved again by the Ugandan example. Spirit possession is basically a belief that there is a spirit possessing you, or submerging your own personality in some way. The identity of this spirit and social attitudes towards it depend on cultural factors. These factors shape the mental content which underlies the personal identification of the spirit.

In western Christian tradition there are two forms of possession by spirits. All Christians in a state of grace are temples of the Holy Spirit and are endowed with charisms or gifts for the service of the community. Such gifts are by no means always extraordinary or miraculous gifts. They include many ordinary forms of service like teaching and administering or natural dispositions such as the gift of tears or supernatural gifts like that of a more than usually intense faith.

Our gifts differ according to the grace given us. If your gift is prophecy, then use it as your faith suggests; if administration, then use it for teaching. Let the preachers deliver sermons, the almsgivers give freely, the officials be diligent, and those who do works of mercy do them cheerfully.[2]

One may have the gift of preaching with wisdom given him by the Spirit; another may have the gift of preaching instruction given him by the same Spirit; and another the gift of faith given by the same Spirit; another again the gift of healing, through this one Spirit; one, the power of miracles; another, prophecy; another the gift of recognising spirits; another the gift of tongues and another the ability to interpret them.[3]

According to St Paul, therefore, there are different levels of teaching and preaching among the gifts of the Spirit. There are also healing gifts and gifts of miracles. Prophecy is the ability to expound Scripture under the guidance of the Spirit, while 'tongues' is the gift of glossolalia or the speech of dissociated people. For the gift of tongues to serve and edify the community there must be someone who can interpret it and reveal the mental content that underlies the phenomenon. The gift of tongues was especially a sign of the outpouring of the Spirit on all the different nations and language groups of the world at the very birth of the Church.[4]

The other form of possession traditionally known to Christians is that by the Devil. Again, one can fall under the influence of evil, perceived as extrinsic and personal, by committing mortal sin, thus subverting one's fundamental option or orientation towards God. A state of mortal sin is by no means necessarily accompanied by psychic phenomena such as a dissociated personality, and where dissociation occurs which is accompanied by a diabolical identification, opinion has varied as to whether it is a consequence of sin or not. Other than in the instances of the Spirit's indwelling and of diabolical possession, Christians are not 'possessed' by spirits, such as those of angels or saints, or by the faithful departed. New syncretist religious movements do sometimes lay claim to possession by angels, saints and souls in purgatory and it may be asked what significance this has. In the Christian west, we are accustomed to the idea of apparitions. It is alleged that the Blessed Virgin, angels and saints have appeared to visionaries. To what extent, it may be asked, is the difference between apparition and possession a cultural one? St Joan of Arc had her 'voices', and visionaries 'consult' the spirits that appear or speak to them in a way that is analogous to the consultation of spirits by mediums.

Spirit mediumship however is proverbially open to manipulation. When religious worship takes the form of spirit mediumship it is often because of a desire on the part of the worshipper for an immediate answer to prayer. It can develop into a way of constraining God, of forcing him into human categories. It is often a means of seeking divine approval and can quickly become a form of divination. 'It is an evil and unfaithful generation that asks for a sign!'[5]

In Maji-ya-Soda's community of affliction everything centres on mental dissociation and glossolalia. This is the vehicle of communication with the water-spirits and the continuous justifying miracle of water-spirit theory. This is frequently the case in such therapeutic communities and even in forms of Christian Pentecostalism. Since the identification of miracles does not ultimately depend on what is, or is not, explicable in terms of western science, it is not profitable to enter into the discussion of whether glossolalia is miraculous or not. It is usually susceptible to scientific explanation as the product of a natural, psychic state. This state, known as dissociated personality or mental dissociation, is not necessarily ecstatic, let alone hysterical or pathological. However, the line between psychopathology and simple psychological needs and drives is not always easy to draw. Glossolalia is the product of an altered state of consciousness in which some of the subject's controls have been relinquished. Phonetic analysis reveals that glossolalia is non-productive and stereotyped, and also that it is non-communicative.[6] It does not transmit a specific message to the listener who has no linguistic code in common with the glossolalist, unless an interpreter or manipulator intervenes to channel the utterances in accord with cultural expectations. Frequently repeated dissociation may lead to an instability of consciousness so that the switch-over from the normal to the altered state can be induced by even a slight stimulus in the manner of a conditioned reflex.

Glossolalia is held by some to have a therapeutic function similar to that of dreaming. If it is not an expression of the collective psyche, it may be a form of group therapy in which mental burdens are unloaded through non-verbal communication.[7] Speaking in tongues is experienced as something refreshing and reinvigorating. It seems often to be followed by a feeling of euphoria. People with the facility for dissociation and glossolalia may, if these phenomena are socially valued, acquire considerable social status and this is one reason why spirit possession can be a form of status redefinition for people in times of social change and collective uncertainty. In the Christian context, besides its latent healing functions, glossolalia is often a form of inchoate prayer or an expression of charismatic or Pentecostal commitment. It is a free utterance symbolic of the Spirit's own freedom. It may be a gift that is actively sought after to the exclusion or down-grading of other gifts. This problem was already present in the early Church and was the subject of a lengthy disquisition by St Paul.

Most of 1 Corinthians, chapter 14 is devoted to this discussion. For Paul, there is a hierarchy in the spiritual gifts. Love is the supreme charism and prophecy is more important than the much sought-after gift of tongues. The gift of tongues is concerned with 'mysterious things' and nobody understands what is being said, not even the glossolalist himself whose spirit prays but whose 'mind is left barren'. However, the one with the gift of tongues 'talks for his own benefit'. He edifies himself. It is a desirable gift and Paul has it himself in greater measure than the Corinthians to whom he is writing. Christians, he says, must be 'mentally adult' and that means using the gift of tongues in such a way that will grow to the benefit of the community. The glossolalist must offer an interpretation himself or use an interpreter. Only one person should use this gift at a time, otherwise, says Paul, an outsider would say 'you were all mad'. If these conditions cannot be fulfilled, the glossolalist must speak to himself and to God. Paul's verdict is nothing if not forthright! 'When I am in the presence of the community I would rather say five words that mean something than ten thousand words in a tongue'.

In rare cases glossolalia may be a parapsychological phenomenon. At the linguistic level it is usually in dissociated persons the distortion of a known language available to the glossolalist and the interpreter. It is suggested that it may also sometimes be the paranormal knowledge of a language ordinarily unknown to the speaker. Evidence is hard to come by, but what there is reveals that it is not limited to Christian Pentecostal contexts. J. M. Robert relates a story which may be a case in point.[8] In 1902 two missionaries from Galula mission in southern Tanzania, one a Flemish-speaking Belgian and one a Dutchman, visited the village of Pakanisya. While conversing with the villagers a person described as 'an old mad woman' joined the group. She was apparently a well-known vagrant in the area. The Belgian missionary enquired: 'Has the harvest been good this year?' The old woman thereupon replied in Flemish, speaking with as pure an accent as one could wish: 'Was it not you who used to steal the best pears from your parish priest in former times, climbing over the garden wall?' The Belgian was visibly shaken and said to his companion, 'Let's get out of here'. The Dutchman had, of course, understood what the old woman said, but in view of the Belgian missionary's emotion, waited till evening before questioning him. 'Didn't that old woman speak Flemish this morning?' he asked. 'Yes', replied the other, 'and this is what she said.' He then repeated the words and they discovered that they had both heard exactly the same thing. Robert had this story from the Dutchman himself and had no reason to doubt it, although it was not revealed if the pear-stealing was a real episode from the Belgian missionary's early life. Pears do not grow in the vicinity of Galula mission, nor indeed anywhere in East Africa, except where they have been introduced by white settlers in highland areas. The old woman could have had no opportunity to learn Flemish or Dutch, since Galula mission had only just been opened in 1901.

What should be the Christian assessment and pastoral

approach to a spirit mediumship phenomenon like that of Maji-ya-Soda's water-spirit community? A case described by Michael Singleton in 1978 puts the dilemma accurately, but points to a solution which I believe to be unacceptable.[9] In 1972 Singleton, then a missionary in Tanzania working in an area some two hundred miles north-west of the village where the old woman had spoken Flemish, was present at an initiation similar in many respects to one of Maji-ya-Soda's sessions. In this case the patient smoked marijuana in addition to being placed under a blanket and over a steaming pot of herbs. The patient was a girl afflicted by spirits as a consequence of having refused to marry the fiancé designated by her father. Under the onslaught of the woman medium, herself also possessed, the spirits who spoke through the girl confessed that she had done nothing deserving of death and that they would merely 'trouble her for a while'. Next morning Singleton decided to offer his own spiritual 'first aid', by playing back to the girl his tape-recording of the spirit-session and adding that he agreed with the spirit-medium. She should have no doubt that the source of her trouble had been identified and she should have no worries for the future. The spirits would not kill her.

The girl clearly believed in the objective personal reality of the spirits that were afflicting her, but Singleton did not, of course, share this belief. For him the spirits were as I have described them above, socio-psychiatric phenomena, the mental burdens of people under stress from social evils larger than the individual, 'factors of fissure in the social fabric'. It would have been a useless enterprise to try to explain all this to an uneducated village girl, so Singleton considered another alternative. He could do what many African Catholic priests of his acquaintance did—impute a diabolical origin to the spirits that afflicted the girl, and exorcize them in a prayer for deliverance. Singleton rejected this course mainly because of his own doubts about the personal existence of angels and devils. With regard to devils, we have already considered this question in Chapter 9. It is worth mentioning in passing a question that Singleton did not consider, namely that the spirits afflicting the poor girl could have been identified as angelical rather than diabolical. Angels appear in both Old and New Testaments inflicting plagues, disasters and epidemics upon humanity, albeit for causes considered just by the sacred writers. However, the fact that the girl's problem was expressed in terms of a conflict between spirits, those 'sent' by her father and fiancé and those controlled by the medium, shows that we have to deal with morally neutral beings not amenable to Christian categories. In any case, in African tradition the human witch takes the place of the Christian's Devil, as the epitome of moral and physical evil. To impute a diabolical identity in this case would be an example of Christian prejudice and an unwarrantable distortion of traditional beliefs.

Are we then in the proverbial 'Catch-22' situation? Singleton's solution to the problem was dishonest as far as his own understanding of the situation was concerned, but he justified his dissimulation in terms of 'client-centred' therapy. Therapists enter into the mental world of their patients in order to help them. However, even in psychotherapy, there are limits to the ways in which a doctor can empathize with a client. The end result of therapy should be a mature and equal relationship between psychiatrist and patient. It should not end in the unequal situation of dissimulation, let alone, of course, the infection of the psychiatrist's own mental health. From the Christian point of view, there is the obligation to evangelize sufferers, to give them a new Christ-centred understanding of the world and not to confirm them in a cosmology which is factually erroneous and subversive of Christian beliefs. The Christian healer has the duty to proclaim the Gospel and to offer the sufferer a direct experience of God's healing love revealed in Jesus Christ. Frames of reference for understanding and coping with misfortune vary from place to place and from time to time. We have seen some of the vicissitudes of Maji-ya-Soda's water-spirit theory. Ultimately, it is a question which is the most satisfying theory. The Christian evangelist, however, need not do violence to a frame of reference which tends to personalize psycho-sociological realities. The actual personalizations are not static and Christians can accept in any case the sign-value of the created order. Christ's personal presence ensures that all human realities are communications of divine healing love. Any experience, however painful or unpromising, can be a gift for human fulfilment and well-being, or it can be a curse and a threat to our existence and our happiness. Which it is depends on our response to the personal encounter that we have with Christ in such events.

Pentecostalism began as a Protestant, Fundamentalist form of Christianity in 1900 and the Pentecostal Assemblies of God quickly became the most important Black American denomination.[10] It spread to various countries of Africa after the Second

World War and holds a considerable appeal, often drawing members from other mission-related churches who experience a need for healing and wholeness that is not fulfilled in their own communions. The Assemblies of God have also exercised considerable influence on African Independent Churches. Catholic neo-Pentecostalism began in 1966 at Duquesne University and has become known as the Charismatic Renewal. It has also begun to flourish in the Anglican Communion and other main-line churches with missions in the Black World.

Charismatic Renewal offers among other things an experience of therapeutic community, with an emphasis on such spiritual gifts as healing and tongues. Such groups are ideally multi-faceted and multi-purpose in the approach to healing, offering a completely integrated ministry in the context of group prayer and commitment. These groups have to resist the temptation of becoming élitist, of catering for sectional interests, for only the educated classes and the religious congregations. On the other hand, they have no wish to degenerate into the 'fairground spectacle' offered by Fundamentalist Pentecostalism in some of its forms, with its neglect of deeper levels of healing, its facile linkage of sin, sickness and sorcery, its naïve adulation of glosso-lalia and its fascination with demonic utterance. In the Church in Africa, the relatively quiet charismatic prayer group, with its regular meetings, often fails to satisfy. There is a growing tendency to emulate popular Pentecostalism and to indulge in mass healing sessions and sessions of exorcism. In many cases these activities cannot escape the charge of deviation from Catholic faith and tradition. Pentecostal healing should be associated with the experience of real community and lived Christianity. The Church is not a travelling circus. It is a fundamental challenge to sick people as sick people—to discover sickness as providential, irrespective of cure. Sickness brings us closer to God and that relationship with him is more valuable and more fulfilling than the expectation of a physical cure.

15

Exorcizing the Devil

In June 1982 the world became aware of the existence of Archbishop Emmanuel Milingo. Mgr Milingo was Archbishop of Lusaka, the capital of Zambia, and he had been called to Rome, so it was officially said, for a rest, for medical examination and for theological reflection. After a year's exile in Rome, Pope John Paul II granted the Archbishop an audience after which it was announced that he had resigned the metropolitan see of Lusaka and had been appointed a special delegate to the Pontifical Commission for Migrants and Tourism. Although the Vatican never offered an explanation for these developments, and although innuendo was far from lacking in Lusaka itself about the Archbishop's personal and episcopal conduct, the world press chose to highlight Mgr Milingo's healing ministry and an alleged missionary resistance to his inculturation of the Gospel in Africa. Archbishop Milingo was headlined as 'witchdoctor', as 'faith-healer', as 'tribal chief'. As we have used the term in this book, 'witchdoctor' is far from being as opprobrious as many people seem to believe. Strictly speaking Mgr Milingo is not a faith-healer, and in his healing ministry he appears much more in the role of a prayerful therapist than in that of a tribal chief.

As a matter of fact, the Archbishop's healing ministry in Lusaka (though not so much his healing journeys to other parts of the world) has been a focus for conflicting emotions. Many people experienced the ministry of Mgr Milingo as an admirable and compassionate form of pastoral care and his removal from office as an incomprehensible and irreparable loss.[1] Articles in the press have cited the 'powerful' Jesuits as the missionary opponents of the Archbishop, but it is a certain fact that foreign priests of other missionary congregations were associated with him in his ministry of healing.[2] Although, in some of his reported statements, Mgr Milingo appears to question the power of the Eucharist, the sacraments of the Church and other traditional

prayers to effect physical healing, he usually conducts his ministry within the context of a western-style Mass, without exuberant singing, drumming or dancing, during which he makes
lengthy intercessions on behalf of the sick people before him,
sometimes laying his hands on them or blessing them.[3] The
major opposition to Archbishop Milingo's healing ministry
seems to have come from his brother African Bishops who
attempted vainly to make him curtail these activities.[4] If he
preserves any rancour it is against his brother Bishops and it may
be the case that—with hindsight—they feel their recourse to
Rome was too precipitate. In many parts of Africa, Europe and
America, there are people who claim to have been healed at Mgr
Milingo's intercession, and the Archbishop himself asserts that
the Pope at his audience in 1983 compared him to the holy
stigmatist, the late Padre Pio.[5] He interprets his new assignment
as a desire on the part of the Holy See to safeguard his healing
ministry and even to extend it throughout the world. Certainly,
he has begun to travel widely and to exercise his healing gift in
many different countries already.

Exorcism of demons plays little part in Mgr Milingo's healing
services outside the African context. In Africa, however, and in
Lusaka especially, the Archbishop exorcized the kind of alien
spirits that were described in Chapter 14, imputing to them a
diabolical identity, and entering, himself, into a mild trance
accompanied by glossolalia.[6] Among the spirits he exorcizes are
the *mashave* or *mashawe* alien or patronal spirits and the *mizimu* or
benevolent spirits of deceased ancestors (who may at times be
held to punish the living with misfortunes of various kinds).[7] The
Archbishop's solidarity with African traditional culture in this
matter consists in an impassioned belief in the objective personal
reality of the spirits, but that is as far as it goes. He refuses to
accept the cultural identities and expectations associated with
these categories of spirit. According to his way of thinking, all
these spirits form a diabolical 'Church of the Spirits'.

The church of the spirits is the work of the Devil and his agents. He gives to his
followers or disciples tremendous powers. For the time being only a few from
the public know the powers, or have seen the display of the powers. The nature
of the powers cannot be explained by any means other than attributing them to
the power of someone above human beings, but a bad one. Many patients are
attracted by the methods of discovery of the diseases and in many instances the
diagnosis is true, because the spirits are intelligent beings, and certainly they are
aware of what is happening in someone's body, and they reveal it. However, it

must be known by those responsible for the welfare of the people of Zambia that the Devil will not heal what he himself has caused.[8]

The Archbishop gives examples of his dialogue with the spirits speaking through the mouths of dissociated clients.

Why do you deceive people claiming that you can heal them when you know that you cause the diseases?
If they follow our instructions some are healed.
But why do you cause diseases and then heal again?
So you know that we are clever.[9]

You have no right to torture this woman, why do you torture her?
She is ours. She is very good, since she obeys us.
Give respect to Jesus Christ who died for her, and so we order you to leave her.
Your Jesus cannot go round as we do. Where is he? You wait. A lot of Christians will come to our side.
You know that we shall overcome you because we are many.
We are too many, we are millions. You cannot count us all, not throughout your life.[10]

This interpretation of the morally neutral spirits of African tradition brings the Archbishop up against two categories of people, the spirit-mediums and traditional healers on the one hand and the missionary and African priests who are anthropologists or psychologists on the other. Like the prophet-founders of the independent churches, Mgr Milingo sees in the spirit-mediums and traditional healers of Africa his chief rivals. They are, in his way of thinking, instruments of the Devil.

It is hard to believe that today's Sing'angas [traditional doctors], taken up by money and deceit, can heal a patient suffering from spirits. The spirits use them as their own agents and the spirits in this case are the causes of the illness.[11]

The devils who have often inflicted so many forms of misery on human beings have been clever by instituting a group of specialists called spirit-healers, who diagnose diseases when they go into a trance. They tell the truth very often, but for their own ends, to win people's confidence. They even prescribe the medicines, which do nothing to the disease, except to develop in a patient dependability [*sic*] on them.[12]

On the only occasion on which I had the pleasure of meeting Archbishop Milingo, in October 1971, he had been invited to preside at the graduation ceremony of the AMECEA (Association of Member Episcopal Conferences in Eastern Africa) Pastoral Institute, then situated in Uganda. The Archbishop's address, delivered to the faculty, students and a number of guests from Makerere University, including the Professor of Educational Psychology, was a lengthy attack on the human sciences and in particular experimental psychology itself. Although this speech was given two years before his inaugurating cure of a 'woman with strange voices' in 1973 and three years before 50,000 people at the Charismatic Leadership Congress at Ann Arbor, USA had prayed for him to receive the gift of healing, his view of scientific explanations was already formed.[13] In 1981 he was to write:

[Many missionaries] have never accepted *Mashawe* as a disease worth healing, since they call it by their own name as a hysterical and psychosomatic disease. They therefore consider anyone engaged in it as an imbecile who chases the wind. It is the problem of inculturation, much more [than?] the refusal to plunge into it.[14]

The priest-graduates and post-graduates of African Anthropology, African missiology, African traditional religions etc. come to us as specialists, fit for teaching their science in high institutes of learning and universities. One wonders as to whether they value their priesthood much more than their chair as lecturers in African universities. One wonders as to whether they intend to convert an African to his own culture or to teach him what he is. . . .[15]

Archbishop Milingo, therefore, imposes a fundamentalist demonological theory on the phenomena of African spirit mediumship. It is a theory which has more in common with the *Malleus Maleficarum* of fifteenth-century Europe than with any tradition to be found in Africa, and it certainly does greater violence to the cultural facts than the socio-psychological theories which allowed Michael Singleton to confirm his client in her literal beliefs (cf. Chapter 14).[16] The Archbishop's demonology is shared by a number of priest healers and exorcists in different parts of contemporary Africa and the best way to recognize the deviations to which their activities may give rise is to consider an example of a session of this kind. It must also be clearly said that many of these priests, like Archbishop Milingo, are certainly endowed with healing charisms and are very much appreciated by the people they serve. The following is a description of a particular session which took place in Tanzania in 1979. It is based on the eyewitness account of an informant who was there. The dialogue with the devils given here was supplied by a second informant who heard it at another healing session in 1975. It is typical of all these dialogues. The description given here is confirmed by my own impressions of the exorcist himself and by conversations with other witnesses and clients.[17]

The famous exorcist and healer, whom we shall call Fr Audax Mwaguzi, had been invited by some lay-people to the diocese of X to carry out his ministry.[18] The Bishop of the diocese was uneasy about the invitation and had reluctantly given his permission, provided that the healer remained for only three days. Rumour travels fast in Africa and when the day for the healing service came a large crowd of people of all faiths and every walk of life had gathered in a kind of natural amphitheatre outside the village. Estimates put the numbers at around 10,000. An altar had been prepared for Mass and there were numerous buckets, gourds, basins and other containers for water beside the altar. Fr Mwaguzi entered the circle, vested for Mass, a small figure with a suggestion of hidden dynamism. He was in complete command. The holy water was blessed and Mass was celebrated in the usual way. The homily, which lasted nearly half an hour, dealt with the cures by Jesus in the Gospels, and particularly with his exorcism of demons.

After Mass, Fr Mwaguzi removed his shoes and ordered everyone to remove theirs. Everyone did so, whether out of human respect or out of a spirit of co-operation and expectation. In any case, it had the effect of making everyone part of the proceedings. The healer then offered a short prayer, asking for the Blessed Virgin's intercession and for God to heal the sick that would be brought to him. While this was going on, sick people were making their way, or being carried, up to the altar where they were seated in rows. The healer then made a few announcements to the crowd. He explained that he had no power to cure people from illnesses that had been caused by evil magic or sorcery and that if his ministry failed in any given case it must be because sorcery was involved. This was a surprising limitation of his powers. However, it provided a built-in explanation of failure, even if it was calculated to strengthen people's superstitions concerning evil magic. He also announced that he would be very shortly sprinkling the crowd with holy water. When this happened, he said, some people would start trembling and shaking. These would be people afflicted by the *majini* or evil spirits and they should be brought up to him for exorcism. This announcement caused a stir in the crowd and an air of tense expectation. It was surprising that he used the term *majini* or Djinns, which are the Islamic demons, considerably more ambivalent and morally neutral than the devils of Christian tradition.

Fr Mwaguzi dipped a branch deeply into one of the buckets of holy water and sprinkled the crowd energetically. The question in everyone's mind was: Who will be the ones to start shaking? Immediately after the sprinkling shouts and screams were heard in different sections of the crowd and struggling people were carried forward to the altar. In some cases there was a total surprise, friends or relatives who had never been afflicted with spirits, or had anything whatever to do with them, were found to be possessed. On arrival at the altar the victims seemed to quieten down until addressed by Mwaguzi. One of them was summoned to him, a young woman in a yellow frock. Holding her by the hair, he drenched her with holy water from a bucket in his other hand and the woman began to scream and go into convulsions. A dialogue ensued between the healer and the possessed woman. The conversation was in Swahili, not the local vernacular.

Leave this woman!
I will not.
I command you to leave this woman!
I will not.
Where do you come from?
Another woman sent me. I cannot leave without her permission.
I command you in the name of Jesus Christ, leave this woman!
No!
What is your name?
My name is Abdallah.

At every refusal of the demon, Mwaguzi poured more holy water on the trembling woman until she was completely drenched. The whole dialogue took about fifteen minutes.

Are you ready to come out now?
I am beginning to be afraid of this being called Jesus.
Are you ready to move?
I am ready.

The final capitulation of the spirit was greeted with cheers and clapping from the audience and the woman was told to go home with some of the holy water in a bottle for her to drink from time to time, as a medicine.

The next demoniac was also a woman, held firmly by two strong men. Fr Mwaguzi again pulled her hair and drenched her with holy water.

Who are you?
I am called Juma.
How many are you?
There are nine of us and I am the chief.
What are you doing here?
We are here to torture her.
How did you come to her?
We were asked by our Master to torture her to death.
When did you come?
We came to her ten years ago when she was in Mombasa.
I order you in the name of Jesus Christ to come out of her.
We will not.

Again, there was the same reluctance of the spirits to depart and repeated drenchings with holy water. The crowd followed the dialogue with laughter and amusement. The spirits begged to be allowed to stay, but one by one they departed, the whole process taking nearly half an hour. All the spirits had Islamic names and some even spoke a few words of Arabic or English. Many professed not to know who 'this being called Jesus' was. There were several more successful exorcisms of this kind, while volunteers continuously fetched water to replenish the holy water buckets. The whole area round the altar was awash with holy water.

Fr Mwaguzi then turned his attention, with less spectacular results, to some crippled people that had been brought up to him. Some Asian parents carried their nine-year-old child to the altar. The child was paralysed and unable to stand, let alone walk. The healer poured holy water over the boy and began massaging his limbs. After five or ten minutes, he lifted the child by the shoulders into a standing position and tried to get him to move. This was too much for the boy. Fr Mwaguzi tried to get the child to stand without support, but each time he let go, the child fell. More and more holy water was poured on him and then the healer forced him to walk by moving his limbs for him. After some time, the child began to take a few steps alone before falling down again. At this point, Fr Mwaguzi called the boy's father to help him walk around, while he attended to other patients.

Another cripple was a girl aged eleven with both legs deformed. She normally walked on the sides of her feet. This was again an Asian child, and again her father was told to help her to walk properly, after she had been duly drenched with holy water. Fr Mwaguzi massaged the girl's feet, stretching them and manipulating them with sensitive hands. Then he took the child a few yards away and ordered her to run to her father. She lurched forward into her father's arms and everyone clapped. Meanwhile an improvised choir had started to sing. Fr Mwaguzi went from patient to patient. When one cripple failed to respond to his ministrations, he turned to another. From the cripples he returned to the demoniacs, and from the demoniacs to the cripples. It was difficult to follow all that was happening or to keep track of who was healed and who was not. Like the expert conjuror, the healer was continually distracting people's attention. Many of the sick and disabled were clearly no better. Some of the possessed took longer to be exorcized than others and Fr Mwaguzi left them for a while. With exorcism, however, he had a near 100 per cent success.

There was considerable movement in the crowd. Some left in order to get something to eat and drink, but Fr Mwaguzi remained there, his small figure leaping around the altar from one patient to another, issuing his commands and pouring his holy water. It was a *tour-de-force*, and it lasted throughout the hours of daylight from around 8.30 a.m. when Mass had begun, until 6.30 when it began to grow dark. At one point an incident occurred in another part of the crowd. Someone was trying to take a photograph of the proceedings and was having difficulty with his camera. Fr Mwaguzi saw him and shouted angrily that he would not allow any camera to function while the healing was going on. At length, he announced: 'Now your cameras will work and you may take photographs'. This was another memorable miracle. After the session, it was rumoured that the healer had predicted that a rainbow would form around the sun at midday and several people claimed to have witnessed this spectacle. Some Muslims who had been exorcized or healed at this session later became Catholics.

The following day there was a similar session and then Fr Mwaguzi departed. This priest is employed by government in the field of religious education and his diocese of residence is not that of his priestly incardination. The Bishop of the diocese in which he resides was embarrassed by Fr Mwaguzi's healing activities and ordered him not to conduct his sessions in church buildings or other mission premises. He was not, however, forbidden to practise elsewhere. Accordingly, he acquired a house in one of the parishes. Here the Blessed Sacrament is reserved and he conducts a healing clinic to which a continuous flow of people come to be exorcized or healed. Many of his clients are people with psycho-social problems, or who are suffering from some kind of social shock or stigma. It is among these that the demons chiefly manifest themselves. Some are experiencing family problems. Some have been victims of robberies or accidents in the home, and some are clearly victims of nervous stress or even psychosis.

I have chosen to describe the healing activities of Fr Mwaguzi, not only because I have met him and some of his clients, but also because he represents a more orthodox and more exemplary type of African priest-healer. There are some who have abused the sacraments and sacramentals of the Church and others whose so-called healings involve acts of indecency. Anyone who has read the *Malleus Maleficarum* by two medieval priest-exorcists will not be surprised at such developments.[19] Fr Mwaguzi, on the other hand, exhibits a personal piety and a zeal in his care for the sick that must earn our admiration. And yet, there are many disturbing aspects to his healing ministry, as there are apparently in that of Archbishop Milingo.

In Chapter 9 we attempted a brief discussion of the mystery of evil in the world and we noted the paradox of Satan's limited victory over the humanity redeemed by Christ. It is important to remember that his victory *is* limited. St Paul, using the demonological and apocalyptic images of his time, speaks of the 'Sovereignties and Powers' and the 'spiritual army in the heavens'.

Finally, grow strong in the Lord, with the strength of his power. Put God's armour on so as to be able to resist the devil's tactics. For it is not against human enemies that we have to struggle, but against the Sovereignties and the Powers who originate the darkness in this world, the spiritual army of evil in the heavens.[20]

In Paul's day, people believed in spirits that moved the stars and the universe itself. They lived in the heavens or 'in the air' and had disobeyed God. They were, so Paul's contemporaries believed, continually trying to enslave human beings to themselves. This is a graphic image of the Christian's spiritual war with the forces of evil in the world, but Christ has already freed us, and armed us with his power; we shall carry off the victory. Paul also speaks about 'the Rebel', 'the Lost One' and the 'Enemy' who in turn becomes the 'Antichrist' of the Johannine writings.[21] Possibly he symbolizes successive historical figures who are the tools of Satan in history. According to Paul, his revolt is restrained until the final apocalyptic battle with the Messiah in his *parousia*. The world is a theatre for spiritual warfare and humanity is deeply flawed by original sin, but Satan, although he is the 'Prince of this world', does not hold the whole universe in thrall, nor is everybody and everything outside the visible Church part of a universal empire of evil.

The nineteenth-century missionaries who brought the Gospel to Africa had a deeply pessimistic view of African religion, culture and tradition. All was under the sway of the Devil and even the good actions of pagans were mortal sins. The world, especially the pagan world, was wholly evil. One African missionary society, for example, enjoined a daily prayer to Our Lady on its members, for the salvation of the Muslims 'and other infidels of Africa'.[22] One line went: 'Have mercy on these unfortunate creatures who are continually falling into Hell in spite of the merits of your Son Jesus Christ'. It was only through the ministrations of an embattled, sacramental Church that salvation was possible. Against this view the Second Vatican Council represents a giant step forward in the development of salvation theology. Not only does it esteem the spiritual and moral values of non-Christian religions and cultures, but it proclaims:

Those who through no fault of their own do not know the Gospel of Christ or his Church, but who nevertheless seek God with a sincere heart, and moved by grace, try in their actions to do his will as they know it through the dictates of their conscience—those too may achieve eternal salvation. Nor shall divine Providence deny the assistance necessary for salvation to those who, without any fault of theirs, have not arrived at an explicit knowledge of God, and who, not without grace, strive to lead a good life.[23]

Moreover, it is not only Christians who are partners in the Paschal Mystery but 'all men of good will in whose hearts grace is active invisibly'.[24] This is a very different picture from the 'empire of Satan' image projected by the early missionaries.

It seems to me that popular exorcism in Africa shares the 'empire of Satan' theory. 'We are too many', said the demons to Archbishop Milingo, 'we are millions. You cannot count us all, not throughout your life.'[25] Popular exorcism encourages dualistic attitudes in which the fear of demons is more real than the healing love of God. Any and every misfortune is capable of diabolical interpretation and, like the witches of African tradition, devils are an unseen presence in the midst of the community, awaiting only the exorcist's holy water sprinkler to manifest themselves. Repeated exorcisms only strengthen people's fears of the demons, in much the same way as the witch-eradicators strengthen people's fear of the witches they eradicate. We do not have any grounds for denying the objective personal reality of devils or even that Satan is a 'king' of devils. Such a denial would even seem to contradict statements of the *magisterium* of the Church. On the other hand, we cannot say with any precision what we mean by describing devils analogously as personal. We cannot even begin to answer Man Friday's question to Robinson Crusoe: 'But if God much strong, much might as the devil, why God no kill the devil, so make him no more do wicked?' We are as puzzled as he was.[26] Does it mean that God loves the Devil, but will not force his loving mercy on him?

Anyway, the condition of certain psychotic people who feel themselves submerged by moral evil in an objectively personal form may very well be evidence for the reality of supra-human powers of evil and form a part of our total experience of them. The Church's official practice of severely circumscribing the use of exorcism and limiting it to such psychopathic and other exceptional cases which can be helped by the prayer for deliverance would seem to be wise and practical. Even so, there is a danger, when entering into the situation of the psychosis, of allowing the mentality of such people to affect our own psychic health.[27] Such exorcism should be used in conjunction with psychiatric treatment. We must not excogitate diabolical fantasies from the psychopathic delusions of people with psychiatric disorders, still less erect them into a systematic demonology or social stereotype. The exorcist's aim would be to minister privately to those who are sick of mind and soul, as individuals.[28]

I have no personal doubt whatever that people such as Archbishop Milingo and Fr Mwaguzi possess God-given healing gifts. These healing charisms in the Church will be discussed in Chapter 17. Fr Mwaguzi, as I have observed him, seems to exhibit a zeal and a love where the sick are concerned which is doubtless experienced by them as healing power. He also has the gift of drawing a potential for cure from the sick people themselves and from others who love them. He seems also to combine these gifts with some of the skills of a physiotherapist. When healing of the body fails, he does not, as some healers do, blame the sufferers themselves for their lack of faith or failure to co-operate in 'claiming' the cure. He is not a faith-healer. On the other hand, his belief in sorcery allows him a loop-hole for failure, though it is not clear to me why his powers should not theoretically be applicable to cases of sorcery. The multiplicity of devils offers another loop-hole to the popular exorcist. If the person remains possessed, it can always be claimed that a partial success has been achieved in removing some of the devils, but not all.

With the devils, however, healers are nearly always successful, and this must be for reasons similar to those which ensure the success of non-Christian spirit-mediums, namely the clients' natural power of dissociation and the manipulation of their glossolalia by the exorcists according to their own demonic expectations and those of the audience. I have no doubt that this manipulation occurs in perfect good faith, as it does, say, in Maji-ya-Soda's community of affliction, and that the outcome is basically therapeutic. However, popular or mass exorcism of this kind runs the risk of causing people to demonize their experience of suffering to an exaggerated degree. Fear of the devil replaces the love of God and a morbid interest in demons is encouraged. People are diverted away from prayer and the sacraments which are regarded as being not sufficiently powerful for the exorcist's purposes. The identification and exposure of devils is not a substitute for growth in the spiritual life and for the practice of love, service and justice in the community. The whole phenomenon may become a dangerous aberration.

In so far as exorcists do inculcate a systematic demonology and really preach the 'empire of Satan', it may be held that they are merely transforming traditional beliefs about possession by alien and patronal spirits, even if the transformation is unhealthy. However, concessions are clearly made to the traditional theory by the Christian exorcists. The Islamic *majini* of Fr Mwaguzi are a case in point. To what extent, it may be asked, is he replacing a Muslim demonology by a Christian one? Or does he accept the Islamic identity of the demons he exorcizes, their Arabic language and their Muslim names? The spirits exhibit all the characteristics of traditional *majini*, being sent by others—even by living human beings—compassing the death of their victims, or simply torturing them for a while according to circumstances. Do Christian exorcists question any of this? Are they no better than a traditional spirit-medium, exercising the role of shaman in the war of the spirits? To this must be added the disturbing consideration that exorcism may also be a platform for a rivalry between Christianity and Islam.

Exorcism can rapidly degenerate into a power-phenomenon rather than a prayer-phenomenon and the healers' feats of strength, their humbling of demons and their 'magic tricks' with cameras, if not with celestial phenomena, pander to the popular fascination with the marvellous. It is doubtful whether such 'shows' really lead people to Christ and to a change of heart. Christ himself discouraged the disciples' rejoicing in exorcism: 'Do not rejoice that the spirits submit to you; rejoice rather that your names are written in heaven'.[29] This raises the further question: What should be the context for the exercise of healing gifts in the Church of the African world? Some answers to this question will be put forward after we have considered the healing character of the Christian sacraments.

16

The sacraments and healing

The idea of a 'Safari Cross' was born in April 1983 at a meeting of
the Eastlands Deanery in Nairobi, capital of Kenya.[1] It was the
start of the extraordinary Holy Year of the Redemption proclaimed by Pope John Paul II and the representatives of the nine
parishes in the deanery were sharing ideas on how to celebrate the
Holy Year. East Africa has given the word *safari* to the world and
Nairobi is the home of the Safari Rally.[2] So why not a 'Safari
Cross'? The idea was a simple one. We would carry a large
wooden cross from one parish to another, until it had circulated
through all the nine parishes of the deanery. The cross would
remain for a week in each parish community, the focus for
celebration, prayer and reconciliation—our own way of sharing
in the Holy Year. The idea was easier to realize in the crowded
Nairobi Eastlands, given the poverty and density of the squatter
populations and their degree of social integration.

The cross was duly blessed by Cardinal Maurice Otunga,
Archbishop of Nairobi, at an impressive concelebrated Mass on
the feast of the Exaltation of the Cross and began its first week at
a parish served by Verona Fathers. From there it was carried to
the parish which is attached to the archdiocesan junior seminary
and on 2 October it reached the parish of the Benedictines. On
Sunday, 9 October, it was to be the turn of our parish, St
Teresa's, Eastleigh, where I had been based since December
1982.

Our special Holy Year week had been prepared very carefully
in the basic communities of the parish. Smaller crosses had been
carried from house to house and venerated at community prayer
meetings. On the Friday before we started our special week, our
large parish church was filled to overflowing for a film projection

of the final episodes of Zeffirelli's *Jesus of Nazareth* with an on-the-spot Swahili commentary. Then the day itself arrived. We started early for St Benedict's outstation chapel to which the cross had been brought the previous night. The chapel is near the parish boundary in an area of the huge shanty-town known as Mathare Valley. For most of us it was our first sight of the by now famous Safari Cross and it was daunting enough—bigger and heavier by far than anything we had imagined. In a brief ceremony the Safari Cross was entrusted to the parishioners of St Teresa's and we surged forward to claim it. At once it was lifted by a hundred pairs of hands and carried high over the bearers' heads. It seemed to float ahead of us borne on finger-tips. Twice during the procession I managed to touch it briefly, but it was difficult to come near it because of the crowd.

And so our *safari* with the cross began. Ahead of it, our banner proudly proclaimed: 'St Teresa's Parish, Eastleigh, Holy Year 1983–1984'. Behind it a huge crowd massed, men and women, people of all ages, priests, religious brothers and sisters. On either side walked sidesmen with yellow sashes. Many of the people had brought crosses they had made themselves, some beautifully carved or painted, some consisting merely of a couple of sticks roughly bound together. As we swarmed through the muddy lanes of the squatter areas, more and more people joined our ranks. A small boy with a home-made cross in one hand thrust his other hand into mine, as we walked side by side. Voices rose and fell with an ever-recurring refrain: 'Come to me all you who labour and are burdened, and I will give you rest'.

There were four stations or stops in the different neighbourhoods through which we passed. The cross was set up against a wall and the people of the basic community led the readings, hymns and prayers. There were moments of poignancy and emotion, as when a reader took his text from Exodus: 'And the Lord said, I have seen the sufferings of my people in Egypt. I have heard their appeal. . . . I mean to deliver them out of the hands of the Egyptians. . . .' Or when Paulo, a paralytic with a speech impediment, laboured at the microphone to make his bidding-prayer. Now we were moving into the crowded Eastleigh estate, skirting drains and refuse heaps, crossing the occasional main road, with the Kenya Police discreetly holding back the traffic. As we neared our parish church, the bells rang out and the Safari Cross was carried into the square where a crowd of some five thousand had gathered for an open-air Mass. After

Mass, the cross was carried into the church and laid before the altar amidst flowers and candles.

We had decided that each day we would take one sacrament as the theme for an evening Holy Year service while the Safari Cross was with us. That Sunday evening we celebrated a baptism in slow-motion, meditating on the ceremony itself and the meaning of its rites. Six children were baptized and parents and godparents were invited to comment out loud on such actions as the signing of the forehead with the Sign of the Cross, the anointing with chrism and the bestowing of the white garment and the burning candle. On Monday evening we had a service of readings, hymns and prayers with the sacrament of confirmation as the theme. Our confirmations were due to take place later in the month, so we invited the confirmation class to the church and prayed over them with uplifted arms. Then, one by one, members of the basic communities stepped up to the microphone to speak of the different gifts of the Spirit and of the particular gifts they discerned in themselves and which they tried to use for the good of the community. One spoke of religion teaching, another of caring for the old and sick and getting treatment for them. Another spoke of reconciling people after quarrels.

Tuesday's theme was the Eucharist and we celebrated a very solemn evening Mass followed by Adoration of the Blessed Sacrament up to midnight. The high point of the celebration was the Lord's Prayer which we began with uplifted arms. At 'give us this day our daily bread' more than a thousand pairs of upturned palms were stretched towards the altar. And at 'Forgive us our trespasses' we joined hands with our neighbours. Communion was given under both kinds, a hazardous undertaking—one might think—in that vast crowd, but no mishap occurred. Wednesday's theme was penance and a very large crowd attended a lengthy penitential rite. Veneration of the cross took place while four priests heard confessions and gave private absolution. The climax was a procession of the resurrection with an icon and lighted candles, carried by children in the darkened church.

For the sacramental anointing of the sick on Thursday we had the biggest crowd yet. Disabled and elderly people had been carried by their communities to the church and given places of honour, and the liturgy was conducted by hospital chaplains from one of the big Nairobi hospitals. Friday's attendance surpassed even that of Thursday. The church was filled to bursting for a solemn evening Mass presided over by the Cardinal who spoke to us about the sacrament of Order, about the Bishop as centre of unity in the diocese and the priest as the same in his parish. After Mass there was a reception in the parish school and people came singing and dancing to greet the Cardinal, while soft drinks were served and the choir sang songs of welcome.

On Saturday evening we took the sacrament of matrimony as our theme. Again, the reflection took place in the context of Mass and several married couples gave testimonies about the need for communication and mutual forgiveness in marriage and all the couples present were invited to renew their sacramental commitment. Then came Sunday 16 October, the day for handing over the cross to our neighbours in the parish served by the Mill Hill Fathers, and the scenes of the previous Sunday were repeated. A huge crowd swarmed around the cross, with banners and loudspeakers, past the food and vegetable kiosks, the open-air mechanical repair shops, the shoe-makers and woodworkers. Again there were stations, and one representative of a basic community compared us all to the apostles after the Ascension. The cross was to be taken from us, but the Lord would still be with us until the end of the world. Finally, the Safari Cross was reluctantly handed over to our neighbours at another open-air Mass in a playing-field at the parish boundary. Five weeks later, on the Feast of Christ the King, the Cardinal presided over a concelebrated Mass and he, together with the clergy of the nine parishes, carried the huge cross from the open-air altar to lay it up in Kariobangi church. It made a brave sight, with us all in red vestments, and a photograph of it fittingly appeared on the front page of a daily newspaper.

The Safari Cross made a great impact on St Teresa's Parish. It was a source of healing, for it brought many people back to the practice of their faith, and many also to conversion and baptism. It brought our communities together, the shanties and the more affluent neighbourhoods. It brought together bishop, priests, religious and laity. It linked up the parishes of the deanery. Altogether, it was a great week of social healing and reconciliation. But even more than that, it taught us about the healing character of the sacraments. We appreciated their community dimension. We saw more clearly than ever before how in the sacraments our human lives and experiences, our earthly realities and all the spiritual and material elements of which humanity is the synthesis, not only speak to us of transcendental reality, but make that redemption available to us. It was a memorable lesson in the relevance of the sacraments to the life and fabric of the community.

At several points in this book already the need has been stressed for a sacramental view of reality. It is only such a view which can make a truly integrated approach to healing possible. It is only such a view that adequately explains our organic involvement with the world of nature and the interaction of all the various levels in the human make-up, physical, psychic, social, spiritual. Integrated healing becomes a reality when every manifestation of healing power is seen to be a part of God's universal healing action and his restoration of our wholeness. The sacraments are actions of Christ and actions of the Church. They are also expressions of our faith and worship. The sacraments are channels of grace. That is to say, they are high points in our transforming encounter with God in Jesus Christ, in our sanctification. But it is a mistake to assume that this transforming encounter holds no consequences for any other level of our life than the spiritual or the moral. It is also a mistake to reject or play down the importance of the sacraments because they do not produce an immediate effect in the area of physical healing. Prayer for healing should not be opposed to the sacraments any more than it should be opposed to medicine. Healing prayer can work miracles of grace and nature, and the sacraments are an eminent form of healing prayer. How many miracles at Lourdes have taken place, not in the baths or through the waters of the spring, but through the blessing with the Blessed Sacrament during the procession on the Esplanade—as if to demonstrate the power of the sacraments to bring about physical healing? However, not every prayer is answered in the way we expect and not every benediction with the Host brings a miraculous cure, yet there is always an answer to prayer, the gift of God's Spirit.

So I say to you: Ask, and it will be given to you; search, and you will find; knock, and the door will be opened to you. For the one who asks always receives; the one who searches always finds; the one who knocks will always have the door opened to him. What father among you would hand his son a stone when he asked for bread? Or hand him a snake instead of a fish? Or hand him a scorpion if he asked for an egg? If you then, who are evil, know how to give your children what is good, how much more will the heavenly Father give the Holy Spirit to those who ask him![3]

Baptism is the foundational sacrament of the Christian life, for it is presupposed by all the others. However, I propose to study the healing character of the Eucharist first of all here, because this sacrament sums up every level and aspect of our existence, because it effects an abiding, localized presence of Christ's healing love among us and because it is the context in which nowadays other sacraments are, or may be, celebrated. The Eucharist also most clearly portrays the whole mystery of Christ's incarnation, life of service, passion, death, resurrection, ascension and outpouring of the Holy Spirit.

St Paul clearly believed that the reception of the Eucharist and reverence towards it were bound up with bodily health.[4] If we examine the post-Communion prayers of the Roman Missal, we find that several of them explicitly envisage 'health of mind and body' as a result of Holy Communion and this is also clearly a motive for bringing Communion to the sick. The prayers at Communion of the sick and in the votive Masses of the sick are understandably explicit.[5] They address Jesus as 'the author of all healing'. They acclaim the body of Jesus Christ as a food 'which can heal forever'. They ask that it may 'make them well' or 'restore their health' and that it may 'turn our anxiety for them into joy'. But the ordinary Sunday prayers continually express aspects of physical healing as well as social and spiritual healing. Many ask for 'strength', even 'strength to face the troubles of life', as well as for protection and the more general desire to experience God's 'healing love', or to have him continue his 'healing work within us'. Some of the petitions are mainly concerned with psychic health. They ask for gifts of understanding, wisdom, new purpose, inner peace, full contentment. In the prayers of the Ordinary of the Mass, the prayer following the Lord's Prayer asks to be delivered 'from every evil' and from 'all anxiety'. A proposed Eucharistic Rite for Tanzania includes a remarkable development of this prayer:

O Lord and King of peace,
grant us your true and lasting love,
so that we may find mutual understanding in our families, our villages and in the whole community. Help us to be rid of our constant enemies: magic, fear, witchcraft belief, quarrelsomeness, stupidity, disease and poverty, so that we can all live in peace and love, in brotherhood and justice, and in all ways contribute to the building of your kingdom, while we wait in joyful hope for the coming of our Saviour Jesus Christ.[6]

At every Mass, before Holy Communion, we make the prayer of the centurion our own: 'Lord, I am not worthy to receive you, but only say the word and I shall be healed'.

The main thrust of Eucharistic symbolism, however, as well as of the explicit petitions in the Eucharistic texts, is towards social healing and reconciliation, the building of the Body of Christ. The actual rite of 'the breaking of bread', by which the Eucharist was commonly known in early Christian times, is an image of the building of Christ's Kingdom. The Didache echoes the words of St Paul:

The fact that there is only one loaf means that, though there are many of us, we form a single body because we all have a share in this one loaf.[7]

In the same way that this bread which is now broken was scattered upon the mountains, and was gathered up again, to become one, so may your Church be gathered together from the ends of the earth into your kingdom.[8]

Again and again the Eucharistic prayers themselves, as well as the collects, prayers over the gifts and the post-Communion prayers, appeal for unity, for one Body and one Spirit, for union with, and growth in, Christ so that there may be a growth in unity with one another. The Eucharist also brings about our organic involvement with the physical environment and the interaction of every level of our existence. If human beings are the synthesis of the universe, the Eucharist makes them even more clearly the priests of creation.[9] Through the Incarnation God united himself with the matter he had created and with all of us embodied spirits, 'flesh of the flesh of the world'. Through the Incarnation and Redemption all of reality is brought into closer union with the Body of Christ. In ourselves we sum up, not only all the elements of the material world, but, by submitting to Christ and being united with him, we orientate the material world towards its final destiny.

The Eucharistic bread and wine are material things, but they are not raw materials. They are offerings 'which earth has given and human hands have made'.[10] They represent human work and productivity and all the concerns, sufferings, achievements and failures that people bring when they offer themselves at Mass. The faithful also join with the presiding priest in consecrating the world and in giving thanks for all earthly realities summed up in God's greatest gift, that of his Son. The Eucharist symbolizes our growth in unity through the self-offering of Christ. It symbolizes all the suffering and loss that we have to endure as a necessary condition of this growth. The Eucharist is, to my mind, the pre-eminently healing sacrament.[11] It is not merely food but a 'medicine of life' which heals at every level and articulates all levels.[12] The Spirit of God who effects the sacrament makes the medicine effective in our persons and communities. Because of this all-embracing nature of the Eucharist, it is fitting that other sacraments be celebrated in the context of a ritual Mass whenever this is possible. It is also appropriate that a minister with the gift of healing, such as Archbishop Milingo, should carry out his ministry in the context of the Mass.

Baptism, which the new code of Canon Law calls 'the gateway of the sacraments', is also the foundation for wholeness or integrated healing.[13] If physical birth is the origin of life and health, sacramental re-birth is the origin of fuller life and more comprehensive health. Baptism has its social dimension of healing and it relates this to the moral dimension. It admits individuals to membership of the community, taking them out of their isolation and giving them the support and love which comes from the Body of Christ. Baptism, indeed, joins them as new members to that Body. It takes away the guilt of original sin, and therefore of social sin which is its consequence. Baptism implies a moral conversion, past or future, and this is expressed in the vows which the candidates make or which are made on their behalf by parents, godparents and community. The healing which conversion brings is a deep re-orientation of our whole existence, a complete change in priorities and values, a healing of the heart.[14] At baptism the candidate is infused with the powerful life of Jesus Christ, the power that vanquishes all sickness and even death itself. This fact should be remembered when the sacrament is administered to the dangerously ill or dying. Nevertheless, it remains true that it is orientated towards the eradication of sin first and foremost. In this eradication a number of images are employed which are borrowed from the treatment of illness and from Jesus' own cures of the sick and possessed. The anointing with the oil of catechumens, as opposed to that with the Chrism, is symbolically related to bodily health and physical prowess in the war with sin, oil making the athlete's limbs supple and strong. The so-called exorcisms are exorcisms in the wide sense, since they do not in any way suggest demonopathic delirium or demonic oppression on the part of the baptismal candidate! However, they do signify deliverance from the moral domination of Satan and the powers of evil. Then there is the Ephphatha, the rite of opening, which is deliberately modelled on Jesus' cure of the deaf and dumb man in the region of Decapolis.[15]

And they brought him a deaf man who had an impediment in his speech; and they asked him to lay his hand on him. He took him aside in private, away from the crowd, put his fingers into the man's ears and touched his tongue with spittle. Then looking up to heaven he sighed; and he said to him, 'Ephphatha', that is, 'Be opened'. And his ears were opened, and the ligament of his tongue was loosened and he spoke clearly. And Jesus ordered them to tell no one about it, but the more he insisted, the more widely they published it. Their admiration was unbounded. 'He has done all things well,' they said 'he makes the deaf hear and the dumb speak.'[16]

With all the 'mumbo-jumbo' of the Galilean witchdoctor, Jesus opens the ears and loosens the tongue of the deaf-mute. The sacrament of Baptism opens our ears to the Word of Christ and loosens our tongue for God's praise and for our confession of faith in Christ, the Saviour.

With the new rites of Adult Baptism, the sacraments of initiation can borrow concepts and images from the initiation rituals of ethnic tradition.[17] This was clearly desired by the Second Vatican Council and many correlations are possible. Chief amongst them must surely be the liminal character of the rite of passage itself. This can be exploited during the catechumenate and it may have a directly therapeutic and reconciling function, in inculcating new moral attitudes and habits of life and in providing social support for the life-crisis through which the baptismal candidate is passing. Since in many cases the baptism of an adult also involves the rectification of an irregular marriage situation or at any rate the Christian recognition of a previously existing marriage, preparation for baptism may involve a far-reaching process of social healing.

By its very name, the sacrament of Confirmation signifies the gift of the Holy Spirit for growth and strength, but this growth and strength is orientated towards service and the use of charisms for the benefit of the community. In the renewed rite of Confirmation, the suggested instruction before the conferment of the sacrament alludes to the fact that the coming of the Holy Spirit in confirmation is no longer marked by the gift of tongues.[18] Presumably there is no reason why it should not be, but it is not part of the ordinary and essential expectation of confirmation. Confirmation is an anointing with chrism, carried out by the laying on of the hand of the Bishop or deputed minister, with the accompanying words: 'Be sealed with the gift of the Holy Spirit'. The gift of the Holy Spirit in confirmation is therefore a sealing of the baptized person's likeness to Christ and a strengthening for office, as priests, prophets and kings were anointed and sealed for office. The extending of the minister's hands over or on the candidates before the actual rite of anointing is accompanied by the prayer for the gifts which will enable the newly confirmed to serve, build and heal the Christian community. Confirmation is not an anointing for the cure of the candidate's own sickness, although it is interesting that in the continuous rites for people who are dangerously ill the laying-on of hands of the Confirmation rite replaces the laying-on of hands which normally accompanies the anointing of the sick, although both anointings are retained side by side.[19] Confirmation, therefore, betokens a witness to the Paschal mystery of Christ and a share in his public ministry, for which he was anointed with the Spirit. That ministry, as we know, is a ministry of healing and revealing in a fully integrated sense.

The sacrament of Penance is a reaffirmation of Christian initiation, particularly of the baptismal vows, which have been broken or endangered by sin. It is a return to one's basic Christian orientation and a constant resource in the struggle which began on the day that the baptizand renounced Satan and 'all his empty promises'. The emphasis in the new rites of penance in the Catholic Church is on the social and reconciling character of the sacrament. Through it we are reconciled to God and to the community of the Church. Not only are the wounds of individual sinners healed, but also the wounds which their sin has inflicted on society, and their contribution to the phenomenon of social sin. The sacrament of penance may now be administered in a general service of reconciliation with either private confession and absolution, or, where the regulations allow, with general absolution. This is a development of immense significance for healing. An emphasis is also now placed in this sacrament on the reading of the Word of God. This too ensures an entry into the mind of Christ and therefore an understanding of the working of his healing power. The healing power of Christ's Spirit is symbolized by the extension of the minister's hand over the penitent, a gesture which is rendered meaningless, if not actually physically impossible, when there is a confessional screen or heavy curtain separating minister and penitent. Less emphasis is now placed on confessional boxes and screens, and this allows for a personal relationship and also for a more obvious healing aspect in the giving of absolution.

Jesus himself linked the absolution of sins with the physical healing of the sick, as is shown in the case of the paralytic who was lowered through the roof.[20] Many confessors have experience of penitents whose sins are linked with physical sufferings, emotional anxieties and unhappy relationships. The further we move away from the 'taboo approach' to sin, the more we find that these areas are interconnected. Even if we consider the area of personal responsibility alone, there is the phenomenon of life-long habits of sin, the sense of confessing the same sins again and again, often a sense of hopelessness and a doubt of true sorrow. All of this calls for healing prayer. The *Passio Domini Nostri* prayer which is retained in the individual rite of penance clearly links repentance for sin with the endurance of suffering, as well as with the performance of good works.[21] The sacrament of Penance is closely linked to spiritual direction and to pastoral counselling, which is why the community celebrations of the sacrament must not be allowed to replace private confession and absolution completely. Penitential rites can sometimes be an excuse for avoiding the personal confrontation which particular confession brings about. This unburdening of oneself to another human being is immensely strengthening and healing, quite apart from the context of faith which sees the encounter as a further guarantee of Christ's healing presence. Anthony Storr's remark, already quoted, is very wise: 'What cannot be fully admitted to another person, cannot be fully accepted by the person himself'.[22]

If one of you is ill, he should send for the elders of the church, and they must anoint him with oil in the name of the Lord and pray over him. The prayer of faith will save the sick man, and the Lord will raise him up again; and if he has committed any sins, he will be forgiven.[23]

This text of St James is the principal basis for our anointing of the sick today and the celebration of this sacrament has recently been renewed. As the Second Vatican Council emphasizes, it is no longer fitting to refer to it as 'the Last Anointing' or 'Extreme Unction'.[24] It is a sacrament for any seriously sick person and not for the dying only. It is therefore to be correctly called the 'Anointing of the Sick'. The effects of this sacrament are not to be seen as wholly, or even primarily spiritual. It is orientated towards the whole health of an individual, towards 'saving' him and 'raising him up', with, as accompanying possibility, the forgiveness of sins and the completion of Christian penance, if he is in a state of sin. The prayers which accompany the rite speak of 'sickness', 'illness', 'suffering', 'pain', 'harm', 'weakness', 'health', 'full health', and they are a direct appeal for healing as well as for forgiveness, for physical as well as spiritual health. Since the sacrament is for ill people to get well, it is also applicable to old people who are in a weak condition, to people about to undergo a serious operation, and to people afflicted by psychiatric disorders, including severe emotional distress. The prayer for healing may not reverse the course of terminal illness or produce a cure in defiance of medical prognosis, but it may distance sufferers from their illness in a remarkable manner, aiding the processes of natural recovery or enabling them to make a calm and comprehensive offering of their life to God. Frequently, the sacrament cures anxiety and emotional distress and removes the fear of death.

The new rites provide for the communal celebration of anointing the sick, either with a community assisting at the anointing of an individual or the anointing of a large number of sick and old people in a congregation, or in a church building and also, if possible, during the celebration of Mass. Although scruples in the matter must not be encouraged, it has to be accepted that only those who are genuinely sick receive the sacrament. It does not seem that the sacrament is designed to ward off sicknesses which have not yet materialized in those who are now enjoying good health.

Finally, in this chapter, let us consider the healing character of the vocational sacraments of Marriage and Order. Marriage has an essentially reconciling character. It is a covenant between man and woman and—in many Third World cultures—between their family communities. Marriage is the 'cement of society' and the origin of all community. As the sacrament of love *par excellence*, it must reflect God's healing and forgiving love. Specifically, married love accepts the burdens of the beloved, and promises fidelity 'in good times and in bad, in sickness and in health', 'for better, for worse, for richer, for poorer'. The community constituted by Christian marriage and the Christian family is an effective image of Christ's covenant with the Church, through his passion, death and resurrection. Married people, therefore, not only exercise a healing role within the family, but that role is ideally exercised even outside the family through the family apostolate and the creation of a familial society in which God's healing and reconciling love is shared as widely and deeply as possible.

The sacrament of Order is a share in the ministerial priesthood of Christ, therefore specifically in his role of healer and revealer, sanctifying, nourishing, teaching and leading the People of God. The task of the ordained deacon, priest or bishop is to be a focus for reconciliation and unity, to build up and to heal the Body of Christ by Word and Sacrament. He is called to be a minister of healing by the very fact that he ordinarily administers the sacraments which, as we have seen, each have their special healing focus.

17

Healing gifts in the Church

John Obiri Yeboa, popularly called John the Baptist, had been a Catholic senior seminarian. He sometimes claimed to be an ordained Catholic priest, though my enquiries of bishops in Ghana, Yeboa's native country, have been unable to confirm this. Yeboa, at any rate, was always immaculately dressed in a black, clerical suit and Roman collar. He also affected an ostentatious gold ring, like a bishop's. I first heard of him when he appeared in Uganda in June 1971 and when he became popularly known there as a prophet and healer. A friend of mine told me that he was divining in the villages around Kampala and that he had revealed that a woman who consulted him had committed fifty murders. What is more, the woman admitted it! It soon became difficult to ignore the Prophet John's activities, as he acquired a house not far from where I was then living and started to conduct healing services and baptisms in Lake Victoria on which my lakeside village was situated. Day after day lorries full of people arrived to receive his ministrations, and it was said that many Catholics were among his followers.

Crowds gathered at the prophet's house where he prayed over the sick and anointed them with oil. He also sold for a nominal fee small bottles of oil which people could take home and use in their continued prayer for healing. It was at the lakeside, however, that his most spectacular services took place and that he earned his name of John the Baptist, although he was not in fact a baptizer himself. At weekends huge crowds gathered on the shore and kept vigil with him until dawn, and the services would end with mass baptisms by immersion in the waters of the lake. There were also rumours of extraordinary celestial phenomena. One young man of my acquaintance claimed that the Prophet

John had caused an immense beam of light to rise over the lake. The light hovered for a time over the water and then seemed to burn itself out over the heads of the crowd. My informant thought it was a trick and it certainly sounded like a para-illuminating flare, such as the army uses to light up enemy targets at night. Yeboa had powerful friends in the Uganda Army and could have obtained such a flare.

Sometimes the prophet held his baptisms on a Sunday morning, and it was on one such morning that I went down to watch the proceedings. There was a crowd of several thousands gathered on the lower and upper shores of the lake. I counted more than seventy cars parked on either side of the road. A choir was singing and the prophet was standing on a piece of high ground, attired in his clerical suit. He held a small crucifix to his lips and with his right hand was signing the foreheads of those he permitted to be baptized. He looked tired and he said no word as he mechanically touched the sick who were brought to him. He looked as if he was in a mild trance. Baptism was an individual healing rite which could be indefinitely repeated. It did not incorporate people into a community. Indeed, the Prophet John had no definable community until the Uganda Government obliged him to register as a church. Those whose foreheads had been signed stood in two rows of men and women, waiting their turn to go down into the lake. At the water's edge they stripped to their underclothes and were then immersed by two baptizers in ragged clothes, who used the Trinitarian formula and tipped the candidates backwards. There was a great deal of splashing and laughter, as the newly baptized swam or struggled back to the shore, and a gang of small naked urchins were frolicking in the water. About a quarter of an hour after my arrival, the prophet left by car and the baptisms continued in his absence.

On 7 July the prophet had achieved such notoriety that he appeared as 'Guest of the Week' on Uganda Television. I watched him being interviewed by a university professor and a Catholic priest. He claimed to have had visions of Christ on numerous occasions and he laid great emphasis on the bodily healing which he believed was a consequence of his baptizing. He took as his charter the closing words of the Gospel of St Mark which he read aloud to his interviewers:

Go out to the whole world; proclaim the Good News to all creation. He who believes and is baptised will be saved; he who does not believe will be condemned. These are the signs that will be associated with believers: in my name they will cast out devils; they will have the gift of tongues; they will pick up snakes in their hands, and be unharmed should they drink deadly poison; they will lay their hands on the sick, who will recover.[1]

This authentic relic of the first Christian generation, which is, however, of doubtful Marcan authorship, summed up Yeboa's whole ministry of preaching, baptizing, casting out devils, speaking with tongues, performing miracles and laying hands on the sick.

A national daily, *The Uganda Argus*, reported on 19 July that the Prophet John had been publicly thanked by the Ugandan President, and given a large sum of money, a Ugandan passport and a return ticket to Ghana.[2] No more was heard of him until 6 September when the same newspaper reported that the prophet had dined with the President and had introduced him to several people whom he had raised from the dead.[3] One had died at 4 p.m. on 4 September and had risen to life three hours later. Early in October I saw the prophet again at a Catholic mission hospital in Kampala. He was at the height of his fame and he strode through the hospital, a tall figure in a black suit, waving his bejewelled hand and scattering blessings. He exuded charisma.

The end of Prophet John the Baptist's ministry in Uganda was somewhat ludicrous. A front page article in the Government daily on 27 September 1973 announced that Yeboa, who had not been seen for a year, had been discovered by Government Intelligence to be a member of the CIA.[4] A Government spokesman instructed the Ghanaian High Commissioner to trace the prophet and declared that this was further evidence of the way in which imperialists are confusing people through religion. Needless to say, nothing further was heard of John Obiri Yeboa in Uganda.

The story of the Prophet John illustrates very well the dilemma of the Catholic Church in Africa and other Third World areas where the healing ministry is concerned. It testifies to the great need people feel for healing and to the success of an integrated approach. However, it is also evidence of how sacraments can be misinterpreted, how categories can be confused, how a cult of the marvellous can develop, how physical and moral healing are often too directly linked, how mass hysteria is encouraged and how insistence on immediate results renders the ministry transient and ephemeral. The Church is strongly drawn to respond to the needs of its sick members, but it fears the deviations which can so easily arise against such a cultural backdrop as we have

been describing in previous chapters. For many centuries the
Church has tended to departmentalize its healing ministry and to
place the emphasis on moral and spiritual healing. Even though
the sacrament of anointing was reserved in those days for the
dying, the Church did not forget to pray for the physical recovery of sick people, nor did it omit to pray for miracles of healing.
Christians tended to leave physical healing to God's providence
and not to think that this providence might be exercised through
gifts bestowed on living individuals. The personality cult was
mistrusted and healing was associated with pilgrimages, apparitions and the cult of saints. Archbishop Emmanuel Milingo is
one of those who believe there is an immense unused power of
healing in the Church which must be reawakened.

[Jesus Christ] certainly left his powers to the Church and it is due to historical
pride that the Christian Church has been deprived of its original powers,
because for a long time it did not confess Jesus Christ as Saviour and Lord. The
Church has been pre-occupied with its structures and organisation, and like the
colonialists, it has been involved in the scramble for regions and people.[5]

In my opinion it is important to pray God to raise [up] among the Christians
genuine healers, who will carry out the work of healing as a ministry among
our people.[6]

The Church today seems to bow its head to so many spiritual uprisings, call
them 'sects'. Some of these are mere enthusiasts who have only smelt Jesus as he
passes by and they are drawn to him. They admire his courage, determination
and the manifestation of his mysterious deeds. Like Simon Magus, they have
secretly gone behind the doors of the Church to learn the spiritual magic for
their own profit. Today, under the false name of being the followers of Christ,
they have attracted thousands and thousands of people. These small men make
a show of their power, which some of them use to make the Church a laughing
stock. Can we blame them? I think it is right to blame ourselves first, since we
have not put in the open the powers of the Church to make everything
new. . . .[7]

Strong words indeed, but how are we to distinguish between the
genuine healers and the 'small men' who 'make a show of their
power'?

The experience of healing associated with pilgrimage should
not be lightly dismissed, nor should its relevance for the peoples
of the Third World or the Church at large be discounted. Pilgrimages in the Catholic tradition are remarkable examples of
integrated social, moral, spiritual and physical healing.[8]
Although they are associated with holy places where miracles

once happened and may happen again, pilgrimages are not a pragmatic or manipulative process like the affliction rituals of contemporary Africa, the spirit mediumship and therapeutic communities of people like Maji–ya–Soda. The miraculous or curative aspect of a pilgrimage is not an end in itself. Miraculous cures are a bonus depending on—in the eyes of the pilgrim—the capricious grace of God. A pilgrimage is a return to the sources of faith. It seeks out a relic or an image or a place of apparition as a kind of window opening on to the heavenly world. The place of pilgrimage brings the wonderful times, events and places associated with Our Lord and the Gospel into the village life of ordinary Christians. In the lives and historical associations of the saints, particularly in the dormition and assumption of the Blessed Virgin Mary, the mysteries of Christ are rehearsed and applied.

Pilgrimages are populist in character, often at odds with ecclesiastical authority—at any rate in their origins. They are voluntary in character, cutting across all the social divisions and classes. Chaucer's pilgrims in *The Canterbury Tales*, for example, are a complete cross-section of fourteenth-century England. The pilgrimage ends in a vast throng, taking part in sacramental celebrations, especially the celebration of the Eucharist, as well as in performing customary actions which are part of the shrine's local tradition. In this throng pilgrims rediscover their own roots as Christians and as human beings without status or structure. To this extent, the pilgrimage is, as Victor and Edith Turner point out, a liminal phenomenon.[9] The pilgrimage helped people to cross frontiers, to experience the universality of the Church, and consequently the pilgrim routes were structures of Catholic communion. The pilgrimage was also a 'way of the Cross', a penitential journey which mirrored the life-journey of individual Christians and of the pilgrim Church as a whole.

At the end of the twentieth century, we still picture the Church as a pilgrim Church. Indeed, this is one of the models of the Church favoured by the Second Vatican Council.[10] In spite of, perhaps because of, the development of communications in the world, pilgrimages are still popular. The post-industrial pilgrimage is centred mainly on Mary, the Woman of the Apocalypse, and universal saint of Christendom. Between 1830 and 1933 there were nine apparitions of the Blessed Virgin in Europe which gave rise to pilgrimages and experiences of healing.[11] Often the apparitions reflected a popular apocalyptic which promised the elevation of the deprived and the distressed. The experience of the First World War especially made the apocalyptic language and imagery more strident.[12] Lourdes, where the apparitions occurred in 1858, has remained the most popular goal of pilgrimage and the one which has received the most official recognition and approval. Bernadette Soubirous is among the very few visionaries in modern times to have been canonized as a saint and it can be said that today Lourdes belongs to the whole world.

From the outset, Lourdes was a place of miraculous healing and more than five thousand inexplicable cures are on the files of the Lourdes Medical Bureau. However, because of contemporary polemics with agnostics, very rigorous investigations were required and, as a result, only 65 of these cures have been declared to be miracles.[13] Two examples may suffice here.[14] Louise Jamain was born at Paris in 1914. In 1927 she underwent an operation for appendicitis after which she spent ten years in hospital with tuberculosis. Her four younger brothers and her mother had all died of the disease. Suffering from an advanced state of tuberculosis of the lungs and intestines and also from peritonitis, she set out for Lourdes on 28 March 1937. She was kept alive only by injections and for three days had repeated oral haemorrhages. After a troubled night, the morning of 1 April found her more calm. At midday she ate a substantial meal, her first since January. Three days later a hospital examination showed a complete absence of pulmonary lesions. In the very same month, she took a job with a printing firm in Paris. Later she married and had two children.

Jeanne Fretel came from near Rennes. In 1938 she underwent an operation for appendicitis. Tubercular peritonitis developed and she had twelve subsequent operations. In spite of this, her abdomen gradually increased in size and became hard and very painful. Her condition worsened and she was put on the pilgrimage train for Lourdes in October 1948 unconscious. On 8 October she was taken, dying, to the Mass for the Sick. After some hesitation, the priest gave her a very small particle of the Sacred Host. Immediately she recovered consciousness and, although her abdomen remained hard and swollen, all pain ceased. After Mass, she was taken to the Grotto, where she felt herself invisibly raised into a sitting position and the abdomen returned to normal. She travelled home by train, on her feet most of the way tending the sick.

When people first started going to Lourdes there were about thirty 'cures' a day of which three or four might be put on the files as possible miracles.[15] Today only about three or four cures are put on the files in a year. This is partly because therapy and medication are so effective that there are fewer 'hopeless cases'. Pulmonary tuberculosis, for example, has been drastically reduced. Medical requirements are so complex nowadays and treatment so universal that it is extremely difficult to establish the ineffectiveness of medical care and so 'prove' that a cure is scientifically inexplicable. The scientific proof of the miraculous has become a pitfall, but whether there is scientific proof or not, people still experience the wonderful healing power of God at Lourdes. It is not science which turns a cure into a miracle. What happens at Lourdes is certainly not at odds with scientific medicine. About two thousand doctors come to Lourdes every year on pilgrimage and the number of pilgrims is steadily rising. In 1950 more than a million and a half visited the shrine. In 1958, the centenary year, there were five million pilgrims. In 1970 there were well over three million and two years later the figure had risen to three million and a half.[16]

Today there are Lourdes Grottoes, by the hundreds and thousands, in every Third World country, although few of them have become places of healing. Pilgrimage shrines have been slow to develop, although in themselves such places are populist and even syncretist in character. This was the case for the ancient European shrines established on previously pagan sites and for the pilgrimage centres of Latin America, like those of Mexico with their Aztec and Ocuiltecan embellishments.[17] When I visited Brazil in 1983, I travelled to the Bom Jesus shrine at Congonhas, where I saw more than two centuries' *ex voto* offerings on display. All the miseries, sicknesses and accidents that had happened to individuals of every class, station or race were there exhibited in graphically detailed pictures and faded photographs. There is little to rival this in the countries of Africa. Places such as the shrines of the Uganda Martyrs, the place of the continuing apparitions at Kibeho in Rwanda, the places where recent apparitions are claimed to have occurred in Kenya, or the tomb of St Jacques Desiré de Laval at Sainte Croix in Mauritius have developed as centres of pilgrimage but scarcely yet as places of healing.[18] This may partly be caused by official fears of popular religious manifestations. It is again the African independent churches which set the example. In many cases, the village of the founder-prophet is the principal shrine and goal of pilgrimage. In life, he resides there to practise his ministry of healing.[19] In death, his grave may be the focus for the expected cures. Often, the prophet's village is given a Biblical name and the geography of the Holy Land is re-created in the African countryside, just as it was in the shrine-villages of medieval Europe, with their 'holy houses', their sacred thorn trees, their 'new Nazareths' and 'Galilees'.

This brings us back to the problem of the genuine healers and Mgr Milingo's 'small men who make a show of their power'. In early medieval Europe when communities were relatively isolated and holy people were made saints by popular acclaim, healers and wonder-workers were multiplied without scandal or contradiction. Today, there is more scepticism and authority exercises a universal and immediate control over such populist tendencies. The Church has been cautious, even sometimes seemingly repressive, with regard to the 'living saints' of our own time. Visionaries have been encouraged to enter enclosed convents. Restrictions were imposed on the stigmatist Padre Pio, and Frère André of Montreal remained his whole life long in his monastic porter's lodge. The assumption has always been that the gift of healing is miraculous, that miracles are proof of sanctity and that the declaration of sanctity is a prerogative of the *magisterium* of the Church. Consequently, popular saint-making is potentially schismatic and the danger is aggravated by the possibility of deviations and unauthorized practices such as are appearing already among some African healers.

The popular understanding of miracle is equivocal, and it is probably best to avoid the term altogether. Whether or not medical science is baffled, people experience healing as a sign of God's power and love. That power and that love operate through the ministry of individuals and the receptivity of their clients. Healing gifts exist and healing takes place in answer to prayer. The problem is how to integrate these gifts into the ordinary life of the Church without cultivating the pursuit of the marvellous, without encouraging a show of power which draws crowds of curious people and which diverts attention from God whose healing power it is to the human being through whose gifts that power is exercised. While there is a place for large-scale healing services at parish level, might it not be in the basic communities that healing gifts should be exercised and sought?

In many parts of Africa today, as in Latin America and parts of

South-East Asia and India, basic Christian communities have come into existence. These are primarily worshipping communities which also undertake pastoral commitments in the parish. Their life centres on a weekly meeting and on a prayerful reading of the Word of God which they endeavour to relate to real life, to their own social problems and concerns. The sacraments are celebrated in these communities where possible, the Eucharist, Penance, Anointing and sometimes Matrimony. Preparation for the sacraments of initiation may also take place in these groups, even Baptism itself. Together, the groups contribute to the liturgical and pastoral life of the parish as a whole. In some cases the first activity of the basic community was care of the sick, and in many communities it has remained the principal activity. The group visits the sick in the neighbourhood and prays over them or with them. Sometimes it is possible to meet with the sick and disabled in their midst and to make them a focus for the weekly prayer of the community. It is legitimate to consider whether healing gifts should not be exercised primarily in such communities along with other spiritual gifts.

The basic Christian community, whether or not it goes in for charismatic forms of prayer (and this, in my experience, is usually not the case), should nevertheless be a therapeutic community in as many senses as possible, without becoming a manipulative community of affliction. However, it might be able to absorb people with a facility for dissociation and who benefit from the therapy of glossolalia. I would offer the following rules where people are afflicted by alien or patronal spirits—the extrapolated forms of socio-psychic experience.

1. In view of their ephemeral and manipulative character, people are to be discouraged from joining communities of affliction that practise spirit-mediumship.
2. Nothing should be said or done to encourage belief in the objective personal reality of, or attachment to, the spirits that are identified as alien.
3. Discussion about the nature of these spirits should be specifically avoided as unproductive, i.e. the discussion as to whether they are objectively personal or psycho-social extrapolations.
4. To avoid putting Christians in bad faith, increasing their fears and falsely attributing misfortunes to direct diabolical intervention, no demonological interpretation should normally be given to these spirits.
5. Instead of being involved in public, mass exorcisms, people who exhibit dissociative powers should be encouraged to join charismatic prayer groups, or other prayer groups, where glossolalia can be practised in an ordered, prayerful and therapeutic way along with other spiritual gifts. In

this way their dissociation can receive an acceptably orthodox and beneficial cultural form.

6. Alternatively, they should be encouraged to channel their dissociative
    powers through the spontaneous prayer of basic Christian communities,
    provided they are able to absorb the phenomenon without scandal and
    under supervision.

7. People who suffer from demonopathic delirium or who are simply con-
    vinced that they are oppressed by moral evil in objectively personal form
    (i.e. they identify it or him as 'the' or 'a devil') as normally understood
    by the Church, should be delivered privately by episcopally designated
    specialists in consultation with a psychiatrist.

I am in agreement with Maddocks and MacNutt and other
standard works on healing that the prayer for deliverance from
demons should rarely be made, always in private and by
specialists.[20] Although a public celebration is more appropriate
for social healing as well as for administering the sacraments in
general, there is always an aspect of healing which must be
exercised in private and which remains personal. Sacramental
absolution normally supposes private self-accusation or confession of sin. Much emotional healing of hurtful memories, much
consolation in bereavement, much of the prayer beside a sick-bed
is normally a person-to-person affair, and enters into the ministry of pastoral counselling.

The sacraments, whether or not they are administered in a
public ceremony or context—as is usually recommended
nowadays—should always be open to the healing dimension.
Besides the special grace of the sacrament, other levels of healing
should be invoked as a matter of course: reconciliation with the
physical environment and the meaning of the actual, material
signs, social reconciliation, healing of emotions and memories as
well as of the body, moral healing and the removal of every
obstacle to love of God and neighbour. The sick should be
constantly prayed for in bidding-prayers, if possible by name.
Although the dream format may sometimes be appropriate for a
sermon (as was the case for Cardinal Hume's intervention at the
1980 Synod), dream material should normally be used in private
contexts of pastoral counselling or spiritual direction, since
dreams are usually a private, not a public, mythology. It should
be stressed again and again that the Kingdom of God is here
amongst us, that God's healing power is available in the Christian community and that we do not have to wait for a future
millennium. The millennium has already been inaugurated.

At parish level or basic community level the sacrament of anointing should be administered to the sick in a public ceremony, if possible in the context of a Eucharistic celebration. This should be done from time to time. The sacrament will more often be a family celebration when the sacraments are given to a bed-ridden or dying person, though even on these occasions the basic community may be represented. Whether they are sick or healthy, Christians should be carefully prepared to participate in the celebration of the sacrament, either as sick recipients of the sacrament or as healthy 'co-agonizers', giving prayerful expression to their compassion and concern.

There should also be room for community healing services, apart from sacramental anointing, in the prayer-life of a parish. At the parish level itself such services will probably be rather rare, and at the inter-parish level I am of the opinion that they should be discouraged lest they develop into a curiosity or show centred on the reputation of a travelling healer. The possibility of visits from itinerant healers is not to be entirely ruled out, and Jesus, after all, was an itinerant healer himself. However, everything should be done to discourage—as Jesus did—misguided crowd reactions and the personality cult of the healer. Jesus dealt tactfully with crowds when he was unable to escape them, and he resisted all attempted adulation of himself as 'king'. Probably, the normal context for healing services should be the charismatic prayer group and the basic communities.

Should such prayer be accompanied by the laying-on of hands? I believe that it should. Love is expressed by touch and when a community lays hands on the sick person this is a symbol of our incorporation in the Body of Christ through which flows God's healing love.[21] The action of laying-on of hands gives greater and more direct expression to the prayer which is recited over the sick and they are made aware of the compassion of their fellow Christians and of their solidarity with them in Christ. In 1976 a Catholic diocese in Tanzania produced a helpful booklet of five prayer services for the sick, all of which included a laying-on of hands.[22] The introduction to the booklet consisted of a careful catechesis. It began with an appraisal of human suffering and its redemptive value, while also recommending the prevention and cure of sickness through hygiene and available medical services. It shows how belief in witchcraft and sorcery, so far from helping to take away suffering, increases mental anguish and robs people of the inner peace which is necessary for recovery. It affirms the

power of prayer where healing is concerned, but discourages the
expectation of miracles and the substitution of prayer for medicine. Finally, it demonstrates the practical ways in which Christians can help the sick by getting them to hospital and by giving a
helping hand at home.

At the time the services were introduced there was some fear
that the gesture of laying-on of hands might be misinterpreted in
a magical sense, but the accompanying texts made the meaning
of the action abundantly clear.

Father, we pray that your will be done. May your will be done in us and in our
sick brother. It is your will, Father, that we praise you in health and happiness,
in sickness and in sorrow. Father, behold our sick brother. We place him in
your hands. Together we place ourselves in your hands. Be praised by us all and
by him with us.
(Here everyone places their hands on the sick person.)
Leader: May your will be done, Father. May we see our brother rise up and
           regain his health like us.
All: Father, your will be done.
Leader: Give him back his health and wholeness, if it pleases you, today.
           Take away from him all suffering of body and soul.
All: Father, your will be done.
Leader: Comfort him in heart and mind; fill his heart with joy and with the
           assurance of getting better.
All: Father, your will be done.
Leader: Protect him from the wiles of Satan, our enemy. Forgive him any
           fault by which he may have offended you since he fell ill.
All: Father, your will be done.
(Here everyone withdraws their hands and prepares to listen to the following
reading. . . .)[23]

The laying-on of hands by the community is the best expression
of social reconciliation focused upon the person of a sick member.

Finally, let us mention an initiative from the diocese of
Abomey in the West African country of Benin.[24] This is a therapeutic movement called Mewihwendo or 'The Black Furrow'.
It borrows its structure from the local communities of affliction
and substitutes Christian practices and sacraments for each of the
traditional stages: divination, public confession, sacrifice,
medication and purification. It develops the African idea that the
body of a human being is symbolically co-extensive with the
cosmos, 'flesh of the flesh of the world'. This idea receives its
fullest expression through our configuration to the risen and
cosmic Christ, in whom all our wounds are healed.

18

Organizing the pastoral care of the sick and disabled

Sengerema is a town with a medical vocation.[1] It is a district headquarters township in Tanzania and much of its activity is focused on the district hospital, originally started by a Catholic nursing order. The town covers a group of low hills surrounding a valley in which the main road from the west of the country divides into two routes to Lake Victoria where ferries convey vehicles and pedestrians to Mwanza town. The population of Sengerema town is in the region of 20,000 and is increasing fast. Most of the inhabitants are engaged in trade, selling food brought in from the rural areas or commodities distributed by government para-statal bodies. There are a great many bars, eating-places and guest-houses, and there are also numerous shops which sell medicines. More than a faint suspicion exists that these medicines find their way illicitly into the shops from the hospital. Besides the hospital itself, there are also numerous clinics, two of which are owned by Protestant Churches with an interest in healing, the Pentecostal Assemblies of God and the Seventh Day Adventists. Both these denominations have their places of worship, as do Anglicans, Lutherans, Muslims and Catholics, with their large mission compound beside the hospital.

The hospital, which dominates the town and straddles one of the roads to the lake, is part of the regional medical system. It contains 250 beds and was founded by the Brothers Hospitaller of St John of God. A community of five brothers lives at the hospital, one brother assisting the matron and another acting as administrator. The hospital, which includes a maternity section, is an imposing collection of buildings. Behind the wards, staff houses line the flying doctor's airstrip. There is also a nurses' training school, with twenty male trainees and eighty female trainees, offering a three-year course plus a fourth year for mid-wifery. Across the road stands the Rural Medical Assistants training school, where a two-year up-grading course is given to eighty male rural medical aides who thereby qualify for running a rural health centre.

The Church provides staff for the hospital and all its training activities. Besides the five doctors, one of whom is District Medical Officer, and some of whom are expatriates hired by the Catholic episcopal conference, Missionary Sisters of Charity work in the hospital and on the staff of the nurses' training school. An African Sisters' congregation, the Daughters of Mary, has several members either working in the hospital or training as nurses. They also run a school for aspirants to their religious life, and the proximity of the hospital affords these girls opportunities for displaying compassion for the sick. Patients are brought to the hospital from distant villages in the surrounding countryside and there is a busy outpatients department catering mainly for Sengerema townspeople. The hospital frequently admits victims of violence and robbery, people cut with machetes or suffering from gunshot wounds.

The pivotal figure in the organization of pastoral care at Sengerema Hospital has been a missionary priest, belonging to the White Fathers' society. Fr Louis Broos is a Dutchman in his mid-fifties with an artificial leg. This disability has not only enabled him to become a full-time hospital chaplain, but it has also brought him psychologically nearer to those he tends. Catholics are the most numerous among the hospital patients, but Fr Louis has made it a practice to visit all the patients every day and to return to those individuals who wish to pray with him or who desire the sacraments. Quite frequently non-Catholics and Muslims ask for prayers and the chaplain adapts his form of words to meet their different religious backgrounds. While the Anglican priest is a faithful visitor to the hospital, the pastors of the other denominations in town are more irregular and the Pentecostals come mainly to disseminate tracts which are often critical of the Catholic Church. Fr Louis was appointed a full member of the hospital staff and has frequently been entrusted with the task of breaking the news to a patient that illness is terminal. His services to dying patients have been very much appreciated.

A constant preoccupation of Fr Louis has been to devise methods of bringing joy and hope to the sick in their distress. One original idea was to invite the girls from the Sisters' aspirants school to sing a few songs every afternoon in each of the wards. This has been immensely popular and the patients eagerly look forward to these visits. Father Louis also started a library with more than 500 volumes in the Swahili language and also a library of recreational and spiritual books. He runs these as a lending library for patients, staff and trainees. Two years ago he started an even more ambitious scheme.[2] With the help of mission funds in Tanzania and Holland, he acquired electronic equipment, 56 loudspeakers, microphones, amplifiers and a cassette recorder. A studio was set up from which Fr Louis could broadcast short morning and evening prayers each day, a recorded news broadcast from Radio Tanzania, music programmes and pre-recorded talks on health and hygiene in the local vernacular as well as in the Swahili language. Special religious programmes were also devised for seasons of the year, such as Christmas or Lent. As Fr Louis put it, 'We hope that electronics may serve the Lord in this hospital and to sing with the Psalmist: O Lord, our God, how great is your name through all the earth'.[3]

Another side of Fr Louis's work has been with the trainees in both the Sengerema medical schools. In both these establishments he has been giving a course in medical ethics. The students study hard and they come into contact with the psychic and social casualties of modern life, as well as the physical casualties of injury and disease. Father Louis has aimed to assist them in the conscientious exercise of their profession and to give them a spirit of vocation as well as a deep respect for human life and dignity. In the person of Fr Louis all the various forms of healing have been integrated and his presence in the hospital has been a constant reminder that medical treatment—even western scientific medicine—is under God's providence and causality. This is something that the African sick readily appreciate.

But God's providence is sometimes beyond comprehension. Shortly after I met Fr Louis for the first time, the doctors told him he was suffering from cancer. For several months he continued with his service of the sick and dying at Sengerema and of the medical community there. Then, just before starting this book, I met Fr Louis at the coast, about to take the plane for

Holland to get treatment for a further stage in his illness. He had been a full-time chaplain in a hospital founded by religious and operating in a Catholic ambit—an ideal situation for pastoral work among the sick and disabled. Yet it was not immediately clear that another missionary could be spared to carry on his work. That work was justly a cause for admiration, but I asked myself: Would Fr Louis perhaps help the sick of Sengerema through his own experience of illness even more than through his bedside ministry and his hospital broadcasts? 'O Lord, our God, how great is your name through all the earth!'

The example of Fr Louis Broos at Sengerema is probably exceptional. Many hospitals in the Third World are far bigger than Sengerema Hospital. Some are served by religious congregations especially founded for the pastoral care of the sick, such as The Servants of the Sick of St Camillus de Lellis. Members of such congregations not only specialize in the medical pastoral apostolate themselves, they are also able to stimulate and organize priests and Christians in the parishes to participate in their apostolate. Large hospitals are usually found in towns and cities and they are, from the Church's point of view, essentially inter-parochial institutions. Widespread co-operation is therefore required if the apostolate is to meet the real needs of the sick. Towards the end of 1982 I visited a number of parishes with hospitals in them in several countries of Eastern Africa.[4] In several places I found that a busy parish priest or curate was also looking after a large hospital, visiting the patients, sometimes with the help of one or two lay-people. Hospital visiting and prayer with the sick is a necessity but it is very time-consuming. It should be possible for the parish with the hospital to liaise with other parishes and to set up pastoral teams to cater for the sick and to call upon the priest for sacramental ministry. This is obviously a second-best, but full-time hospital chaplains are usually a luxury that cannot be afforded.

In one African town parish that I visited there were two large hospitals and a clinic run by Mother Teresa's Missionaries of Charity. Visiting the sick in the hospitals was organized by the parish through the basic Christian communities. There was a weekly roster read out in church at Sunday Mass. The possibilities of this teamwork were not yet fully exploited, but clearly much can be done. Bishops are often reluctant to sanction the commissioning of extraordinary lay ministers of the Eucharist, and especially of empowering them to carry Communion to the sick. In some places religious sisters are carrying out this ministry, but not lay-people. The extension of this ministry and its incorporation into hospital visiting teams would seem to be a necessity in many places. The interest of basic Christian communities in visiting their own sick members who are hospitalized is insufficient, since the attempt should be made to serve all the sick without any discrimination. A specialized team could be trained in the various aspects of the ministry: prayer for and over the sick, bringing Communion, comforting the distressed, speaking of death where necessary and where others find it difficult, sitting with the dying, helping would-be suicides, contacting the bereaved and the families of seriously sick people to help them confront the realities of sickness and death.

The Church's record where medical care in Third World countries is concerned is good. Not only do the dioceses and deaneries cater for the pastoral care of the sick through specially appointed committees and representatives, but many hospitals have been founded or funded by Christian organizations. Funds are obtained and medical staff provided through the national medical commission of an episcopal conference or through interdenominational Christian Medical Commissions responsible to National Christian Councils. In Third World countries, as we have already seen, hospitals are centres of a health-care programme for an entire region, embracing many hundreds and thousands of square miles. Doctors are virtually only to be found in hospitals and health-care is hospital-centred. At the lower levels the Church can probably make its most important contribution. This is being done in many fields: primary health care, nutrition, baby homes, homes for the aged, dying and destitute, leper villages, schools for the disabled, the blind, deaf-mutes, refugee camps and treatment centres for the victims of famine. Many organizations, not all of them Church-based, are at work: Mother Teresa of Calcutta's Missionaries of Charity, Jean Vanier's communities of *L'Arche*, Group-Captain Cheshire's Homes, Help the Aged, Save the Children, Lepra and so many more. Today, when foreign exchange is hard to come by and efficient distribution is hard to ensure, the Church is one of the major channels for obtaining medical supplies from abroad. There have also been the Christian 'spectaculars': Dr Albert Schweitzer who returned to his ruined hospital of Lambaréné in Gabon in 1924; Cardinal Léger of Montreal and his sojourn among the lepers of Cameroun; 'Docteur Lumière', the French missionary in West Africa, Father Goarnisson, who trained hundreds of medical assistants to perform a simple eye operation and save a whole tribe from blindness. Such people have been the meteors that left a dazzling trail across the sky, but most of the heroes of Christian medical work in the Third World are unsung.

Third World leaders often praise the religious nursing orders and mission hospitals in their public utterances; and among ordinary people mission hospitals often enjoy a better reputation than government hospitals, even though they are not able to give their services completely free of charge. The Church probably makes its greatest impact where medical care is concerned in the inculcation of attitudes, attitudes of responsibility for health and hygiene among ordinary people and professional and vocational attitudes among doctors, nurses, and health and social workers. Criticism is very frequently voiced about neglect, about poor treatment and about rudeness in hospitals and clinics. During the first five months of 1984 a Kenyan national daily carried a lengthy correspondence on the subject of the rudeness of midwives.[5] Hardly an issue appeared without a further contribution on this subject and most of the letters agreed that midwives *were* rude. It was only the occasional midwife herself who attempted to defend her colleagues and the reputation of her profession. People have great expectations of their doctors and nurses, but there are also great pressures and temptations. Tribalism, favouritism, corruption and fraud are particularly tragic when they occur in the medical profession. Unfortunately, this is one area where social justice needs to be urgently applied.

Missionary organizations have been known to abuse their role in medical work also at times. In southern Africa it has not always been easy to evade the government's policy of apartheid, as it applies to hospital work, although the extreme cases of dying black patients being refused admittance by all-white hospitals are probably rare. More often missionaries have been guilty of subordinating the care of the sick to proselytism for their own denominations. The health worker who makes all the patients sing a hymn before she opens the door of the clinic or dispensary is still quite common. More serious abuses, such as preventing patients receiving the ministrations of pastors from their own denomination, are—in my experience—becoming rarer. In the late 1960s I used to visit patients in a large African hospital run by missionaries of a Protestant denomination. All the doctors in the hospital were also ordained ministers of the

Church in question and patients were obliged, often against their will, to participate in daily religious services in the wards. Furthermore, all literature other than the tracts and periodicals of the Church was banned. The moment of truth came when several Catholic patients whose confessions I had heard unobtrusively wanted me to bring them Holy Communion. Since ministers of other Churches were strictly forbidden by hospital rules to hold services on the premises, there was no course but dissimulation. Rightly or wrongly, I arranged to bring the Blessed Sacrament to a small utility room indicated by a Catholic male nurse and the communicants who could be moved were brought there singly to receive Communion. As I recollect, there was only one patient who had to remain in bed and I managed to give her Communion without being discovered. It was not at all the right atmosphere in which to administer the sacraments! Fortunately, the hospital was eventually taken over by government and proselytism was no longer possible.

Just as it is important in prayer for the sick to stress that medical treatment is still necessary, it is equally important to pray for doctors, nurses and health workers. In the expectation aroused by healing gifts and by community prayer for healing, they are all too easily forgotten. Yet the God who heals by means of scientific diagnosis, medication, surgical operations and skilled nursing is the same God who heals in answer to prayer and who reveals his loving power in healing gifts and in the receptivity to them on the part of the sick. Prayer is not 'alternative medicine'. It carries with it the commitment to use the means which God has put at our disposal in nature and in human reason and skill. When we pray for the sick we should not forget to pray for those who exercise the nursing profession. They are the free and responsible agents of God's healing power. They must always have something of the Good Samaritan about them, as Pope John Paul II has reminded us.[6] Doctors and nurses need the gifts of compassion and sensitivity. They need to be generous and available. Their love must be unleashed by the suffering which they encounter and which they seek to alleviate. They must come to understand that 'man is health' and that sickness cannot be treated as if it were detached from real people, with real emotions and a real destiny in God.[7] They need the prayer of the Christian community in its concern for health and wholeness.

Equally, those who pray for and with the sick and those who attend healing services and celebrations of the sacrament of

anointing need to acquire something of the skills and the compe-
tence of the medical profession in their handling and care of the
sick. They need something of the *brancardier* spirit of those who
help the sick pilgrims at Lourdes if they are to help bring the sick
and the disabled to church or to community gathering. At the
bedside of a sick person, they need to show genuine concern for
the physical well-being of the one over whom they pray, to make
him or her comfortable, to be sensitive about not tiring the
patient or overstaying visiting-hours. Integrated healing means
that no aspect of wholeness is overlooked, even though healing
is being conducted at one level and the levels are clearly dis-
tinguishable. In the parish community everything has to be done
to integrate the chronically sick, the incurables and the
handicapped into normal Christian life. They should be helped to
participate in the important liturgical celebrations, to have their
say in decision-making, to make their contribution to parish
structures and associations. Special forms of recreation for them
could also be devised, like the African pop group founded by Fr
Arnold Grol WF for disabled youngsters in Nairobi.[8]

Old people's homes and hospices for the dying are beginning
to appear in Third World countries, particularly in the urban
areas where family life is often breaking down and people no
longer have the means to help their relatives die with dignity. To
my way of thinking such hospices could usefully develop not
only as places where the dying are cared for and the dying process
'hidden', as it were, but also as centres from which the care of
people dying in their own homes could be organized. Teams of
people with training and experience could thus be available to sit
up with the dying and to help them make their last lonely
journey, dying into the love of God. Religious sisters who carry
out this work make an increasingly valuable contribution.

Jesus Christ is the source of integral healing and wholeness. In
him resides the perfection of Godhead or the 'fullness of divinity'. The Letter to the Ephesians goes so far as to call the Church,
which is Christ's Body, 'the fullness of him who fills the whole
creation'.[9] Scholars have argued for centuries over the precise
meaning of this *pleroma* or fullness. Is it that the Church is filled
with Christ's own fullness, as his instrument continuing his
mission in the world? Or does the Church somehow com-
plement even Christ's fullness? Does he find new scope, new
applications for his divine perfection in the new creation, the
cosmic rebirth of which the Church is the symbol and the

beginning? Perhaps we could hold on to both interpretations of *pleroma*.

And when everything is subjected to him, then the Son himself will be subject in his turn to the One who subjected all things to him, so that God may be all in all.[10]

The final wholeness promised by Christ is Heaven itself.

For you who fear my name, the sun of righteousness will shine out with healing in its rays.[11]

You see this city? Here God lives among men. He will make his home among them; they shall be his people, and he will be their God; his name is God-with-them. He will wipe away all tears from their eyes; there will be no more death, and no more mourning or sadness. The world of the past has gone.[12]

The throne of God and of the Lamb will be in its place in the city; his servants will worship him, they will see him face to face, and his name will be written on their foreheads. It will never be night again and they will not need lamplight or sunlight, because the Lord God will be shining on them. They will reign for ever and ever.[13]

The many peoples of the world, especially the black races and the peoples of Africa, who use the sun as one of their images of God, have no difficulty in grasping the imagery of these texts from Malachi and Revelation. The sun burns, the sun sweetens, ripens and heals. In the new creation the divine sun will shine on the just with healing, and not with burning, rays. God himself will shine on them and there will be no more sadness. Heaven is where God is—the closest possible communion with him. The wholeness promised by Heaven has to be proclaimed. People want to hear about Heaven, even if the mere thought of it leaves the mind swinging. The promise of final wholeness lures us on and takes away our fears. Those who are resuscitated after cardiac arrest speak of their experience of the 'Being of Light' and of their extreme reluctance to return to earthly life.[14] It seems that after such an experience they are never again afraid of death. If we can but glimpse Heaven, nothing will hold us back. Pastoral catechesis should include the subject of healing and the hope of future wholeness in Heaven. In the adult catechumenate, and especially perhaps in the post-baptismal mystagogy, also in the preparation of children for Holy Communion and Confirmation, the relationship of healing and wholeness to our heavenly fulfilment should be explained.

However, it is not enough simply to proclaim the promise of
Heaven. The Kingdom of Heaven must be inaugurated on earth.
This is the true millennium which has already begun and which
will be consolidated when earth and earthly life have ended. To
inaugurate Heaven on earth is to engage in integral healing.

Then they brought to him a blind and dumb demoniac; and he cured him, so
that the dumb man could speak and see. All the people were astounded and said,
'Can this be the Son of David?' But when the Pharisees heard this they said,
'The man casts out devils only through Beelzebul, the prince of devils'.

Knowing what was in their minds he said to them, 'Every kingdom divided
against itself is heading for ruin; and no town, no household divided against
itself can stand. Now if Satan casts out Satan, he is divided against himself; so
how can his kingdom stand? And if it is through Beelzebul that I cast out devils,
through whom do your own experts cast them out? Let them be your judges,
then. But if it is through the Spirit of God that I cast devils out, then know that
the Kingdom of God has overtaken you.'[15]

The curing of sickness and disability, together with the removal
of oppressive evil forces, is a sign that the Kingdom has overtaken us. Whether Satan fights against himself, or whether the
Kingdom of God triumphs over him, as the miracles of Jesus
demonstrated, the kingdom of evil is destroyed either way. A
pastoral programme of integral healing must have as its objective
a foretaste of the joys, the security and the certainty of Heaven, as
well as the assurance of the conquest of evil—the assurance that
Satan is conquered before he begins.

Heaven is a new creation, a new cosmos, the world of the
future. The conservation of our earthly environment is not at all
irrelevant to this cosmic rebirth. Heaven reaches out to us
through earthly realities, and these realities, as we have seen,
communicate the ultimate reality of Heaven to us, through the
sacraments and through the prayerful and rational use of medical
material. Physical healing is no less relevant to our heavenly
fulfilment, for our resurrection to eternal life is in a very real, and
yet very mysterious, sense a bodily resurrection. We are embodied spirits and the resurrection will be for us a continuation
of our identity as spirits with a 'spiritual body'.[16] What physical
medicine does for the well-being of the whole embodied person,
it does for the one who is ultimately glorified. Indeed, it can be
said to be a part of the whole integral development of the human
person towards heavenly fulfilment.

The writings of the New Testament, and particularly the
Pauline writings, often speak of the goal of humanity in terms of

social reconciliation. It is a reconciliation in Christ, through whom we are reconciled to God. We become all in all, because God becomes all in all.[17] Social healing has important positive consequences for physical healing, as we have seen earlier in this book. However, it also extends into emotional and moral levels of healing. Emotional distress and psychiatric disorders are a result of unsatisfactory relationships. Human beings need each other in order to be themselves and, as Anthony Storr has shown, isolation leads to mental disintegration 'as starvation leads to death'.[18] The satisfactory relationship is a living relationship and love is the Christian vocation. 'No one has ever seen God; but as long as we love one another God will live in us and his love will be complete in us.'[19]

Moral disorders are typically anti-social. They endanger or even break relationships—our relationships with others and through others, with God. But moral healing is also an inner healing, besides being an outward reconciliation. It is a rediscovery of God in ourselves, confronting our own being in freedom and responsibility, discovering the root of our own personality. By living our lives to the full and using our God-given talents and faculties, we affirm God's loving presence and we experience his healing power. This healing centres on his forgiveness, his tenderness, his mercy. In God we find ourselves and we find others. We enter into the communion of saints earthly and heavenly. A pastoral catechesis of integral healing enables the Christian to understand the spiritual life as the initiation of a heavenly existence, as beginning to transcend earthly life on earth itself. It destroys the fear of sickness, of sin, of death. It sweeps away those paranoid social fears which make human beings impotent before the powers of evil, the nightmares of a cosmic conspiracy of witches or of demons. Such a pastoral catechesis can draw on many positive aspects of Third World experience, as we have shown in this book, and it should underlie all that is done for healing in the medical, social, moral and spiritual fields.

Matthew and Dennis Linn tell us that a hurtful memory is not healed by suppressing it, by denying it, by the attempt to forget it, or by any other attempt to 'kill' it.[20] Hurtful memories are healed because good is drawn out of them. I think this applies to every level of healing. Being healed means that there has been a sickness or disorder and that there may be scars and traces of the experience in ourselves and in others. However, the experience has been transcended and health and wholeness have been wrested from it. It has been a purification. The author of the Letter to the Hebrews, in describing our heavenly vocation, makes the comparison between the blood of the murdered Abel pleading from the ground for vengeance and the precious blood of Christ which brings a new covenant with God and which pleads more insistently than the blood of Abel. The glorified Christ pleads for us at the right hand of God with his wounds still visible and his blood still, as it were, freshly outpoured. He is the wounded healer.

What you have come to is Mount Zion and the city of the living God, the heavenly Jerusalem where the millions of angels have gathered for the festival, with the whole Church in which everyone is a 'first-born son' and a citizen of heaven. You have come to God himself, the supreme Judge, and been placed with spirits of the saints who have been made perfect; and to Jesus, the mediator who brings a new covenant and a blood for purification which pleads more insistently than Abel's.[21]

We are all of us healers. As we discovered, in discussing the sacrament of Confirmation, we are called to participate in the healing ministry of Christ, to heal ourselves and others. With Christ we are healers and that means that we are wounded healers like him. After the Resurrection Christ showed the wounds in his hands and his side to the apostles. It was a proof of the continuity of his identity, but it was also a sign that he had drawn victory and glory from those wounds. For us, too, God is able to draw good out of evil and glory from our wounds, even the wounds that are self-inflicted.

Crown him the Lord of love:
Behold his hands and side,
Rich wounds yet visible above
In beauty glorified:
No angel in the sky
Can fully bear that sight,
But downward bends his burning eye
At mysteries so bright.[22]

Notes

Chapter 1: Jesus and the witchdoctor

1 Robert 1949, 151–152; and cf. 1 Kings 18:20–40
2 Gorju 1920, frontispiece caption
3 Schoffeleers 1972, 73–94; Sundkler 1961, *passim*. M'Bona was a spiritually powerful ruler who was killed in pre-colonial times. His spirit is still believed to dwell in the Zambezi valley and Christ-like characteristics are now commonly applied to him
4 Mk 7:34; cf. Nineham 1963, 204
5 Jn 9:6
6 Mk 7:35; cf. Nineham *loc. cit.* and Maddocks 1981, 37
7 Mk 5:27–29; Ac 19:11–12
8 Mk 6:12–13; Lk 10:34
9 Mk 9:14–29
10 Mk 5:30
11 Mk 2:5
12 Jn 5:6
13 Jn 11:11–15
14 Maddocks 1981, 101–102
15 Jn 9:3
16 Lk 13:1–5
17 Mk 2:1–12
18 John Paul II, *Salvifici Doloris*, 1984, 8
19 Mt 5:3–10
20 John Paul II *op. cit.* 23
21 Isaiah 53:5
22 John Paul II *op. cit.* 26
23 Barrett 1968

Chapter 2: Flesh of the flesh of the world

1 Zahan 1979, *passim*
2 Goetz 1965, 117–125
3 Soyinka 1976, *passim*
4 Between 1964 and 1970 I did field research among the Kimbu with subsequent visits in 1978 and 1979. The organic universe here described is more fully set out in Shorter 1980, 189–195

5   Greene 1978, 122
6   Zahan 1979, 156
7   Hopkins in Pick 1966, 404, also 16
8   The Liturgy of the Roman Easter Vigil
9   Gen 1:28
10 Rom 8:19–23
11 2 Cor 5:1–5
12 Haenchen quoted in Jeremias 1976, ii, art. 'King'
13 Cf. Taylor 1972, whose ideas I follow in this section

Chapter 3: The scandal and scope of sickness

1   Jn 9:3
2   Cf. Job 38:1–42:6
3   Jn 5:14
4   Turner 1969, 94–203
5   van Gennep 1960
6   2 Sam 24:1–17
7   Mk 2:5
8   Mt 27:42

Chapter 4: Sickness unto death

1   Soyinka 1973, 147–232
2   Fortes and Dieterlen 1965, 105
3   Hinton 1982, 47
4   Phil 1:21–24
5   2 Cor 5:8
6   Phil 3:10–12
7   Eliot, *Four Quartets, East Coker* III
8   *Ibid.*

Chapter 5: Sickness and society

1   Maclean 1971, 24
2   Harjula 1980, *passim*; Maclean 1971, 18
3   Douglas 1970, 65–81
4   Evans-Pritchard 1951, 51
5   Beattie 1964, 34, 61. Beattie was using an idea of A. N. Whitehead
6   Achebe 1962
7   Turner 1969, 94
8   Soyinka 1973, 113–146
9   Abega in Fasholé-Luke *et al.* 1978, 601
10 Geertz 1966
11 Evans-Pritchard 1956, 112
12 Jn 15:12

13 Mt 18:35
14 Mt 6:14
15 Eph 2:13–16
16 2 Cor 5:18–20

Chapter 6: Psychiatric and emotional disorders

1   Maclean 1971, 24
2   Storr 1970, 70
3   Orley 1970, 34
4   Stengel 1970, 35–36
5   Storr 1970, 68
6   Maclean 1971, 27
7   Naipaul 1978, *passim*
8   Orley 1970, 43
9   Storr 1970, 117
10 Cohn 1959
11 *King Lear* Act III, scene ii, 1–3, 6–9
12 1 Sam 10:10–11
13 Turner 1969, 109–110
14 *Ibid.* 111
15 Mk 3:20–21
16 Turner 1969, 201
17 Linn and Linn 1978, 10
18 Storr 1970, 91
19 Linn and Linn 1978, 57
20 Stengel 1970, 113–116, 126–127
21 *Ibid.* 140
22 *Ibid.* 143
23 Hinton 1982, 79–93
24 *Ibid.* 81
25 *King Lear*, Act V, scene iii, 322–323
26 2 Cor 4:13
27 Mt 11:28–30

Chapter 7: Sickness of the soul

1   My Maori friend quoted a proverb from his own culture to sum up our
    intercultural exchange: *nau to rourou naku te rourou ka ora te manuhiri* ('The
    produce from my basket and from yours for the betterment of all'). On
    taboo see Steiner 1956, *passim*
2   Freud 1950
3   Gibran 1976, 49
4   This passage uses Clifford 1974, 18–22, 30–92
5   Lk 18:13
6   Phil 3:13–15
7   Rom 7:15, 18–19, 24–25

Chapter 8: Human sources of evil

1 Story told by Angelo Manyanza, Mazimbo village, 18 January 1966, recorded by the author
2 27 August 1975, to be exact
3 Mt 5:38–39
4 A celebrated line spoken by Gandhi in Richard Attenborough's film of that name, released in 1983
5 Cf. Cohn 1959; Cohn 1975
6 Aquinas, *Summa Theologiae*, I, 51, 3, ad 6, supp. 58, 2
7 Gregory IX, *Vox in Rama*, 1233; Innocent VIII, *Summis Desiderantes Affectibus*, 1484
8 Sprenger and Kramer (1486) 1968
9 Evans-Pritchard 1937

Chapter 9: Non-human sources of evil

1 Cf. Bastide 1978, 264–265
2 2 Sam 24:1
3 1 Chron 21:1
4 Cf. Tylor 1891
5 Beattie 1961, 29
6 Tempels 1959
7 Mulago's criticism of Tempels is discussed in Kagame 1979; it originally appeared in K. Dickson and P. Ellingworth, *Biblical Revelation and African Beliefs*, London, 1969
8 Mt 16:23
9 Job 1:6–12; 2:1–7
10 This quotation is from *Lucifer Démasqué*, by Mme 'X', Paris, 1895; it was reproduced in *L'Ami du Clergé* 1921, p. 501. The translation from the French is my own
11 Sacred Congregation for the Doctrine of the Faith, July 1975
12 Iliffe 1979, 32
13 Blixen 1980, 29
14 Storr 1970, 136

Chapter 10: Scientific and pre-scientific medicine

1 Field 1961, 114
2 *Ibid.* 115
3 Mawinza 1968, 45
4 Gelfand 1962, 107
5 Maclean 1971, 91–92
6 Pepys' *Diary*, 3 February 1667
7 Harjula 1980
8 Maclean 1971
9 It was 14 April 1969
10 In November 1970

11 Nichols 1981 discusses some of the problems posed by charismatic groups today
12 *Macbeth* Act V, scene i
13 *Ibid.* Act V, scene viii
14 *Daily News*, 14 January 1975
15 This idea was given to me by Rev. F. B. Welbourn
16 Harjula 1980
17 Swantz, L., 'The Medicine Man in Dar-es-Salaam', unpublished thesis submitted to Dar-es-Salaam University
18 Cf. Kabeya 1978
19 Mk 1:40–42
20 Linn and Linn 1978, 59
21 MacNutt 1977; Linn and Linn 1978
22 Jn 5:7
23 Maddocks 1981, 32
24 Mk 9:22–24
25 2 Cor 4:6

Chapter 11: Magic and anti-Church

1 Lev 19:26b, 31
2 Mk 5:25–34
3 Lk 7:39
4 Geertz 1966
5 1 Sam 4:1b–11
6 Storr 1970, 129
7 Ac 8:9–13, 18–24
8 Ac 13:6–12
9 Simson 1974, 9; Mk 6:45–52; Jn 6:16–21; Mt 14:22–33
10 McHugh 1973, 89–90

Chapter 12: Dreaming and healing

1 The incident occurred in 1973
2 The dream occurred in 1974, but I did not refer to it in my article: 'Dreams in Africa', *AFER (African Ecclesial Review)* 1978, 20, 5, pp. 281–287, from which this chapter draws freely
3 Freud 1977, 61
4 Dunne 1927, 37ff., 50, 59
5 Rycroft 1979, 36
6 Jung 1977a, 556
7 Rycroft 1979, 53, quoting Hall
8 Storr 1970, 176
9 Sundkler 1980, 98
10 *Ibid.* 98–112
11 Communications from B. A. Ogot and A. Wipper, 1974
12 de Craemer 1977, 69
13 I made a personal study of the Bachwezi movement at the request of the Bishop of Mbarara, Uganda, in 1971

14 Programme broadcast during the course of 1977
15 Rycroft 1979, 128
16 Freud (1958) 1977, 96–97
17 Cf. Harjula 1980
18 Cf. Jung 1956, 7, on the 'healing dream'
19 Hussein 1975
20 Rycroft 1979, 148–149
21 Jn 1:51
22 Mt 1:20; 2:12; 2:13; 2:22; 27:19
23 Mt 27:19
24 Ac 12:6–11
25 Ac 16:9–10; 23:11
26 The late Victor Turner noted Francis' predilection for dream symbolism:
    Turner 1969, 142
27 Ac 16:9–10
28 Hussein *op. cit.*
29 Jung 1977b, 192, 556–557
30 Kuper 1979, 645–662
31 Rycroft 1979, 83–85
32 Reported in *AFER*, 23, nos. 1 & 2, 26–27
33 *Ibid.* 27
34 Laye 1959
35 Laye 1972
36 Laye 1971

Chapter 13: Yearning for the millennium

1   My first visit to Papua New Guinea took place in August 1983 at the
    invitation of the Director of the Melanesian Institute
2   Lawrence 1964
3   The account was recorded at Mazimbo village in Tanzania on 18 January
    1966
4   Dan 2:1–13
5   Shorter 1979a, 141–142
6   Ranger in Ranger and Weller 1975, 45–75
7   Sundkler 1961
8   Barrett 1968, 23
9   *Ibid.* 184
10 Barrett *et al.* 1973, 188
11 Bucher 1980
12 Turner 1967
13 Dillon-Malone 1978
14 Martin 1975
15 2 Pet 3:3–9
16 See e.g. Okolo in Shorter 1978, 68–71

Chapter 14: Spirit healing

1   Accounts of the water-spirit community have appeared in: Shorter 1970,

Shorter 1979a, Shorter 1979b. This chapter makes use of further material supplied to the author in 1980 by the spirit-medium's son Patrick, and in further interviews with the spirit-medium himself

2 Rom 12:6–8
3 1 Cor 12:8–10
4 Ac 2:1–21
5 Mt 12:39
6 Cf. Goodman 1969 and Richardson 1973
7 Kelsey quoted in Hollenweger 1972, 342ff.
8 Robert 1949, 152–153
9 Singleton in Fasholé-Luke *et al.* 1978, 471–478, 'Spirits and Spiritual Direction'
10 Cf. Hollenweger 1972

Chapter 15: Exorcizing the Devil

1 This was an impression I gained in talking chiefly to missionaries during a visit to Lusaka in March 1984
2 Cf. Manigne in *L'Actualité Religieuse* 1984, no. 9, 15 February, 42–43; missionary solidarity with Archbishop Milingo in several cases emerged in my Lusaka interviews. For a sympathetic account of the Milingo case which reveals something of its complexity, cf. Mona MacMillan's Introduction and Epilogue to Milingo 1984
3 Manigne *loc. cit.*; interview of Archbishop Milingo with the *Weekly Review*, 9 December 1983, 10–14. The Archbishop is reported as saying about the celebration of Mass and confession in the case of a sick woman in 1973 that they brought 'no improvement'
4 *Weekly Review, loc. cit.*
5 Milingo 1981; and *Weekly Review, loc. cit.*
6 *Weekly Review, loc. cit.*
7 The *mashave* or *mashawe* spirits which originate in Zimbabwe have been the subject of several studies, e.g. by Colson and Gelfand
8 Milingo 1978, 4–5
9 *Ibid.* 5
10 *Ibid.* 8
11 *Ibid.* 5
12 *Ibid.* 19
13 Manigne *loc. cit.*; *Weekly Review, loc. cit.*
14 Milingo 1981, 128
15 *Ibid.* 134
16 *Malleus Maleficarum* (1486), Sprenger and Kramer 1968; Singleton in Fasholé-Luke *et al.* 1978. Even Mona MacMillan finds it difficult to draw a clear line between 'devil' and 'evil spirit' in the thinking of Mgr Milingo: cf. Milingo 1984, 7
17 Communication from Mr Julius Rugambwa and Mr Erasto Shayo
18 I have preferred not to name the diocese or the village where the healing sessions took place
19 Cf. *Malleus Maleficarum, op. cit.* 195 for the exorcism of one who is bewitched: 'He is to remain bound naked to a Holy Candle of the length of Christ's body or of the Cross'. There are frequent injunctions in the

Malleus to strip and anoint the naked bodies of demoniacs. A Catholic priest in another diocese of Tanzania was publicly denounced by his Bishop for exorcizing in this manner in 1979

20 Eph 6:10–12
21 2 Thess 2:3b–4; 1 Jn 2:18; 2 Jn 7; Rev 13:1–8
22 This prayer featured in the prayer book of the Society of Missionaries of Africa until the offending phrases were removed in 1957
23 Vatican II, *Lumen Gentium* 16
24 Vatican II, *Gaudium et Spes* 22
25 Milingo 1978, 8
26 Defoe (1719) 1972, 206
27 Hollenweger 1972, 381
28 Cf. MacNutt 1977, 200, who upholds the idea of 'demonization' or demonic oppression but believes exorcism should be private
29 Lk 10:20

Chapter 16: The sacraments and healing

1 The description which follows is based mainly on my article in *The Tablet*, 29 October 1983, 1070–1071, 'Stations of the Safari Cross'
2 The word *safari* is Swahili for 'journey'
3 Lk 11:9–13
4 1 Cor 11:28–32
5 ICEL 1976, 475–479; and Roman Missal
6 *Mtindo wa Ibada ya Misa kwa Nchi ya Tanzania* (mimeographed), 13, my tr. from the Swahili
7 1 Cor 10:17
8 Prayer from the Didache, included in the Thanksgiving of the Roman Missal
9 Culliton 1983, from which several ideas for this section have been taken
10 Offertory prayer in the Ordinary of the Mass
11 This is the opinion of Maddocks 1981, 113, with which I agree. It is also, with less emphasis, the opinion of MacNutt 1977, 265
12 I introduced the phrase 'medicine of life' into my All-Africa Eucharistic Prayer, although this was a cause of argument at the time; cf. Shorter 1973, 116
13 Can. 849 (New Code)
14 Hetsen and Wanjohi 1982, 23
15 Also written Ephphetha; the rite is optional for infant baptism
16 Mk 7:32–37
17 The main adaptation specifically foreseen (e.g. ICEL 1976, 55) is the application of the minor exorcisms to the renunciation of the worship of false gods, magic, witchcraft, and dealings with the dead, in so far as this renunciation does not give offence to adepts of non-Christian religions. While explicit renunciations are welcome, this suggestion raises a number of difficulties, already touched on in this book
18 ICEL 1976, 307
19 *Ibid.* 617
20 Mk 2:1–12, and parallels

21 ICEL 1976, 363
22 Storr 1970, 91
23 Jas 5:14–16, but cf. also Mk 6:13
24 *Sacrosanctum Concilium* 73; cf. the excellent discussion on Anointing of the Sick by Maddocks 1981, 116–121, and MacNutt 1977, 251–261

Chapter 17: Healing gifts in the Church

1   Mk 16:16–18
2   *Uganda Argus*, 19 July 1971
3   *Ibid.* 6 September 1971
4   *Voice of Uganda*, 27 September 1973
5   Milingo 1978, 8
6   *Ibid.* 8
7   *Ibid.* 16
8   Cf. Turner and Turner 1978
9   *Ibid.*
10 e.g. *Lumen Gentium* 14: 'the Church, a pilgrim now on earth . . .'
11 Turner and Turner 1978, 209
12 Cf. some of the words ascribed to Mary at Fatima in 1917
13 Manigne 1984, 34–36
14 'Miraculous Cures at Lourdes' (mimeographed), Ottawa, 1958
15 This paragraph is based on Manigne *op. cit.*
16 Turner and Turner 1978, 230
17 *Ibid.* 40–103
18 I visited Namugongo, Mityana and many of the shrines in and around Kampala, Uganda, during my years in that country, 1968–1975. I visited Sainte Croix in Mauritius in 1976
19 Cf. Sundkler 1961, 291–294
20 Maddocks 1981, 127–130; MacNutt 1977, 189–210
21 Maddocks 1981, 121–123
22 *Ibada kwa Wagonjwa* (mimeographed), Muhinda-Mulera-Kasumo, 1976
23 *Ibid.* 7–8
24 Adoukonou 1984, 44–45

Chapter 18: Organizing the pastoral care of the sick and disabled

1   I studied Sengerema, its hospital and the apostolate of Fr Louis Broos in 1982 in connection with the Urban Pastoral Project of the White Fathers' Tanzania–Kenya region; cf. Shorter 1983b
2   Fr Louis described this scheme himself in 1982: 'Electronics Praise the Lord', *Flashes* (White Fathers' mimeographed bulletin), no. 3, 1982
3   Psalm 8
4   Shorter 1983b, 86–88
5   *The Daily Nation*, Nairobi
6   John Paul II, *Salvifici Doloris* 1984, 29
7   One of the educative government slogans in Tanzania is *mtu ni afya*, 'man is health'

8   Fr Grol founded in 1975 the *Undugu* (Solidarity) Society of Kenya which has started many initiatives in the poorer areas of Nairobi City
9   Eph 1:23
10 1 Cor 15:28
11 Mal 4:2
12 Rev 21:3–4
13 Rev 22:3–5
14 Cf. Moody 1975
15 Mt 12:22–28
16 1 Cor 15:44. This is the literal meaning of the Greek *pneumatikon*; cf. *Jerusalem Bible,* note 1 to this text
17 2 Cor 5:18–20; 1 Cor 15:28
18 Storr 1970, 36
19 1 Jn 4:12
20 Linn and Linn 1978, 53 and *passim*
21 Heb 12:22–24
22 M. Bridges (1800–1894), 'Crown him with many crowns'; cf. *The Westminster Hymnal,* London, 1965, no. 98.

Bibliography

(Published works cited in the text)

Abega, P., 1978: 'Liturgical Adaptation' in Fasholé-Luke *et al.*, 597–605.
Achebe, C., 1962: *Things Fall Apart*, London (1958).
Adoukonou, B., 1984: 'Le Sillon Noir', *L'Actualité Religieuse*, no. 9, February, 44–45.
Barrett, D. B., 1968: *Schism and Renewal in Africa*, Nairobi.
Barrett, D. B., *et al.*, 1973: *Kenya Churches Handbook*, Nairobi.
Bastide, R., 1978: *The African Religions of Brazil*, Baltimore and London.
Beattie, J. H. M., 1961: *Bunyoro, an African Kingdom*, New York.
    1964: *Other Cultures*, London.
Blixen, K., 1980: *Out of Africa*, London (1936).
Bucher, Mgr H., 1980: *Spirits and Power*, Cape Town.
Clifford, W., 1974: *An Introduction to African Criminology*, Nairobi.
Cohn, N., 1959: *The Pursuit of the Millennium*, London.
    1975: *Europe's Inner Demons*, London.
Culliton, J. T., 1983: 'The Mass: Its Personal Meaning in Daily Life', *The Furrow*, July, 417–429.
de Craemer, W., 1977: *Jamaa and the Church: A Bantu Catholic Movement in Zaire*, Oxford.
Defoe, D., 1972: *Robinson Crusoe*, London (1719).
Dillon-Malone, C. M., 1978: *The Korsten Basketmakers*, Manchester.
Douglas, M., 1970: *Natural Symbols*, London.
Dunne, J. W., 1927: *An Experiment with Time*, London.
Evans-Pritchard, E. E. Y., 1937: *Witchcraft, Oracles and Magic among the Azande*, Oxford.
    1951: *Social Anthropology*, London.
    1956: *Nuer Religion*, Oxford.
Fasholé-Luke, E., *et al.*, 1978: *Christianity in Independent Africa*, London.
Field, M. J., 1961: *Religion and Medicine of the Ga People*, London.
Fortes, M., and Dieterlen, G., 1965: *African Systems of Thought*, London.
Freud, S., 1950: *Totem and Taboo*, London.
    1977: *The Interpretation of Dreams*, Harmondsworth, Middx (1953).
Geertz, C., 1966: 'Religion as a Cultural System' in M. Banton (ed.), *Anthropological Approaches to Religion*, London, 1–46.
Gelfand, M., 1962: *Shona Religion*, Cape Town.
Gibran, K., 1976: *The Prophet*, London.
Goetz, J., and Bergounioux, F. M., 1965: *Prehistoric and Primitive Religion*, London.

Goodman, F. D., 1969: 'Phonetic Analysis of Glossolalia in Four Cultural Settings', *Journal for the Scientific Study of Religion*, Vol. 8, no. 2, 227–239.

Gorju, J., 1920: *Entre le Victoria, l'Albert et l'Edouard*, Rennes.

Greene, G., 1978: *The Human Factor*, Harmondsworth, Middx.

Harjula, R., 1980: *Mirau and his Practice*, London.

Hetsen, J., and Wanjohi, R., 1982: *Anointing and Healing in Africa*, Gaba, Kenya.

Hinton, J., 1982: *Dying*, Harmondsworth, Middx.

Hollenweger, W. J., 1972: *The Pentecostals*, London.

Hussein, Sheikh Yahya, 1975: *Siri za Ndoto—Secrets of Dreams* (Swahili and English), Nairobi.

ICEL (International Commission on English in the Liturgy), 1976: *The Rites of the Catholic Church*, New York.

Iliffe, J., 1979: *A Modern History of Tanganyika*, Cambridge.

Jeremias, J., 1976: *The New International Dictionary of New Testament Theology*, London.

John Paul II, Pope, 1984: 'On the Christian Meaning of Human Suffering', Apostolic Letter *Salvifici Doloris, L'Osservatore Romano*, N.8 (822), 20 February.

Jung, C. G., 1956: *Symbols of Transformation*, London.
    1977a: *The Symbolic Life*, London.
    1977b: *Memories, Dreams and Reflections*, Harmondsworth, Middx.

Kabeya, J. B., 1978: *Daktari Adriano Atiman* (Swahili), Tabora.

Kagame, A., 1979: *La Philosophie Bantoue Comparée*, Paris.

Kuper, A., 1979: 'A Structural Approach to Dreams', *Man*, Vol. 14, no. 4, 645–662.

Lawrence, P., 1964: *Road Belong Cargo*, London.

Laye, C., 1959: *The African Child*, London.
    1971: *The Radiance of the King*, London.
    1972: *A Dream of Africa*, London.

Linn, M., and Linn, D., 1978: *Healing Life's Hurts*, New York.

McHugh, J., 1973: 'The Origins and Growth of the Gospel Traditions', *Clergy Review*, February, 91.

Maclean, U., 1971: *Magical Medicine*, Harmondsworth, Middx.

MacNutt, F., 1977: *Healing*, New York (1974).

Maddocks, Bishop M., 1981: *The Christian Healing Ministry*, London.

Manigne, J. P., 1984: 'Lourdes: Le Piège du Scientisme', *L'Actualité Religieuse*, no. 9, 15 February, 34–36.

Martin, M. L., 1975: *Kimbangu, an African Prophet and his Church*, London.

Mawinza, J., 1968: 'Reverence for Ancestors in Tanzania' in *Theory and Practice in Church Life and Growth* (mimeographed), Nairobi, 44ff.

Milingo, Mgr E., 1978: *The Church of the Spirits—Is it to Blame?*, Lusaka.
    1981: *The Demarcations*, Lusaka.
    1984: *The World In Between*, London.

Moody, R., 1975: *Life after Life*, Covington, Georgia.

Naipaul, S., 1978: *North of South*, London.

Nichols, P., 1981: *The Pope's Divisions*, Harmondsworth, Middx.

Nineham, D. E., 1963: *The Gospel of Saint Mark*, Harmondsworth, Middx.

Okolo, C. B., 1978: 'Christ is Black' in Shorter 1978, 68–71.

Orley, J. H., 1970: *Culture and Mental Illness*, Nairobi.

Pepys, S., 1825: *Diary*, 'suitably edited' by N. Braybrooke, London.

Pick, J. (ed.), 1966: *A Hopkins Reader*, New York (1953).

Ranger, T. O., 1975: 'The Mwana Lesa Movement of 1925' in Ranger and Weller, 45–75.

Ranger, T. O., and Kimambo, I. N. (eds), 1972: *The Historical Study of African Religion*, London.

Ranger, T. O., and Weller, J. (eds), 1975: *Themes in the Christian History of Central Africa*, London.

Richardson, J. T., 1973: 'Psychological Interpretations of Glossolalia: A Re-examination of Research', *Journal for the Scientific Study of Religion*, Vol. 12, no. 2, 199–208.

Robert, J. M., 1949: *Croyances et Coutumes Magico-Religieuses des Wafipa Païens*, Tabora, Tanzania.

Rycroft, C., 1979: *The Innocence of Dreams*, London.

Schoffeleers, M., 1972: 'The History and Political Role of the M'Bona Cult among the Mang'anja' in Ranger and Kimambo, 73–94.

Shorter, A., 1970: 'The Migawo—Peripheral Spirit Possession and Christian Prejudice', *Anthropos*, Vol. 65, 110–126.

1973: *African Culture and the Christian Church*, London.

1978: *African Christian Spirituality*, London.

1979a: *Priest in the Village*, London.

1979b: 'Spirit Possession and Christian Healing in Tanzania', *African Affairs*, no. 4, 45–53.

1980: 'Creative Imagination and the Language of Religious Traditions in Africa', *Kerygma*, no. 35, 189–195.

1983a: *Revelation and its Interpretation*, London.

1983b: *Urban Pastoral Project*, Tabora, Tanzania.

Simson, P., 1974: *Gospel Miracles*, Gaba, Uganda.

Singleton, M., 1978: 'Spirits and Spiritual Direction: The Pastoral Counselling of the Possessed' in Fasholé-Luke *et al.*, 471–478.

Soyinka, W., 1973: *Collected Plays*, Vol. 1, Oxford.

1976: *Myth, Literature and the African World*, Cambridge.

Sprenger, J., and Kramer, H., 1968: *Malleus Maleficarum*, London (1486).

Steiner, F., 1956: *Taboo*, London.

Stengel, E., 1970: *Suicide and Attempted Suicide*, Harmondsworth, Middx (1964).

Storr, A., 1970: *The Integrity of the Personality*, Harmondsworth, Middx (1960).

Sundkler, B. G. M., 1961: *Bantu Prophets in South Africa*, London (1948).

1980: *Bara Bukoba*, London.

Taylor, Bishop J. V., 1972: *The Go-Between God*, London.

Tempels, P., 1959: *Bantu Philosophy*, Paris.

Turner, H. W., 1967: *History of an African Independent Church*, Oxford.

Turner, V. W., 1969: *The Ritual Process*, London.

Turner, V. W., and Turner, E., 1978: *Image and Pilgrimage in Christian Culture*, Oxford.

Tylor, E. B., 1891: *Primitive Culture* (2 vols), London.

van Gennep, A., 1960: *The Rites of Passage*, London.

Weekly Review, 1983: 'Milingo Defends his Healing Mission', Nairobi, 9 December, 10–14.

Zahan, D., 1979: *The Religion, Spirituality and Thought of Traditional Africa*, Chicago.

Bible references are to *The Jerusalem Bible*, London, 1966, published and copyright 1966, 1967 and 1968 by Darton, Longman and Todd Ltd and Doubleday & Co. Inc., and are used by permission of the publishers.

Canon Law references are to: Canon Law Society of Great Britain and Ireland, *The Code of Canon Law*, London, 1983.

Vatican II references are to: A. Flannery, *Vatican Council II*, Dublin, 1975.

Thomist references are to: St Thomas Aquinas, *Summa Theologiae*, Editiones Paulinae, Rome, 1962.

Shakespeare references are to *The New Temple Shakespeare*, London, 1946 ed.

References to T. S. Eliot's *Four Quarters* are to the Folio Society edition, London, 1968.

Index